Formed Together

SRTD

STUDIES IN RELIGION, THEOLOGY, AND DISABILITY

SERIES EDITORS

Sarah J. Melcher
Xavier University, Cincinnati, Ohio

John Swinton
University of Aberdeen, Aberdeen, Scotland

Amos Yong
Fuller Theological Seminary, Pasadena, California

Formed Together

Mystery, Narrative, and Virtue in Christian Caregiving

Keith Dow

BAYLOR UNIVERSITY PRESS

Cover design and typesetting by Kasey McBeath
Cover image courtesy of Callahan/Shutterstock

Library of Congress Cataloging-in-Publication Data

Names: Dow, Keith, 1982- author.
Title: Formed together : mystery, narrative, and virtue in Christian caregiving / Keith Dow.
Description: Waco : Baylor University Press, 2021. | Includes bibliographical references and index. | Summary: "Investigates the ethical motivation and formation of caregiving in Christian social service environments with people with intellectual disabilities"-- Provided by publisher.
Identifiers: LCCN 2020040104 (print) | LCCN 2020040105 (ebook) | ISBN 9781481313216 (hardcover) | ISBN 9781481313988 (pdf) | ISBN 9781481313971 (mobi) | ISBN 9781481313230 (epub)
Subjects: LCSH: Church work with people with disabilities. | Caring--Religious aspects--Christianity. | Caregivers.
Classification: LCC BV4460 .D677 2021 (print) | LCC BV4460 (ebook) | DDC 261.8/32--dc23
LC record available at https://lccn.loc.gov/2020040104
LC ebook record available at https://lccn.loc.gov/2020040105

Series Introduction

Studies in Religion, Theology, and Disability brings newly established and emerging scholars together to explore issues at the intersection of religion, theology, and disability. The series editors encourage theoretical engagement with secular disability studies while supporting the reexamination of established religious doctrine and practice. The series fosters research that takes account of the voices of people with disabilities and the voices of their family and friends.

The volumes in the series address issues and concerns of the global religious studies/theological studies academy. Authors come from a variety of religious traditions with diverse perspectives to reflect on the intersection of the study of religion/theology and the human experience of disability. This series is intentional about seeking out and publishing books that engage with disability in dialogue with Jewish, Christian, Buddhist, or other religious and philosophical perspectives.

Themes explored include religious life, ethics, doctrine, proclamation, liturgical practices, physical space, spirituality, and the interpretation of sacred texts through the lens of disability. Authors in the series are aware of conversation in the field of disability studies and bring that discussion to bear methodologically and theoretically in their analyses at the intersection of religion and disability.

Studies in Religion, Theology, and Disability reflects the following developments in the field: First, the emergence of disability studies as an interdisciplinary endeavor that has impacted theological studies, broadly defined.

More and more scholars are deploying disability perspectives in their work, and this applies also to those working in the theological academy. Second, there is a growing need for critical reflection on disability in world religions. While books from a Christian standpoint have dominated the discussion at the interface of religion and disability so far, Jewish, Muslim, Buddhist, and Hindu scholars, among those from other religious traditions, have begun to resource their own religious traditions to rethink disability in the twenty-first century. Third, passage of the Americans with Disabilities Act in the United States has raised the consciousness of the general public about the importance of critical reflection on disability in religious communities. General and intelligent lay readers are looking for scholarly discussions of religion and disability as these bring together and address two of the most important existential aspects of human lives. Fourth, the work of activists in the disability rights movement has mandated fresh critical reflection by religious practitioners and theologians. Persons with disabilities remain the group most disaffected from religious organizations. Fifth, government representatives in several countries have prioritized the greater social inclusion of persons with disabilities. Disability policy often proceeds based on core cultural and worldview assumptions that are religiously informed. Work at the interface of religion and disability thus could have much broader purchase—that is, in social, economic, political, and legal domains.

Under the general topic of thoughtful reflection on the religious understanding of disability, Studies in Religion, Theology, and Disability includes shorter, crisply argued volumes that articulate a bold vision within a field; longer scholarly monographs, more fully developed and meticulously documented, with the same goal of engaging wider conversations; textbooks that provide a state of the discussion at this intersection and chart constructive ways forward; and select edited volumes that achieve one or more of the preceding goals.

Contents

III Responding to the Call

Acknowledgments

This book would not be possible without my encounters with people with intellectual and developmental disabilities and their families. I am grateful for their lives, experiences, and the ways that their journeys have shaped and directed my own. Through their stories, prompting theological questions, I met Hans Reinders who graciously welcomed me into the Ph.D. program in theology at Vrije Universiteit, Amsterdam. Reinders' guidance and writing helped to form the trajectory of my dissertation, "Call, Encounter, and Response: Loving My Neighbour with Intellectual Disabilities," the basis for this book. Thanks to Tom Reynolds for his insight, review, and encouragement. Thanks also to Christian Horizons, offering support as I navigated working full time and writing my dissertation, and to my work supervisor Neil Cudney for his constant encouragement, flexibility, and friendship.

With the inevitable disclaimer that I can never thank all of the people with whom and for whom I have been formed, I want to express my appreciation and love for my wife, Darcie, and children, Isaiah, Lucy, and Charity, who inspire and sustain me through times of discouragement or stress. I am grateful for my father, Ernest Dow, and the patient care he demonstrated with my mother for many years before her death. Finally, this book is dedicated to my mother. She was my teacher from my earliest years both academically as we homeschooled and in practices of care, giving herself to us and on our behalf. May she rest peacefully in the divine care that sustains us all.

Introduction

Giving a Careful Account

> The whole trouble lies in that people think that there are conditions
> excluding the necessity of love in their intercourse with man, but such
> conditions do not exist. Things may be treated without love; one may
> chop wood, make bricks, forge iron without love, but one can no more
> deal with people without love than one can handle bees without care.
>
> **Leo Tolstoy**[1]

Writing an introduction offers the briefest taste of omniscience; that moment
where the author has read through to the end and returns to give a full
account. Even so, parts of what follows are already a dim memory. The
account is never complete. Along the way, our greatest discoveries are found
at the relational intersections of the stories we tell: the accounts that we give
of our lives and experiences.

Many people struggle to "give an account" in the way expected of them.
This may be because of a speech impediment or difficulty with traditional
forms of communication. Perhaps someone has a mobility challenge that prevents her from *getting to* a place where her story might be heard. Someone
may have an IQ considered lower than "normal" among the population and
so not deliver his account in the way that one might expect.[2] Many people are
not able to express their intentions, their actions, or their plans as coherently
or intelligibly as is demanded of them.

Through this book, you will encounter "accounts." Many of these accounts
are of my own experiences, often of supporting people with intellectual

disabilities. Any of these accounts or stories are problematic if taken in an authoritative or definitive sense. Yet all reflect the ways that the people I have known have helped to write this book.

GIVING AN ACCOUNT: NASSIM

I saw Nassim almost daily for four years when I worked as a direct support professional. He was a large man and hairy everywhere except on the very top of his head. He would saunter around his home swaying and singing or laughing with short, gulping chuckles—as though in response to a joke that only he understood. When Nassim became anxious or upset, he would pace quickly. His vocalization became louder and more agitated. He would hit himself on the side of the head. I worried that his colostomy bag might get caught and come undone, leading to a messy and possibly dangerous interaction.

When Nassim was happy, though, he would take you by the arm. At times, he would play with his fingers on your hand, tapping on your palm as though he were sending telegraphs to the remote regions of space. Perhaps to those who heard and laughed along with his inside jokes.

Nassim loved food. One of his favorite activities was to go each week down to the local Lebanese restaurant and gulp down shawarma. They knew him well there. His preference for shawarma tied him to his cultural and social roots. The restaurant workers did not know his grandmother, though. Nassim's grandmother was a short and feisty woman who had raised one grandson with a significant developmental disability and Nassim's father, who had recently passed away.

Nassim's grandmother didn't just call him Nassim. It was "my Nassim." She doted on him in a way I have only seen mothers do with newborn children. She would make sure that his care was top-notch down to the smallest details. One might surmise the blessing and curse of this for those who supported him. There would be moments of intense preparation as we headed out the door to take Nassim to his grandmother's house for the weekend. We needed to match every sock perfectly without signs of grime or dust. We had to be ready to answer for every aspect of the care he had received in the past week. Yes, he had been taking his medication. Yes, he had enjoyed his shawarma. Yes, Nassim had been a "good boy."

As time passed, Nassim's grandmother was no longer able to take him for the whole weekend as she had previously. She was growing older, and Nassim was just as strong as he had always been. She was not able to handle his times of anxiety and distress anymore. It was remarkable that she was able to support him for as long as she had. Love is miraculous that way.

To those who knew Nassim well, his life may have revolved around food, but his food pointed to his deeper roots in his culture and, more specifically, in his close and sustaining relationship with his grandmother and his father. To observe his relationship with his grandmother was to see his life, his personality, and his interconnectedness with the world.

THE AIM OF THIS BOOK

What does life look like for Nassim now that his grandmother is no longer able to care for him? These natural relationships lie at the very core of *who he is*. Once these roots are severed, who will be grafted into Nassim's identity? Nassim's grandmother and father are irreplaceable. Nevertheless, those who are with Nassim and care for him most hours of the day also play an integral role. How might these care providers contribute to Nassim's sense of identity and fulfillment? More specifically, what does it mean to *care well*, to fulfill one's moral responsibility to Nassim?

The purpose of this book is to explore accounts of caregiving and related philosophical, theological, and biblical resources to locate the appropriate motivation for, and formation of, ethical Christian care provision.

Many of the experiences here are from my time as a direct support professional with people with intellectual disabilities in a Christian service agency. However, the implications of this work extend beyond the field of intellectual disability. Paying attention to the caregiving encounter with people with intellectual disabilities is a uniquely revealing exercise. These encounters expose the reliance of Western morality on intellectual ability and myths of transparency. We think we are good, because we think that we know—all too well—who others are, who we are, and who God is.

What if our intellectual hubris was called into question?

Can we be good in the absence of knowledge?

What, then, might it look like to love and care for each other?

A BRIEF OVERVIEW

Part I: The Call to Care

The first part surveys the ethical resources of vocational language professed by caregivers. People providing care often express a sense of "higher calling" *to* people with intellectual disabilities, whether they describe this using religious language or not. This *call to* others is a potential source of ethical motivation.

Chapter 1 ~ Vocation and Transcendence: Called to One Another

Chapter 1 examines the ways in which Martin Luther shaped the direction of vocational language in his *consecration of the ordinary*. In comparing and contrasting his perspective with that of Søren Kierkegaard, this chapter establishes that *belonging* and *distance* are integral factors in resilient vocational caregiving.

Chapter 2 ~ Vocation and Immanence: Called by Each Other

Chapter 2 goes on to unpack the nuances of belonging and distance in direct caregiving relationships. Building on a personal account of supporting Michael, it is shown that a kind of "eternal equality" is necessary to maintain ethical distance. However, we are also *called by* those whom we support into relationships of belonging. "True care is mutual care," but care providers must navigate the complexity of being called *to* support (a transcendent call or a sense of distance) and being called *by* the people they support (a sense of belonging).[3]

Chapter 3 ~ A Theological Story: The Limits of Professional Ethics

Chapter 3 inquires into current approaches to caregiving ethics as established in the name of professionalism. Do these practices equip caregivers to practice resilient, ethical care? Following Alasdair MacIntyre's critique of "managerial effectiveness," I will demonstrate these approaches to be insufficient to explain or support ethical motivation and formation. To adequately address the sense of being "called to" and "called by" others, Christian care provision requires a fuller understanding of theological anthropology and account of human flourishing.

Part II: Encountering My Neighbor

The second part argues that an adequate understanding of *calling* in the Christian tradition entails recognizing that *all people*—including those with intellectual disabilities—have intrinsic value, being created in God's image. However, preceding intellectual recognition, we first *encounter* one another as image-bearers of God.

Chapter 4 ~ Traces of the Divine: The imago Dei and Human Ability

Chapter 4 provides an overview of existing approaches to the *imago Dei* and disability. We *receive* our ethical obligation to one another before we develop any theoretical moral system. We are responsible to one another precisely *as* created in God's image. However, we *live into* the fullness of this image through the *imitatio Dei*. Within the Christian tradition, ethical formation involves conforming to the nature of Christ. This is where we come to appreciate the mystery and revelation bound up in our encounter of others, ourselves, and God.

Encountering one another as created in God's image is not a simple task because of the barriers we face and the presuppositions we carry with us.

Chapters 5 through 7 examine three myths of recognition that underlie these barriers:

Chapter 5 ~ Seeing You through Me: The Myth of the Transparent Other
Chapter 6 ~ The Stories I Tell: The Myth of the Transparent Self
Chapter 7 ~ A Mysterious Revelation: The Myth of a Transparent God
To presume that recognition of the *imago Dei* is easily accessible to our intellect is to presume that our knowledge of one another and ourselves is easily accessible as well. Narrative ethics in the vein of Alasdair MacIntyre look for intelligible accounts that comply with the *tyranny of transparency*—a transparency that is unattainable. We need a moral responsibility tied not to myths of transparency but to the shared opacity of our stories and lives.

Part III: Responding to the Call

The final part sketches the posture that is *called for* by Christ once we encounter one another as created in God's image—both revelatory and opaque. It unearths several *virtues of care* and concludes where the project began, with an exploration of the Source of this mysterious calling.

Chapter 8 ~ Formed Together in Love: Toward an Ethic of Christian Care

Within the Christian tradition, caregivers respond to their calling out of an overflow of God's love, already received. It is only out of this love that care arises out of gift rather than solely in response to an ethical demand. "We love because he first loved us."[4]

Chapter 9 ~ The Virtues of Care: Discovering Who We Are

The virtues of courageous humility, loving mercy, of confession and forgiveness, of lament and morning, and of quiet attentiveness arise not out of an overreaching estimation of intellectual prowess but out of deep humility. In this way, we encounter everyone, including people with intellectual disabilities, as full moral agents capable of rich human flourishing.

A NOTE ON METHODOLOGY

> What is reasoning? It is the result of doing away with the vital
> distinction which separates subjectivity and objectivity.
>
> **Søren Kierkegaard**[5]

This book does not claim detached impartiality or even objectivity in its approach. Its reasoning arises out of a broadly phenomenological or existential tradition. I frequently relay the way experiences of care provision *present themselves* and then attempt to make sense of these experiences in light of diverse theological and philosophical frameworks. In short, I aim to take seriously the vital distinction and interplay between subjectivity and objectivity. My arguments and critical analysis arise not apart from my experience in direct support but precisely out of these encounters and experiences. The people I have met and known have shaped the ways I think. I will share "accounts," stories of my interactions with others, and proceed to analyze the ways that relevant theories and the Christian tradition might critically interpret these interactions. [6]

One might note that Søren Kierkegaard, Emil Brunner, Henri Nouwen, Emmanuel Levinas, Alasdair MacIntyre, and Judith Butler are diverse thinkers in their interests, areas of expertise, and conceptual frameworks. Each contributes important insights to the overall project. Occasionally I will highlight where they complement or critique one another. Note that my use of their writing is primarily constructive, drawing from their work precisely in those areas that intersect with the questions of this book.[7]

My commitment is to investigate a distinctly theological ethical motivation for caregiving and its posture toward people who receive care.

- *Motivation* can be understood as the "inner or social stimulus for an action."[8] Motivation is closely linked in the pages that follow to a fundamental *obligation* or *responsibility* to one another.

- Where *posture* is an embodied stance toward others, the positioning of one's body or one's attitude or approach, it relates closely to *formation*. Posture is the resulting shape of one's approach in response to the way that one has been *formed* to do so. In this way, posture will be used in conjunction with a sense of formation throughout this book. *Formation* speaks to those interactions that shape us into an *image* or *form*.[9] Personal formation occurs particularly through those voices and encounters that inspire us, breathing life into our experiences.

Within the Christian tradition, we are *always already* responsible to one another as people created in the image of God. Ethical motivation refers back to this call to love my neighbor as myself. Our posture toward one another is then formed in response to the love of God already received, in the example of Christ through the *imitatio Dei*. We are formed together in the virtues of care as much out of the partial opacity of our shared stories as out of the revelation of who we are *through* our stories.

Pastoral Deconstruction

In response to God's love, no ethical system or theory is adequate. Systems privilege intellectual ability in a way not reflective of our encounter with God or one another. The intellect is a sharp scalpel, proficient at dissecting the world. Our calling in care is to work to stitch the world back together. This book does not set out to establish an ethical system. It is, instead, an act of *pastoral deconstruction*: in response to a pastoral calling, and out of respect for the people I have known and cared for, I seek to *question* and to *unsettle* assumptions regarding the privilege of intellectual ability in the accounts we give of our shared humanity.

Insofar as we have been given intellectual ability, it is true that our rationality is to be directed to seek the Good and to love God. "Love the Lord your God with all your heart and with all your soul and with all your mind and with all your strength."[10] However, as we are formed to "love our neighbors as ourselves," loving God with our minds is no more virtuous than loving God with any other aspect of who we are. Our neighbors with intellectual disabilities frequently demonstrate the virtues of care relayed in this book without requiring the ability to articulate them.

THE END OF THE BEGINNING

This book is born partially out of a desire to tell my story, to give an account that inspires care for one another. Madeleine L'Engle observed that "story makes us more alive, more human, more courageous, more loving."[11] I agree that stories *can* do this. I only pray that this particular story is one that does so. I hope that it is a testimony to the far-reaching impact of people with intellectual disabilities on my life and faith and a witness to the ways that God has changed me *through* these friends who are often relegated to the margins of society and the church.

I hope that, upon arriving at the epilogue, you will have a new appreciation for how our shared stories are significant—not because of their intelligibility but because of their relationality. Our partial, shared opacity to ourselves and others binds us together, forms us together. The accounts that we give gesture toward our goals, projects, hopes, and dreams. These acts of revelation structure us and define us in ways new and old. They help make sense of (reveal) our experience and hide (conceal) aspects of it simultaneously. Our stories offer a mysterious revelation of our origin as people created in God's image, formed in our encounters with one another.

The story that I gave of Nassim's life is only a short account of who he is from the time that I was fortunate to share with him. It is not exhaustive. It is a way of pointing, gesturing, and alluding to Another whose life and love have roots deeper than I can understand. I pray that this book points beyond itself to the fabric of this passing gift we call "life" and the richness of those encounters that we call "care."

I

THE CALL TO CARE

1

Vocation and Transcendence

Called *to* One Another

Everything calls. We live in a world infused with stimuli that demand our attention, our investment, our *care*. Scrolling through my social media newsfeed, I was struck by the phrase *"This is your calling."* Investigating further, the post turned out to be an ad for creating an online storefront. I kept scrolling. Perhaps I have now missed my vocation in life.

At one point in the not-so-distant past, the language of "calling" was restricted to a life of devoted service to God and the church. The *One who called* was understood to be a transcendent deity, and not everyone could expect to hear this summons to set-apart service. Now, everybody is expected to pursue their calling—whatever this may be. We are no longer sure of who or what *calls*, only that advertising companies compete to generate the most compelling demands on our time and our lives.

Every sense stimulus, every notification, every person or thought cries out for our concern and interest. Is it possible that anything and everything is a calling? If so, we risk succumbing to care fatigue, overwhelmed by the constant mental noise and the demands of modern life.

Related questions emerge:

- Might any occupation or job be a vocation?

- What are the moral implications of the language of vocation?

- What might be the resources here for considering ethical caregiving in the Christian theological tradition?

- Is there any right or wrong way to pursue one's calling?

11

The pages that follow ask whether, amid all the cries for our attention, there is still space to hear a call to care for one another—a call that transcends the demands placed on us by everyday life. Perhaps the language of vocation still carries ethical connotations that motivate and sustain care provision.

WHY VOCATION?

Interpreting one's work as a calling is not unique to Christian caregiving. In light of contemporary nonreligious conversations that also touch on vocation, "calling" may seem to bear little relation to a theological-ethical inquiry. Why does it make sense to begin by considering vocation?

As mentioned in the introduction, this book cannot be detached from my own journey and experiences of caregiving. Friedrich Nietzsche once observed that every great philosophy so far has been "a confession of faith on the part of its author, and a type of involuntary and unself-conscious memoir."[1] As I reflect on my experience of caregiving with people with intellectual disabilities, some aspects of this book are not so involuntary or unselfconscious after all. While many aspects of my caregiving journey remain mysterious to me, a clear sense of being called to others remains.

Giving an Account: Called to Encounter

Coming to the end of my undergraduate studies in philosophy at a Canadian Catholic university, the shelves in my small room were lined with works by Aristotle, Plato, Thomas Aquinas, David Hume, and Immanuel Kant. They were the cheap paperback versions, of course—the ones I could afford. Each thinker had his own views on how to live a moral life, how one might live into full human flourishing. Even as I sought to understand these diverse frameworks and perspectives, I struggled with the detached theory of it all.

As a Christian, the existentialism of Søren Kierkegaard gave words to some of these tensions for me. It was not enough to *know*. One must *act*. Kierkegaard's critique of Christian scholarship is that it often serves to complicate ethical matters so that one might avoid potentially life-changing ethical demands. "Take any words in the New Testament," he suggests, "and forget everything except pledging yourself to act accordingly. My God, you will say, if I do that my whole life will be ruined. How would I ever get on in the world?" This is where theory and theology come to the rescue: "Christian scholarship is the Church's prodigious invention to defend itself against the Bible."[2] The irony that Kierkegaard highlights goes beyond Christian thought and writing. Ethical discourse without corresponding action accomplishes little.

Encountering others in right relationships is just as—or more—important than having the right answers. If I was not acting on what I already knew to be good, continuing to pursue an ethical framework would have little lasting effect.

Out of this realization, and an awareness of the biblical mandate to serve the marginalized and work toward justice in the world, I felt called to find work that had a meaningful impact on the lives of people in need. This call—together with a philosopher's desperation for reliable income—led me to work with a Christian organization serving people with intellectual disabilities.

In this instance, it was philosophy that drove my autobiography. I knew that to live out my desire to live a "good life," I needed to make decisions that embodied my beliefs. I was invited to apply to be a direct support professional by a friend, someone who believed that I would be able to make a positive difference in the lives of people with intellectual disabilities. This all took place before I really knew anything *about* the people whom I would serve. It was not a well-reasoned ethical system that prompted me to act; it was a dissatisfaction with ethical theory alone, a calling to encounter people who had been marginalized, and the more particular "call" of a friend who saw potential in me that I had not seen in myself.

My experiences in the years that followed, working with people with intellectual disabilities, have since driven my philosophical and theological inquiry. Neither is complete without the other. Experiences prompt questions that were at first hidden, just as my studies opened me to experiences that put my ethical beliefs to the test. What began as detached study became personal and meaningful. In turn, I seek to uncover those extractable principles from my own experience that may be transferable to others. As Henri Nouwen describes, "What is most personal is most universal."[3] It is the interplay between recognizing the subjectivity of our experiences and exploring transferable principles that constitute any possibility of "objective" understanding. To deny subjectivity is to compromise truth.

In my caregiving journey, it has been a calling that I cannot fully comprehend or articulate that compels me forward. I had little to no understanding of what I was "getting myself into." Calling does not come with a job description. Even Christ's disciples had little idea where they were headed when they followed him. There may have been an unsettling from where they were, but, more significantly, there was a draw to the person of Christ who called them to follow.[4] In the structure of the call, then, we see that it is not a prerequisite to be fully aware of that *to which* one is called.

All I knew is that this was a "higher" calling in the sense that I experienced it as a demand with which I must comply; it was a calling that drew me, pulled me, and pushed me beyond my own immediate projects and purposes to encounter *another*.

Vocation as a Shared Experience

The language of *vocation* (from the Latin *vocare*, "to call") captures a fundamental aspect of my journey toward caregiving. As I investigated this instinct through dissertation research, it turns out that my account is not isolated. Robert Hickey's work with Canadian direct support professionals reveals the prevalence of an experience of motivational calling. Most of these caregivers relay a desire to *do good* through their work, described as "prosocial motivation." Whether inspired by religious factors or not, prosocial motivation is an indicator that many direct support professionals view their work as more than a job, more than simply a way to make an income. Their desire to *do good* may take the form of a spiritual calling, like my own, or that of a more generic draw to help people without a clear sense of religious motivation.[5]

After working in direct support, I spent several years as a recruitment and hiring manager. In this role, I conducted several hundred interviews. As part of each of these interviews, I asked some form of the question, "Why do you want to work with people with disabilities?" These exchanges further confirm Hickey's research. The draw of prosocial motivation and the language of "calling" resonates with new applicants as well as with experienced caregivers. Care provision *draws* people. Many interviewees had limited knowledge of the precise responsibilities of the day-to-day job yet felt a strong sense that they had been called to work with vulnerable people. In the context of a faith-based organization, many of these interviewees identified their calling as arising from religious motivation, referring to God as the *One who called*.

IMMANENCE AND TRANSCENDENCE

The history of vocational language helps us to understand the impact of religious and nonreligious thought through the years. Work as calling has a convoluted history. Originally intertwined with religious implications, contemporary research often attempts to separate "calling" from its transcendent connotations. The framework for these definitions is confined to the *immanent*, claiming no access to a "higher power" or reference to the divine.[6]

Current research may control for the importance of religion or simply state that "this concept of a calling is not to be taken in any traditionally religious sense."[7] Definitions, likewise, vary depending on the presence or absence of spiritual principles. One example defines calling as "a consuming, meaningful passion people experience toward a domain."[8] It views calling as a *psychological construct*, existing "within individuals' minds and reflect[ing] the sentiments people experience toward a domain."[9]

Psychological motivation serves as a cornerstone in this example. Calling exists only within an immanent frame of reference, within individuals' minds. Calling involves finding meaning in one's work and a passion *toward* one's work. Nonreligious definitions incorporate the thoughts and emotions that someone might experience. These sentiments can then be relayed in further research and studies, and so—in being confined to an immanent frame—can be quantified and measured in the literature.

Frederick Buechner, a Christian author, preacher, and theologian, connects the summons from a transcendent Caller to the place *to which* one is called: "The place God calls you to is the place where your deep gladness and the world's deep hunger meet."[10]

It is understandable that these descriptions differ in their reference to the divine. One is articulated from the perspective of academic psychology, while the other is intended for a relatively devout lay audience. Where the former reduces its focus to measurable aspects, Buechner has no hesitation in identifying "God" as the One who calls, and "profound need" as the place to which God calls.

THREE ASPECTS OF VOCATIONAL BELONGING

In pursuit of the ethical foundation of direct care provision, three aspects stand out in the similarities between these descriptions. Each relates to *belonging*.

Experiencing Belonging in a Domain or Place

Each description emphasizes an aspect of calling as belonging to a "domain" or to a "place." In Buechner's account, the attachment comes in the form of "deep gladness," while the former study identifies "a consuming, meaningful passion." This place or domain may or may not be where one currently *is* or *in which* one is engaged. Buechner's "to" implies a sense of being drawn somewhere new or perhaps outside of one's comfort zone. Being directed "toward a domain," in the former psychological definition, does not exclude one from being actively engaged in the domain. In either case, though, the "to" or "toward" indicates forward movement—a deepening commitment within a domain if not an actual change *of* domain. When we are called, we experience a new or deeper sense of belonging to a domain or place—an attachment to the space of our vocation.

Experiencing Belonging within Oneself

Each definition references the importance of finding *belonging with oneself*. Whether the authors refer to the individual's disposition or the "you" who experiences the call, vocation is not separate from *who one is* or *where one finds oneself*. One cannot simply pursue a vocation as one might a goal or an objective.[11] Vocation relies on a tension between the truth and values of one's own identity and an unsettling toward where one is *called*. Everyone experiences limits. Everyone offers gifts to the world. Whether in relation to ability or other dimensions of who we are, finding belonging with oneself means coming to terms with one's own limits and vulnerabilities as well as one's capacity and giftedness.[12] To be called means that I encounter my own vulnerabilities and strengths, channeling the range of my embodiment toward the meaningful difference I might make in my world.

Experiencing Belonging with Others

Finally, secular and religious perspectives reference the importance of *finding belonging with others*. Calling involves a crucial intersubjective dimension. This may be referenced in terms of "social comfort." Social comfort is the relational or interpersonal aspect of domain involvement, specifically in feeling *comfort, enjoyment,* and *fit* being around others.[13] It is in our work with others that a sense of unity and purpose is either reinforced or eroded.[14] To be called is to be called *with* and *to* one another, to meet each other's needs and to cultivate meaningful relationships with other human beings through the course of our activity and engagement.

In summary, to experience one's work or occupation as a calling involves a deep sense of belonging to *one's place*, to *oneself*, and to *one another*. Vocation engages a person's identity, including her strengths and limits. Within this calling we discover deep gladness in meeting the needs of others, and we experience the social comfort of being with others in a place or domain.

A Divine Call?

Where much can be learned from the similarities among diverse views on vocation, they do not necessarily offer insight into the distinctly theological-ethical dimension of calling. While some studies control explicitly for religion so that they do not "skew" their results, theological authors will typically identify the one who calls as *God*. The former studies beg the question of *who* or *what* "calls." They may refer to a nebulous summons of some kind without referencing the divine. Does receiving one's calling from a "higher power" impact its ethical significance?

VOCATION AS A SPIRITUAL CALLING

It would be an understatement to say that Martin Luther shaped the historical conversation on vocation. His writing shifted the language of vocation
from the sense of a "spiritual calling" to an "occupation or profession," as
the timing of an etymological shift bears out.[15] Where using "vocation" in
the sense of a spiritual calling or obligation dates back to the thirteenth century, it was not until the 1550s that it first came to mean "one's occupation or
profession."[16]

Prior to Luther, to have a vocation described the sacred or set-apart call
by God to the full-time devotion of a religious order. Luther protests this
special status of priests, monks, and nuns by emphasizing the spiritual calling
of *all* occupations: "What seem to be secular works are actually the praise of
God and represent an obedience which is well 'pleasing to him.'"[17] In hyper-
bolic fashion, Luther elevates housework above monastic pursuits: "It has
no obvious appearance of holiness, yet . . . household chores are more to be
valued than all the works of monks and nuns."[18] Luther has extended God's
call to all of ordinary life.[19] He continues to understand calling as being *from*
God to work done *for* God, except there is now no "set-apart" sacred work.
Throughout Luther's writing, one discovers a consecration of the ordinary.
Just as Luther identified each Christian believer as part of a "holy priesthood," all work was now "God's work."[20] Even in this context, vocation was
securely attached to the *God who calls* and only found its fulfillment in the life
of the baptized community.

In the centuries that followed, however, religious overtones of vocational
language faded into undertones. Max Weber traces this transition through
Calvinism and other Protestant influences, but it is difficult to get a clear
sense of exactly how this transition happened.[21] We now find ourselves in a
society where management scholars largely dismiss claims that calling carries
moral or sacred connotations and where the language of calling is used in
diverse and divergent ways.[22]

An increasing emphasis on rationality and choice in the philosophical
tradition also played a role in shifting terminology away from the mysterious
sense of a divine calling toward an understandable and rational occupational
choice.[23] As theologian John Swinton observes:

> Within a secularizing culture that was gradually beginning to allow sci-
> ence and reason to usurp ideas about God, reason came to replace the
> idea of vocation. . . . To have a vocation is to receive something from
> outside of yourself, to have your life profoundly shaped and directed by
> forces beyond your own control and comprehension.[24]

If reason truly replaced the role of vocation, though, one might wonder why the language of calling persists over time—particularly, in the writing of management scholars, health service professionals, and researchers. Perhaps that which we receive *from outside of ourselves* is an inescapable foundation for ethical care provision. Perhaps, even without being willing to identify a transcendent moral framework or reference religious beliefs, research employs vocational language in an attempt to capture the aspects of our lives that are "profoundly shaped and directed by forces beyond [our] own control and comprehension."

These incomprehensible and uncontrollable forces shape our lives in diverse ways, many of which do not require religious belief. Disability is one such example. Even if we understand aspects of many of the genetic or historical factors that lead to our embodied conditions, their forces are generally beyond our control. Our bodies are formative in our experience of the world. We all experience limits, just as we each possess gifts and attributes that may "direct" us in certain ways or establish us with a propensity or aptitude for certain activities. Simply experiencing these forces is not sufficient to establish an ethical calling, however. The language of calling elicits not only dispositions based on determinative factors but also an obligation to respond to a call toward a greater good. "Calling" implies not only an *is* but an *ought*. It makes little sense to speak of "calling" if rational deliberation is the only determinant of our actions. One cannot "call" oneself, so the very notion of call and response takes us outside of ourselves and beyond those forces we control or comprehend.

Ethical care provision that is experienced as a vocation requires reference to a transcendent moral obligation or responsibility of some kind. What has yet to be determined is how this calling transcends one's immediate reality. At a basic level, to be called is to be summoned toward something *other*. The transcendent, experienced as a "higher calling," is a specter that continues to haunt vocational language.

In contemporary professional literature, the specter of transcendence takes form as a mysterious sense of purpose or meaning, along with the choices one makes and actions one takes in pursuing this purpose. From a theological perspective, vocation points to God's transcendent call on our lives and the ways in which we respond to this calling.

A Dangerous Ghost: The Dark Side of Vocation

So far, our emphasis has been on whether vocational language offers ethical resources for caregiving. However, it may also be asked whether a sense of calling might work *against* ethical caregiving. Several detrimental aspects to viewing work as a calling are identified in the literature.[25]

- People who view their work as a calling can develop "career tunnel vision." They might resist feedback from others or demonstrate a lack of adaptability in their work.

- A sense of calling might come with much personal sacrifice and at the expense of other aspects of one's life.

- People with a sense of calling may be at higher risk of having their work and dedication exploited by their organization.

- Viewing work as calling can result in a higher degree of burnout due to heightened expectations for one's own performance and the performance of others. Nurses, for example, experience burnout more readily if they are first "on fire," or passionate about nursing.[26]

Studies on compassion fatigue further validate the potential "dark side" of work as calling. Compassion fatigue is a type of burnout specifically related to caring professions, defined as "fatigue, emotional distress, or apathy resulting from the constant demands of caring for others."[27] Worn down by the "cost of caring" for the people whom they support, caregivers can be left with nothing to give. Besides experiencing overwork and fatigue, people undergoing compassion fatigue are at risk of depersonalizing the people for whom they provide care. This can result in caregivers interacting with people as they would with tasks or objects. In compassion fatigue, caregivers may be incapable of mustering the emotional resources necessary to engage on a deeply human level.

Hickey has conducted extensive research into the nature of burnout and compassion fatigue. Overall, his results make one thing clear: "The most striking finding in this initial review is how much people enjoy working with people with developmental disabilities."[28] He records that direct support professionals "truly enjoy working with people with developmental disabilities and appear deeply committed to the nature of direct support work."[29]

Hickey finds that while prosocial motivation and "value-based behaviours at work" help to buffer the support relationship from stress and emotional exhaustion, "the desire to do good was found to also be related to employees feeling more emotionally drained as they experienced the conflict between service idealism and service reality."[30] In imperfect systems and contexts of inadequate funding or challenging situations, a frustrated desire to provide excellent care results in compassion fatigue.

One observes in Hickey's work the dangers of a sincere desire to *belong* in one's vocation without a corresponding sense of progress or achievement. This lack of fulfillment may be due to the constraints of the system around the caregiver. It may be due to not seeing growth in the people for whom she cares.[31] Perhaps the caregiver feels deeply the health setbacks of people she supports or a lack of progress toward the goals that people have set for their own lives. It is often an accumulation of small losses, of minor setbacks, and of frustrated progress that leave the deeply caring person with "nothing left to give."

A sense of calling in one's work increases the attachment and commitment to one's work. In helping professions, then, calling enhances the depth of care provided. Yet deep care is accompanied by deep loss at setbacks and suffering in the lives of the people one cares about. Too often, those providing care fail to recognize the impact of these interpersonal losses in their own lives. The calling or caring does not cause burnout or compassion fatigue directly. These commitments lead to a heightened engagement, which makes experiences of grief or frustration that much more pronounced and crucial to address. As Rachel Naomi Remen observes, "We burn out not because we don't care but because we don't grieve. We burn out because we've allowed our hearts to become so filled with loss that we have no room left to care."[32]

If a passionate attachment to one's work may lead to compassion fatigue and burnout, the question becomes whether there is a way to experience one's calling that promotes resilience and ethical engagement. Before answering this question, though, it is important to consider the potentially negative impact of understanding one's calling as a *divine* vocation in addition to the more general concerns raised above. To do so, we must return to the history of viewing work as calling in the writing of Martin Luther. Viewing one's *place* or *domain* as a divine calling has had tragic implications when not paired with a corresponding ability to stand back and critique the projects to which we belong.

Luther and the Demands of Providence

> For there is a perennial nobleness, and even sacredness, in Work. . . .
> The latest Gospel in this world is, Know thy work and do it.
>
> **Thomas Carlyle**[33]

The language of calling has transitioned from that of a distinctly religious vocation to Martin Luther's consecration of *the ordinary*. Following Luther, any activity or occupation can be understood as God's call on one's life. In this conviction, Luther espouses a strong sense of God's Providence. Luther's writing reflects a "divine destiny" that leaves little room for flexibility. Max Weber observes:

> The stronger and stronger emphasis on the providential element, even in particular events of life, led more and more to a traditionalistic interpretation based on the idea of Providence. The individual should remain once and for all in the station and calling in which God had placed him, and should restrain his worldly activity within the limits imposed by his established station in life.[34]

Weber goes on to maintain that in the development of orthodox Lutheranism, "the only ethical result was negative; worldly duties were no longer subordinated to ascetic ones; obedience to authority and the acceptance of things as they were, were preached."[35] This view of Providence does not permit an adaptable sense of vocation. It leaves little room for the understanding that God's plan does not depend upon every person remaining in their particular station in life, in the occupation in which they find themselves.[36] In Luther's writing, one discovers an oppressive Providence that confines each person to the "forces beyond one's control and comprehension."[37] "Is" becomes "ought" without having the distance or perspective from which to call into question one's situation as ethical or otherwise. After all, each person is where God has placed him, doing the work that God has given him to do. To "abandon one's post" would be to neglect God's plan for his life.

The religious psychology of this perspective of calling related to care provision might be surmised. Caregivers already feel a deep sense of compassion for the people whom they support. On top of this, in a strong view of Providence, caregivers may experience the added pressure that pursuing any *other* direction is to abdicate their God-given responsibility.

A Call to Obedience, a Call to Quietude

Reflecting on Romans 13, Luther instructed that human authorities were understood to be agents of God's will. As such, Christians were to obey New Testament principles in their interactions with one another, yet these might need to be set aside in the domain of secular authority as instituted by God.[38]

> You should esteem the sword or governmental authority as highly as the state of marriage, or husbandry, or any other calling which God has instituted.[39]

In Luther's time, and in the centuries that followed, the effects of his theology became evident. The call of God became conflated with the interests of the state. Luther acknowledges that rulers are often foolish and corrupt. However, as long as they are not dictating the beliefs of a soul and are "only" acting as "executioners and hangmen," they are *God's* executioners and hangmen. As such, God desires "that everyone shall copiously accord them riches, honor, and fear in abundance."[40]

What is striking is that these passages are found in a document explicitly designed to *limit* the powers of temporal authority. Here, Luther ordains rulers' power as divine will and reinforces subjects' duty to obey temporal authority as a duty to God. He also gives explicit permission for subjects to continue in obedience even if they are unsure whether a ruler is acting ethically or not.

It has been argued that Luther's theology of vocation led to a Germany composed of "quietists" and "yes-men" who felt compelled to obey the dictates of government as if obeying God.[41] His writing shaped the prominent Lutheran tradition in Germany at the time of the Nazi rise to power in the twentieth century. Karl Barth notes the implications of this: "The German people suffer under [Luther's] error of the relation between law and Bible, between secular and spiritual power."[42]

A culture that understood its submission to authority as divinely ordained, and its rulers as "God's executioners and hangmen," was ill-suited to stand up to one of the most oppressive and evil regimes in history. According to the government, physicians who were part of the Akton T4 program were providing a "mercy death" to patients "deemed incurably sick, after most critical medical examination."[43] This program alone killed more than seventy thousand people, most of whom were disabled.

A strong view of God micromanaging every action and interaction may leave much of one's calling outside of one's *control*, but in terms of *comprehension*, it professes that everything that happens is exactly as God would have it. The transcendent will of God seems to become "transparent" to us, yet we are left wondering how God could be good in light of the suffering and evil around us.[44]

Stepping Back to Gain Perspective

Now, how does this historical account connect to a "higher calling" born out of religious commitment? Luther's consecration of *the place where one finds oneself* and divination of civil obedience led, at least in part, to the widespread quietude of German society when confronted by injustice.

A sense of belonging in one's work, care, and calling can offer a rewarding and fulfilling experience. To *only* belong to one's immediate occupation, without the capacity to step back and question one's environment, engagement, or the authority for whom one works, is a dangerous position. Belonging is a double-edged sword. In the context of sustaining relationships, it is life giving and frees us to flourish. Without the flexibility to pursue other paths, though, belonging takes the form of crushing servitude. To experience *only* belonging without a sense of perspective or distance from one's care and calling can be catastrophic, especially when received as a divine command. Within Christian caregiving, support providers often relate their calling to the divine. Here, there is a real need to establish resilient theological "distance" from the weight of a strong view of Providence.[45]

Even in nonreligious contexts, an elevated sense of vocation can lead to "career tunnel vision," to great personal sacrifice and burnout. In caring professions, a "consuming, meaningful passion" can result in depersonalization and compassion fatigue.

Diverse religious and nonreligious contexts use the language of calling. Even outside of religious usage, "calling" is haunted by an etymological and theological ghost of ethical obligation. This obligation falls outside of that which can be controlled or comprehended, transcending rational calculation and one's immediate environment and situation. Whether used religiously or otherwise, if a perspective of distance—the ability to "step back" from one's immediate obligation—does not balance the closeness of belonging, then vocation can become oppressive.

Any position from which one might sustain resilient ethical caregiving must incorporate this distance of perspective. In the Christian tradition, a theology of caregiving must also make sense of the way God calls not only *to* others but *through* others. Perhaps in hearing the call of our neighbors, we will discover a kinder Providence than Luther's, encountering a God who calls us not only to one person or situation but to be with our neighbors in relationships of radical equality.

2

Vocation and Immanence
Called *by* Each Other

The following account explores one particular caregiving relationship. This encounter demonstrates how relational connection with people fosters an experience of *being called* that holds in check one's obligation to professional expectations and imperfect systems and structures. We are called *to* our neighbor in care, but we are also called *by* the person whom we support. In these relationships we experience a form of belonging with the potential to sustain our ethical obligation and commitment.

BELONGING AND DISTANCE IN DIRECT SUPPORT

Giving an Account: Michael

I had already been working direct support for a couple of years when I became the coordinator of supports for a man in his forties whom we'll call Michael. Michael sported oversized square-frame glasses that he kept pushing up on his nose to keep in place. He loved to joke around, sidling up to support staff and jovially elbowing them as he wisecracked about the day or their unique personalities. It was his way of connecting with others, as someone who found his identity in relation to those around him. Michael had a mild intellectual disability and wrestled with depression. He was offered supports in a group living environment where he had a large basement apartment-type setting to himself. He had friends and family outside the group home and regularly participated in events and social gatherings, taking the bus and operating with a relatively high level of independence. Michael had difficulties with impulse control concerning food and money, and friends and family often took advantage of his generosity. I grew to appreciate and care for Michael. I frequently accompanied him to appointments and events.

Every so often, Michael would move out. That is, he would decide that he no longer wanted to live in the group living environment or receive caregiver support. Despite having a relatively independent living arrangement and the freedom to come and go as he chose, he struggled with the idea of receiving help at all. The cycle continued for a while: Michael would move out to a friend's house only to return and admit that he needed the assistance that supported living provided.

In our province, there were—and still are—close to twenty thousand people with intellectual disabilities in need of various kinds of additional support. Due to this systemic pressure, it was untenable for the organization to keep this space and support open to Michael if he chose to keep leaving services. It was determined that if he decided to leave again, we would no longer be able to keep his apartment for him upon his return. Someone else would quickly move into that living space.

It should be noted that this was a limited model of care, one constrained by a system providing a particular kind of all-inclusive service. Supported independent living in apartment settings was becoming more common, but most service options were still group-living settings. People were no longer sent to institutions but did not yet have a range of options available to them.

Michael understood that if he left again, he was leaving for good. Several months later, he was gone. Knowing that he was saying goodbye, we helped him to move out and to settle in the community. We knew that he had the potential to live successfully on his own, yet we doubted that he would continue to have the positive influences in his life that would encourage healthy decision making and financial responsibility. Having spent a couple of years as his primary support worker, I experienced a real sense of loss in seeing him go. We advocate for self-determination, yet it is never easy to see people we have come to care about make life-altering decisions with potentially significant negative implications.

Michael and I kept loosely in touch over the years that followed. Communication became difficult, though, as he moved frequently. It became challenging to know where he would be at any given time. We heard rumors that he was living on the street, either as a result of financial mismanagement or giving what little he had out of his generous and somewhat gullible spirit. When he came to us, he was significantly overweight. Through encouragement and support, he had learned to make healthier decisions and to lose weight. When Michael left services, his support system was gone. He quickly regained the weight he had worked hard to lose.

As an idealistic young man, I took my sense of vocation seriously. I became a support worker to respond to the call of God on my life to make a positive difference in the lives of people who had been marginalized by society. Through my relationship with Michael and others, vocation took on the reality of "belonging." I cared about Michael. He was delightfully funny and genuinely kind and unassuming. The support relationship was reciprocal in that we received mutual enjoyment from the time we spent together. I am grateful to Michael for his patience with me as I figured out how to provide support and empower him to make decisions. I'll never forget how he would lumber over in his Ottawa Senators T-shirt with a goofy grin on his face and jostle me when we were kidding around.

I wish that this story had a happy ending. Perhaps I assumed that a strong sense of vocation would lead to fulfilling outcomes for all involved. The goal was to see Michael grow and learn to make decisions toward a full and rewarding life.

Unfortunately, it turned out that Michael still needed a supportive community that did not take advantage of him. Michael had many friends, but I'm not sure anyone was close enough to him to impact his life in this way. Michael went back and forth between support systems on the streets of Ottawa and friends and family. He put on weight and was unable to manage his finances successfully. We lost track of him for a while. One day I heard the devastating news that Michael died from a heart attack while living on the street.

As we gathered together to celebrate Michael's life and remember him together, I wrestled with the knowledge that, for a period, I had been his primary support. There are so many things I could have done differently. Maybe his death could have been prevented?

In these moments the rose-tinted perception of vocation that brought me to the field to serve and support others seemed to shatter. I found myself in systems and structures of support with limited funding, tight governmental regulations, and formats of service that didn't allow for enough flexibility to meet Michael's needs. What if this had been different? What if I had advocated more strongly for Michael's independence and particular needs? What if . . . ?

In this experience with Michael, it was a sense of calling and a close relationship of "belonging" that made his eventual death that much more heartbreaking. It was not just a calling *to* Michael that made his death difficult, it was the sense of being called *by* Michael himself—my identity had, in a way, become entangled with his own.

The sense of loss at Michael's passing was not only related to a calling that was beyond control and comprehension; it was due to systems and structures that were also beyond any particular caregiver's control. Funding and service constraints meant that we were not able to provide the kinds of tailor-made support that could have helped Michael navigate his world and impulses successfully.

I'm sure that I could have done more to advocate for Michael's needs. Perhaps this would have opened up opportunities for others, as well, to have their particular needs for independence and self-direction met. Yet going back to change this was not an option. All I could do was be open to how this experience might shape my posture toward others in the future.

Looking back, I think it was the understanding that God had called me not just to Michael but to all the people I supported that gave me the perspective I needed to keep on going. I was not ultimately responsible for Michael's life or decisions. Rather than crushing my sense of calling, Michael's passing was a reminder to invest wholeheartedly in the lives of the people I continued to support.

The pages that follow demonstrate that, together with the experience of belonging, a humble appreciation for the equality of each person *before God* is a constituent element of a resilient ethical vocation. There are three aspects to being "before God" that impact the ethical relation of vocational care, or a *higher calling*:

1. The self before God as eternal responsibility.
2. The neighbor before God as eternal equality.
3. Neighbor-love as the antidote to love of preference.

The Call of Eternity: The Self before God

It was evident that the system we were a part of was not able to provide the best support for Michael. Pressures for others to receive services forced a difficult choice. If one's calling is to one's organization, or even to a larger system of care provision, there is little perspective from which to "stand back" and critique it. If one's fundamental obligation is to the place where one finds belonging, then the constraints of that place can become oppressive. Within the Christian tradition, one's obligation is ultimately to God. Unless one holds the strong view of Providence that Luther expressed, this obligation transcends one's immediate projects and institutional commitments rather than being bound up in them.

To be a human being *before God* is the fundamental and definitive Christian ethical relation.[1] As Dietrich Bonhoeffer expressed, the incarnation of the divine makes this possible: "God enters into created reality, that we may be and should be human beings *before God*."[2] This God-relation is an *eternal* relation. As such, temporal projects and relationships must find their meaning in relation to the divine, not the other way around. Our responsibility to God takes a transcendent priority over any particular or immediate priority we might have. From this perspective, in relation to the experience shared above,

a. I was not responsible for controlling Michael's life or the service system of which we were a part and,
b. my higher obligation was to God, to whom I was ultimately accountable.

This obligation included a duty to Michael directly yet goes beyond Michael; it is a responsibility that extends into eternity.

The eternal relation of the self before God is what brings Søren Kierkegaard to the topic of occupation in *Purity of Heart Is to Will One Thing*. The driving question of vocation, he asserts, is "whether your occupation is great or mean, is it of such a kind that you dare think of it together with the responsibility of eternity?"[3] He suggests a thought experiment. Imagine that someone you had deep respect for in their life visits you from beyond the grave. You find yourself "before" her or him in your present occupation. Do your commitments continue to be meaningful and worthwhile as you explain them to this visitor from eternity?[4] Consciousness of one's eternal responsibility before God

> does not demand that you withdraw from life, from an honorable calling, from a happy domestic life. On the contrary, it is precisely that consciousness which will sustain and clarify and illuminate what you are to do in the relations of life. You should not withdraw and sit brooding over your eternal accounting. To do this is to deserve something further to account for. You will more and more readily find time to perform your duty and your task, while concern over your eternal responsibility will hinder you from being "busy" and busily having a hand in everything possible—an activity that can best be called: time-wasting.[5]

Kierkegaard goes on to stress that eternal responsibility must be considered not only in the *end* or *result* of one's occupation but in the means that one uses to attain the end. "There is only one end: the genuine Good; and there is only one means: this, to be willing only to use those means which genuinely are good."[6] The perspective of eternity is a reminder that one's ethical responsibility is not measured after a particular result but in and through each aspect of one's occupation.

Viewing one's occupation from the perspective of the eternal inspires a "lightness" or a kind of distance in engaging in temporal affairs. It is no longer the demands or crises of the moment that determine meaning and success. Neither, as Kierkegaard observes, are the *results* of one's actions of paramount importance. This is not a utilitarian ethic of care. The demands of eternity weigh equally on the means as they do on the ends.

Kierkegaard presents a nuanced theological distance from which to view our calling. Each person's responsibility *before God* provides perspective from which to assess and question certain projects and pursuits. Within this distance lies a strange tension between the weight of ethical responsibility and a "lightness" regarding temporal affairs and immediate concerns. Rather than simply being detached or caught up in "eternal accounting," however, we can intimately engage in *lasting* vocational practices rather than the activities that make for short-term success. The light of eternity illuminates those areas where traps of busyness or an obsession with temporary success might otherwise catch us.

At the time, I would not have used Kierkegaard's words to describe my processing of Michael's death. In hindsight, though, it was my conviction that I invested fully in my time spent with Michael—despite his eventual decision to leave—that prepared me to process grief at his passing and frustration over the circumstances that led to his death. I understood my vocation in the context of the Christian tradition. It was not a calling only to Michael or to the particular service organization or system of which I was a part but a responsibility to God in light of eternity. This theological vantage point offered the perspective from which to recognize the constraints of the system of which I was a part without despairing that my calling was confined to or negated by these constraints.

The Call of Equality: The Neighbor before God

> It is easier to love humanity as a whole than to love one's neighbor.

Eric Hoffer[7]

The second aspect of a transcendent calling that provides perspective in Christian caregiving builds on the first. Just as the God-relation defines one's vocation, so the God-relation defines every other relationship. Every neighbor (or "near one") is similarly positioned before God and is defined by this eternal equality.[8] One human being cannot be considered of greater worth or value than another since each person's defining relation is their standing *before God*. This fundamental equality remains no matter one's station in life, profession, or range of abilities.

Defining human relationships by this transcendent relation is the only way to conceive true equality, according to Kierkegaard. Without an eternal criterion, one might judge other people by their similarity to or difference from oneself. For Kierkegaard, the neighbor becomes the category of equality, defined by each person's posture before God:

> The neighbor is every person, since on the basis of dissimilarity he is not your neighbor, nor on the basis of similarity to you in your dissimilarity from other people. He is your neighbor on the basis of equality with you before God, but unconditionally every person has this equality and has it unconditionally.[9]

In unconditional equality, the category of the neighbor, a "neighbor" also crucial to Luther's theology, becomes a subversive challenge to any ableism, racism, sexism, or other form of bigotry or prejudice.[10] Before God, "there is neither Jew nor Gentile, neither slave nor free, nor is there male and female."[11] In Kierkegaard's words, it is through this relation that the neighbor "is the absolutely true expression for human equality."[12]

An unwavering commitment to eternal human equality and dignity grants vocation the perspective from which to question one's place or one's domain when ethical integrity is at stake. The basis for this commitment is also crucial, as it must supersede one's immediate projects, duties, or other obligations—such as to one's institution, organization or to the state. Kierkegaard's articulation of our relation to our neighbors emphasizes each person's eternal responsibility and responsibility *for* others who are equally defined by their posture before the divine.

The Call of Neighbor-Love

Love your neighbor as yourself.

Matthew 22:39

The third aspect of a higher calling builds on the eternal equality of the neighbor to describe the ways in which *neighbor-love* transcends *preferential love*. It is natural for human beings to come to "prefer" some people over others. This may be because of shared interests, shared priorities, or shared time. When we come to know people well, preferential love often emerges. Jesus' command to love God and to love my neighbor as myself compels me beyond immediate preference to other *near ones*, those whom I do not initially prefer. This is love established by our shared position *before God*: "Love for the neighbor is . . . the eternal equality in loving, but the eternal equality is the opposite of preference."[13] The eternal equality of love calls us beyond the love of preference to *every other* neighbor.

Where preferential love is an intimate aspect of finding belonging in one's vocation, neighbor-love provides the caring commitment that draws each of us beyond our immediate preferences or inclinations. Preferential love *pulls* us toward another, whereas neighbor-love *pushes* us toward those whom we may not yet know. In preferential love, we are *called by* the human other; in neighbor-love, we are *called toward* our neighbors by the divine Other. The eternal equality of neighbor-love transcends immediate preferences to call us into the lives of others.

ADAM: THE JOURNEY OF PREFERENTIAL CARE

Henri Nouwen's *Adam* expresses feelings that many new caregivers experience when they first step into their role. Nouwen recalls being asked to support Adam as part of the L'Arche Daybreak community near Toronto. "I was aghast! I simply didn't think I could do this. 'What if he falls? How do I support him as he walks? What if I hurt him and he cannot even tell me? . . . So many things can go wrong. Besides, I don't know the man. I'm not a nurse."[14] There is a fear, a hesitation, an initial repulsion, even, to encounter Adam as a neighbor. Nouwen feels inadequate and unprepared.

The response Nouwen receives from experienced staff is reassuring. There will be plenty of time to feel comfortable. He will come to know the routine. Perhaps, most importantly, "you will get to know Adam and he will get to know you."[15] In the early days, Nouwen saw Adam as "someone who was *very* different from me."[16] Nouwen is constantly nervous about his role and his ability to support Adam. Why was he given this role? Why was he supporting a man with so many needs? The answer was always the same, "So you can get to know Adam."[17] Adam was limited in his communication, and Nouwen failed to understand how he could ever truly "get to know Adam." Nouwen constantly needed to call on others for help. His fellow workers always encouraged him, "Keep at it, Henri. . . . You're just getting to know him. Pretty soon you'll be an old hand! Pretty soon you'll love him." Nouwen could not imagine what it would mean to love someone like Adam.

One can imagine how the story goes: "Gradually, very gradually, things started to change."[18] As a professor whose life had been shaped by words and books, Nouwen had to get to know Adam in a new way. He began to meet

Adam in the time they shared together and in the silence of the rhythms of Adam's day. Nouwen recounts, "I began to talk to Adam.... It didn't seem to matter to me anymore that he could not respond in words. We were together, growing in friendship, and I was glad to be there. Before long Adam became my much trusted listener."[19] The remainder of the book explores the many things Nouwen learned about himself, his world, and his faith from the gift of his friendship with Adam. Most new support workers experience a transformation similar to Nouwen's, yet few go on to express it in the way that Nouwen was able to. Nouwen followed his calling to get to know Adam, yet it was not until he faced his fears that this friendship started to grow. What at first was only a commitment to get to know Adam became a sincere appreciation for and love for Adam. Nouwen developed a preferential love for Adam because of the time they had shared together.

Nouwen's encounter with Adam reveals how neighbor-love as a caring commitment, based on eternal equality *before God*, can lead to preferential love. This is not always the way relationships progress. Sometimes, the person to whom we provide care is not someone for whom we come to care. Love of neighbor (the call of God *to* love one another) often leads to preferential relationships, whereby we experience being called *by* the person whom we support. However, it does not always do so. In those instances where preferential love does not emerge, it is the love of neighbor that sustains ethical accountability as a higher calling to *every* other near one, including the person I have difficulty relating to or understanding.

CALLED TO REMAIN

Giving an Account: Jason

> I met Jason in gym class. Jason had Asperger's syndrome, one of the manifestations of autism syndrome disorder. He had no social awareness, no filter. He did all the worst things a person can do in a grade 9 gym class. He stared too long and stood too close. He said the wrong thing at the wrong time and always very loudly. He was far too free with his laughter and his tears. He assumed the friendship of all and raised no walls around his open heart. In a culture where the highest ambition was to go unnoticed, Jason was anathema. And so he became, of all the pariahs a high school contains, the most rejected.
>
> Our teacher made Jason my partner for the semester and so became the voice I had been waiting to hear. It was a call I neither wanted nor recognized, but I had just enough of Christ in me not to reject it outright.

As the semester passed that call grew steadily clearer within me. My relationship with Jason began to extend beyond the mandated eighty minutes
of gym class. I began to sit with him at lunch and join him in the library,
where he spent his breaks. Sitting with Jason, I learned the meaning of
loneliness, of isolation, of otherness. I also learned how easily those dark
spells can be broken by the simple, intentional presence of another human
being. A friendship formed between us that lasted beyond the end of the
semester, and he returned to the segregation of the special education classroom where he spent the rest of his time at school.

Jason introduced me to the rest of that class, a separate nation more
removed from the high school mainland than its most ostracized clique. As
the grades went by I spent more and more time among its inhabitants: kids
with Down syndrome and cerebral palsy, autism and acquired brain damage. I discovered the world of the Other, there outside the city walls, and
the great and unique beauty, the incredible joy and the courageously borne
grief that exists there. I saw the deep wounds that daily rejection causes and
how easily that pain could be eased by even the smallest acts of empathy. I
was welcomed in a way that I had never been welcomed before. I received
gifts I had not known I needed.[20]

Michael Bonikowsky, who shared the story above, describes himself as a
professional caregiver and an unprofessional stay-at-home dad. He gradu-
ated from high school, then went to the "big city" and studied at a Christian
university. He still did not feel as though he had found his "calling" and
was increasingly filled with anxiety about his purpose and direction. Eventually, a friend invited him to apply to work at an organization supporting
people with developmental disabilities. "Remembering the peculiar joys of
Jason's class and having exhausted all other options, I applied and was hired."
Michael goes on:

As soon as I walked through the door of the group home, I knew that
I had come home. It was brutal, exhausting work, full of heartache and
conflict and unanswered questions. But more than any of that, it was holy.
Here was my calling, unrecognized and ignored for so many years, now
ringing loud and clear through the secret places of my heart. This was a
place where I could serve and give of myself in the ways that I had longed
for. But more than that, and so unexpectedly, it was the place where I was
served and given to in a hundred necessary ways I hadn't known I needed.
We healed one another's hurts. It was then that I realized that my friendship with Jason was, in many ways, the best and truest part of my life. It was
the voice of God calling me home, to him and to my true self. [21]

Nouwen and Bonikowsky relay experiences of vocation that connect the transcendent call of God to being called *by* a person, or the people, with whom they provide care. Sometimes the call comes first through an unsettling *toward* another, and sometimes the call is first recognized in the presence *of* another. For Christian caregivers, though, this intertwined sense of being called *to* and being called *by* is by no means an isolated experience.[22] The profound realization sinks in that, as Nouwen describes, "you are not only you; others belong to you too."[23] It is in *moving toward* one another that what is initially received as a nebulous higher calling becomes real and particular. Our love for humanity "in general" becomes affection for people specifically. It is in *moving toward* one another that we experience belonging. This belonging must be held in tension with the transcendent call of God to our other neighbors. As we draw close to others, we realize our shared eternal equality before God. Working eight or more hours a day with the same people, professional support staff may spend just as much time with those receiving support as with their own families. We learn their joys and sorrows, and we become invested in their goals and dreams. We realize that we are not so different, after all. We come to know and love others as Henri came to know and love Adam, and as Michael came to know and love Jason.

THE BEAUTY AND DANGER OF PREFERENTIAL CARE

Preferential care carries real significance. It is love that has come to know and value *another*. We see something *in* the other that we appreciate, that we care for, that we prefer. Friendship is an example of this, frequently arising out of shared interests, hobbies, or activities. Family love also falls into this category, with shared experiences, DNA, and heritage. We are *like* them. Love for one's partner falls into this category as well. Kierkegaard writes, "Erotic love is undeniably life's most beautiful happiness and friendship the greatest temporal good!"[24] These are to be highly valued and not to be taken for granted. There is beauty in these moments of human connection with people with whom we experience natural love.

The challenge lies in the human inability or lack of desire to know everyone in this way. Each of us carries an inclination to love people who are similar to us, yet we struggle to love people we perceive to be radically dissimilar or "other." There are countless people we never get to know even to the extent that we discover what similarities might exist. In this way, each form of preferential love is a *temporary* good but fails to meet the demand of an *eternal* good. Note how, for Kierkegaard, erotic love is *life's* most beautiful happiness, and friendship is the greatest *temporal* good. One might recall here Kierkegaard's emphasis on our "eternal responsibility" before God. The question remains whether loving someone because we prefer them sufficiently meets this ethical demand.

The dark side of preferential love is its inability to encounter those beyond its "likeness." Those who live on the margins of society face stigma and prejudice that distance them from experiencing the preferential love of those around them. The love of neighbor, a love that is commanded and takes seriously the neighbor's eternal equality before God, is necessary for an ethical Christian perspective on calling. Indeed, even those whom we prefer—or whom we have once preferred—will fall out of favor at times. In those moments, it is neighbor-love that maintains our ethical relationship with them *regardless* of passing (temporal) preference.

The category of the neighbor is the "eternal equality" of encountering every other as *before God*. When central to a passionate sense of calling, neighbor-love opens caregivers to acknowledge that *every other* is worthy of love. For caregivers who become frustrated in their current obligations, the call of neighbor-love can provide a necessary corrective. Neighbor love is what draws us to others even when similarities are not initially evident. For Nouwen and Bonikowsky, this commitment opened them to draw close to Adam and Jason to discover the beauty from which then preferential care developed. For others, it may mean carrying on in dedicated support even when preferential love is an ever-elusive affection. Neighbor-love releases the pressure of feeling as though everyone we support needs to be an "Adam" or a "Jason." It describes the commitment we have toward one another as people who are equal *before God*.

TOWARD TRUE CARE

> True care is mutual care. If their only reward had been the small salary, their care would soon have become little more than human maintenance.
>
> **Henri Nouwen**[25]

As it relates to calling and vocation, preferential love for care partners—whether evident from first meeting or hard won, as it was for Nouwen—is a beautiful reality of finding *belonging* in direct support work. Nouwen's quote above emphasizes that reciprocity is a sustaining aspect of meaningful care provision. When there is no initial respect for people receiving care, or when depersonalization begins to occur because of compassion fatigue, care provision becomes nothing more than "human maintenance."[26]

The neighbor-love that Søren Kierkegaard emphasizes does not depend on, and will not always develop into, preferential love. However, the initial ethical demand of neighbor-love should always lead to an increased appreciation for the dignity of the person whom one *shall* love.

Perhaps the most pressing need for social service organizations is to attract and retain care professionals who view their work as more than the maintenance of human bodies. Care providers must be ethically committed to the people who receive support and who find themselves in vulnerable circumstances. Caring professionals must not only practice this ethical commitment with people toward whom they have a sense of attachment in the form of preferential love. There will be people, there will be days, and there will be periods of time during which caregivers feel more or less preference toward the people they serve. Even feeling a *high* degree of preferential love toward people who receive care, without a sense of perspective and ethical distance, can quickly lead to burnout and, in turn, depersonalization.

DISTANCE IN PROFESSIONAL SERVICES

The need for distance or flexibility in one's sense of calling is not unique to religious or Christian caregiving. In the words of one nurse:

> People that have a calling just are willing to take what the assignment brings. You know, you're willing to adjust. You're willing to go the ways it needs to be. And you don't get all uptight over that stuff. [Those who can't adjust] are the people that, you know, who get the ulcers, the people that are all up in a wad about stuff every day.[27]

What this nurse identifies is a kind of *flexibility* in one's perception of work as calling. Flexibility requires being able to make comparisons of one's present commitments and activities in light of other potential options. It requires a "degree of readiness to initiate change or to demonstrate plasticity in response to life events and circumstances."[28]

Flexibility, then, "allows individuals to adapt to or bounce back from setbacks and challenges, and even to engage the environment more proactively" and "allows individuals to account for the needs of others and use adaptive strategies to respond to workplace challenges and adversity."[29] Flexibility means that one is not tied too closely to a single set of ideas or overly invested in one way of doing things. Flexibility requires a sense of distance from the immediacy of one's work.

While research on vocational caregiving acknowledges the *behaviors* that help mitigate compassion fatigue, burnout, and depersonalization, it does not articulate a motivation or viewpoint from which these behaviors are likely to arise. Without a framework for ethical motivation, one cannot describe how caregivers *might arrive at* a well-balanced outlook on vocation. Adherence to particular tradition is required from which to approach the moral formation of caregivers. As this nurse has done, however, it is possible to explain what a healthy sense of calling "looks like" on a day-to-day basis. Flexibility is the behavior where support workers are "willing to adjust" rather than being "all up in a wad about stuff every day."

In Kierkegaard's writing, neighbor-love and preferential love are *postures* toward one another rooted in Christ's commands and human nature, respectively. These dispositions were formed from within the theological and anthropological principles of the Christian tradition. This is the same Christian tradition within which I found myself when I heard that Michael had died. Here, I found the resources with which to continue caring for others, even while mourning Michael's death. I was able to understand that I could not control the systems I found myself a part of, nor was this my responsibility. My calling was a transcendent call, a responsibility before God to care for my neighbors. It was a blessing to be close to Michael for a time. His life influenced my own, and I pray that my care had a positive impact on his life as well. Rather than experiencing devastation at his passing, my Christian faith and fundamental responsibility to God equipped me to give thanks for the time that we had together and resolve to continue to pour my efforts into supporting those who were then near. Had I not found myself within this tradition, I doubt that I would have had the resilience to continue in the way that I did.

Christian caregiving involves a "call *to*" serve people together with being "called *by*" the people one encounters. A responsibility that transcends one's immediate inclinations or temporal obligations is required to establish an ethical calling. To provide resilient care, both a sense of belonging and appropriate distance are necessary. Within the Christian tradition, Kierkegaard points to the call of eternity, the call of equality, and the call of neighbor-love as perspectives from which to draw this critical distance. In being defined not by our similarities or differences to one another but by a radical equality *before God*, the call of eternity helps to situate particular concerns and areas of calling within a larger perspective of Christ's command to *love our neighbors as ourselves*.

The question remains, though, whether these same possibilities for ethical distance can be found in professional caregiving guidelines and behavioral expectations. What resources for Christian caregiving might be discovered in contemporary professional ethics?

3

A Theological Story
The Limits of Professional Ethics

> Service systems can never be reformed so they will "produce" care.
> Care is the consenting commitment of citizens to one another. Care
> cannot be produced, privileged, managed, organized, administered
> or turned into a commodity. Care is the only thing a system cannot
> produce. Every institutional effort to replace the real thing is a
> counterfeit.
>
> **John McKnight**[1]

A challenge for care providers is that, as organizations, they are ill equipped
to endow employees with or sustain them in a deep sense of ethical motivation
from which to encounter the people whom they support. As observed in relation to the language of "flexibility," these organizations can identify behaviors that "work" yet fall short of articulating a framework out of which those
behaviors might arise. The ethical framework that *is* provided is superficially
"immanent." Certain behaviors are expected because they are expected. They
are expected because they lead to what are deemed satisfactory results. They
are expected because they align with what is considered to be a professional
approach. Higher moral principles such as motivation toward human flourishing, a spiritual calling, or moral imperatives are welcomed on an individual or personal level, yet they are not explicitly acknowledged because of
the absence of a defined anthropology. In short, as McKnight's quote above
powerfully conveys, service systems cannot care. People care. Some organizations do better than others in fostering environments where people can be

committed to one another in caregiving relationships. Others attempt to produce care by creating systems and structures that actually *prevent* caregivers from responding to their sense of calling.

We discover clues as to how organizations and institutions arrive at this place through the language of "profession." In many ways, "profession" traveled a path similar to that of "vocation." Just as vocation began as a religious concept to describe the work of full-time service of God, so "profession" specified the work of clergy. In the twelfth century, "profession" meant "vows taken upon entering a religious order." This finds its roots in the Latin *professionem*, meaning "public declaration."[2] Since that time though, "profession" has expanded to include any occupation with a governing body and a set of declared standards. In some cases, it simply refers to a "body of persons engaged in some occupation."[3]

There are subtle transitions that took place between clergy and the establishment of other professions, such as lawyers. As the Roman Empire fell, clergy began filling in for the crumbling legal system.[4] The adoption of professional commitments by specialized lawyers with no clerical obligations was a natural development. In time, physicians also became *professionals* according to such "professions" or declarations as the Hippocratic Oath. These transitions led to Irving Zola's observation that the red cloaks of bishops gave way to the black cloaks of lawyers and then to the white cloaks of doctors.[5]

While the impact of the religious roots of "vocation" has become ambiguous in many studies, the religious or spiritual connotation of "profession" has all but vanished. The original *profession* was made to God and one's Christian brothers and sisters in the form of religious vows. It has since become a generic *profession* to the public or clients that one has the skills and competencies associated with a claimed occupation. A governing body then verifies one's profession through a piece of paper, references, or compliance with a set of standards.

As is the case in much of Western moral language, the grammar of "call" and "profess" carries a lineage deeply indebted to Judeo-Christian ethical thought. Where these terms initially carried the weight of a rich tradition of thought and practice, they have become disconnected from the contexts that gave them meaning. Yet, to describe oneself as a "direct support professional," as an example, is precisely the way in which one makes an ethical claim about one's responsibilities to the people with intellectual disabilities whom one supports. To be a professional is to commit to a specific set of behaviors or *competencies* that one will display in every situation, with every person. In the field of developmental services, the process of professionalization attempts to provide a kind of *distance* or a perspective of ethical objectivity. This, in response to the *belonging* experienced in caregiving relationships with people with intellectual disabilities, is a way of articulating a commitment to following ethical standards with each person, regardless of the professional's personal relationship with that person.

Without recourse to underlying beliefs, professionalism expects care providers to display, consistently, certain behaviors in pursuit of immediate or particular ends. Behavior in this context has no higher *telos* that arises out of a full picture of human flourishing. The resultant message is that the intention or motivation of caregivers is secondary and perhaps even superfluous to the behaviors they demonstrate. Similarly, the *good* toward which professionals work either remains undefined or merely reflects current trends in social service theory. Agencies are left to determine what "human flourishing" looks like for the people that they support, often without being aware of how they are situated within a defined philosophical or faith tradition. Because of this, many simply adopt the values that are handed to them by the culture of which they are a part. Unfortunately, some of these values—such as an unmitigated emphasis on individualism, autonomy, and performance or achievement—contribute to the marginalization of the very people they claim to serve.

The language of *professional*, when denied its teleological roots and unhinged from its obligation to ethical motivation, adopts philosophical and ethical presuppositions from the field of bureaucratic management. Neglecting to address intention and motivation is not a value-neutral approach. Values continue to be formed within a tradition of which agencies may be entirely unaware—an emphasis on *effectiveness* that directly undermines a "higher call" of ethical responsibility that is formed in the Christian theological tradition.

One may question whether cultivating moral motivation and formation is even of interest to organizations providing support. If caregivers demonstrate the necessary behaviors, does it matter how they arrive there? One difficulty lies in the ongoing expectation that professionals act as moral agents *even when* the answers and behaviors are not clear or defined. In times of transformation and change, the ability to prioritize, question, and respond to moral dilemmas is a crucial element of ethical support provision. A robust anthropology is needed, which for Christian service organizations is a *theological* anthropology. Without this framework, people providing care are either set up for ethical failure or at least for unquestioned compliance to a semi-arbitrary set of behaviors. Morality without anthropology denies people providing care access to the depth of their humanity—the place from which moral decision making derives its significance and the place from which genuine care arises.

PROFESSIONALISM: PERSPECTIVE WITHOUT PURPOSE

Direct support professionals working with people with intellectual disabilities are caught between two realities. One is a commitment to an almost poetic ideal of completely person-directed supports provided by an unlimited employee base of qualified professionals. This is nothing more than a romantic fiction given the systemic and financial constraints of the field. The other is of a practical nature: limited funding and recruitment base, and the pressure of retention of competent employees.[6] To respond genuinely to existing needs means abandoning ideal support provision. The following account is not a personal one. It is an account of the professionalism of developmental services in Ontario, Canada.

Giving an Account: Ontario Developmental Services

A crisis had been looming for some time in Ontario: an inability to attract or retain enough employees to provide care with people with intellectual disabilities. Pay was meager, and it was not a job that many people knew of or thought of when choosing a career. The human resources strategy group for developmental services issued a cry for help: "Finding people with the skills and enthusiasm to work in developmental services is getting harder. High turnover and an aging workforce mean that we have to change how we promote and grow this field."[7]

One recommendation that came out of this work to figure out how to "promote and grow" the field was the establishment of core competencies—behaviors that could be expected of each person hired to provide care. This was an aspect of helping the position of direct support professional become a "career of choice" in Ontario, with the belief that increased professionalization would establish consistency and recognition of these positions.[8] The core competencies would become the basis for training, hiring, and career progression within the sector.[9]

The Hay Group was a "global management consulting firm" that was called upon to develop these core competencies.[10] The Hay Group conducted seventeen focus groups with 188 people to assess the characteristics, traits, and motives that distinguish top performers from average performers.[11] In their words, "Competencies enable top performers to demonstrate critical behaviours: more often, in more situations, and with better results."[12] The competencies they established for direct support professionals were advocating for others, collaboration, creative problem solving and decision making, fostering independence in others, initiative, interpersonal relations and respect, and resilience.

Rather than focusing primarily on skills and technical knowledge, the core competencies gave recruiters a framework from which to assess the behavioral aspects of direct support work. Core competencies referenced *how* a person approached their work related to elements such as social role, self-image, traits, and motives instead of merely acknowledging what skills and knowledge a person needed to possess.[13]

The core competencies identified by the Hay Group serve the purposes of professionalization by identifying a behavioral or ethical code for direct support professionals to follow. This ethical code helps to persuade potential stakeholders or clients that the care providers hired will act ethically and that the organization itself can be trusted.[14] The competencies are one way of "professing," or declaring, to people and families receiving services that there will be no preferential treatment—each person can expect to receive the same standard of care, as based on defined behaviors.

Along with the practical reality of a transient workforce, developmental services face an ongoing challenge to provide innovative, individualized services that are compatible with flexible models of living and working in communities.[15] In this rapidly changing environment, agencies need to adapt. Service providers must know that they can depend on direct support professionals to flexibly make day-to-day decisions that align with organizational values and ethics.

Behavior-based competencies, as standards of professional ethics, fail to provide the framework necessary for adaptive and transferable moral decision making. While competencies indicate what *were known to be* the most effective behaviors in direct support when they were established, they lack the underlying motivational and moral formation necessary to fully equip the direct support professional and their organization to respond in times of service transformation.

In other words, ethics as best conceived by professional standards in caregiving lack the deeper philosophical or theological background that make moral decision making possible.

From Descriptive to Prescriptive: The Limits of a Process

The Hay Group, devoted to "management consulting," had no direct ties to developmental services. It was commissioned to conduct extensive focus groups and interviews to assess key indicators of competencies of "outstanding performers" in developmental services. In doing so, they provided their best estimation of *effective* care provision a decade ago. Based on this process, the *descriptive* competencies then became the *prescriptive* basis for assessing incoming direct support professionals. These core competencies now form the basis of ongoing performance evaluations for direct support professionals.

Whether or not one is particularly interested in the development of care provision with people with intellectual disabilities in a province in Canada, there are several aspects here that demonstrate why a more robust framework for ethics is needed than professional competencies afford.

Measuring "right" behavior in a certain time and place, even if it is ethical behavior in that setting, may no longer be ethical behavior when the situation or context changes. The process of assessing the competencies occurred within a specific narrative—a particular story or account—at a certain point in the transformation of developmental services.

The following pages explore this narrative:

1. Alasdair MacIntyre's critique of the ethics of managerial effectiveness show that just because something is *effective* does not make it *right*. There must be an understanding of what is good for the person with an intellectual disability to know whether the ends toward which core competencies are effective are "good." In this sense, effectiveness is a moral fiction.
2. As a set of guidelines established in a particular time and place, core competencies cannot provide the ethical formation required for care providers to adapt to change. Knowing the good toward which one works is the start of ethical formation that will equip the person providing care to respond flexibly to new situations and services.

The nuances of these dynamics can then be observed within the tension between the competency of *fostering independence in others* and a commitment to *fostering belonging*. To be ethical, behaviors must be considered in the context of a transcendent standard or "higher calling." In Christian care provision, theological anthropology is needed.

EFFECTIVENESS AS MORAL FICTION

The core competencies are described as "characteristics that distinguish the top performers in a particular job from average performers."[16] The concept of effectiveness is implicit in the identification of *performance*. Some people perform better than others and so are considered more effective at their job.[17]

It should not come as a surprise that a "global management consulting firm" relies upon what Alasdair MacIntyre calls "the peculiarly managerial fiction embodied in the claim to possess systematic effectiveness in controlling certain aspects of social reality."[18] What does come as a surprise is that this claim is a *moral fiction*. MacIntyre observes that we do not generally doubt that effectiveness of managers, and we do not generally think of "effectiveness as a distinctively *moral* concept."[19]

MacIntyre's objection to bureaucratic management is that the managerial approach is to not question the "end" toward which one is working, only the most effective way to arrive there.[20] This perceived effectiveness is understood as good in itself, regardless of the end, *telos*, or goal toward which work is directed. Going further, implicit in managerial effectiveness is the expectation that managers *will not* challenge or question their ends. This is not seen as their role or responsibility. Effectiveness is portrayed as a form of excellence while simultaneously embodying *a-morality*. Managers are assessed based on their ability to produce results toward the end that has been passed down to them, rather than being treated as moral agents in themselves. In this way, effectiveness takes on the morality of whatever end it happens to be directed toward.[21]

Looking back at the process of establishing professional ethics based on core competencies, a critique of managerial effectiveness brings the inadequacies of the process to light. A team of global managerial consultants, deliberately selected to be "outside" the framework of caregiving, was selected to identify behaviors of top performers—the most effective workers. As a distinct entity from the organizations it serves, the Hay Group did not evaluate the ends toward which these organizations worked. These ends would be considered outside of its scope. Accepting these ends as given, the Hay Group arrived at a set of effective behaviors that organizations then adopt as a basis for hiring and performance. The moral fiction of *effectiveness* has subtly embedded itself, through this process, into the professionalization of care.

EFFECTIVE COMPETENCIES VS. ETHICAL FORMATION

Now, if the ends or aims of care provision continue to be *good* for the person with intellectual disabilities and for society in the years and decades that follow the initial assessment, then one might argue that effectiveness continues to be directed toward an ethical end. That is, so long as the particular set of behaviors identified in core competencies also continue to be the most effective way of achieving these ends.

However, even if one grants that these *were* the most effective behaviors toward the goals expressed at the time and were adequately assessed, a decade later the field has fundamentally shifted. The aims of agencies providing care are no longer what they were thanks, in part, to a strategic priority to transform developmental services.[22]

As services adapt and change, care professionals are expected to respond appropriately and ethically in dramatically shifting situations. Organizations must have the capacity to assess and critique professional behavioral standards toward organizational ends. One approach would be constantly to update expected behaviors. However, without a clear understanding of the ends toward which they work, professional behavior would always be one step behind the current state of the field. A far better direction is to equip caregivers to be reflective moral agents, able to assess the current situation and adopt behavior that best meets the ends toward which they work.

Rather than assuming the moral fiction of effectiveness, caregivers need to be equipped to question and critique current practices and actions in order to best support the flourishing of the people they serve. Service agencies themselves are not homogeneous. A "top performer" as defined by one organization may fail to work toward the established goals or conception of human flourishing espoused by another agency. When some organizations approach care from a faith-based perspective and others do not, these differences become especially pronounced.

The Story of Service

"The goods" of caregiving have been understood in diverse ways throughout history, as can be observed in developmental services. Various traditions have differing perspectives. Each organization, agency, or institution has its own account of what it is working toward, as understood in the context of its history and organizational culture. These are "stories of service," *accounts* that are provided to explain the objectives of care provision. Although these stories differ, themes emerge even in the specific context of intellectual disability:

- In the not-so-distant past, the narrative around ethical service provision argued that people with intellectual disabilities are best cared for outside of the public eye, in a place where they can all be "looked after" together.

- As problematic aspects of institutional living came to the fore, another account of service argued that group home settings were the best place to care for people with intellectual disabilities, places where they can engage with the community and see their family and friends in an environment of constant support.

- As time went on, the limiting nature of providing *too much care* became the emphasis. Agencies recognized that each person requires different forms of support and that group homes are not the ideal environment for everyone.

- In times of increasingly individualized supports and little to no increase in government funding, it can be difficult to know whether a goal of human flourishing or of financial sustainability is the primary objective, especially as human flourishing becomes increasingly difficult to define without a shared framework or tradition from which to understand anthropology. It becomes difficult to separate the aims of maximizing cost-benefit ratios from an emphasis on "independence" as a human good.

In the past decade or so, accounts of *flourishing* as a human good assert that people with intellectual disabilities need maximum self-determination, an abundance of choices, and the ability to make their own decisions in as close to an independent environment as possible. One might note the ways in which this view of flourishing dovetails neatly with capitalistic influences and power dynamics: *the human being as consumer*. In many ways, this is the account of the good in which core competencies arose. As such, the defined behavioral expectations of employees meet a real need for *fostering indepen- dence in others*, for example. In the Core Competency Dictionary, there is a strong emphasis on "enabling others to be self-sufficient," in reference both to staff and to people supported.

Goods can be understood in diverse ways. Goods that provide pleasure, for instance, or goods that serve a purpose. Goods particular to a practice or occupation. Goods for society and goods for each individual.[23] One begins to see how the goods of care provision become complex. It is one thing to deter- mine what the goods of the profession are in relation to society. Over time, much of modern Western society has come to recognize the value of involv- ing and including people with disabilities in communities, for example. This recognition has shaped the goods internal to the practice of direct support. Each developmental services organization, however, has its own history and organizational culture that further determines the priority it places on par- ticular goods. Faith-based organizations often arise out of a long tradition of what is "good" that, to a greater or lesser degree, influence the goods internal to their practice. One of the more recently acknowledged fundamental goods of care provision is that each person receiving support is to determine the role that particular good will play in her life and support.[24]

Depending on the tradition or history of an organization, it will draw to varying extents from societal principles around it, from particular models of understanding disability, or from varying religious or cultural traditions. Priorities will vary significantly, especially as methods of support become more diverse and innovative. There will be times when certain "accounts" of the good are incommensurable with or even contrary to others in the same field, or with those that came before them. It is in wrestling with these incommensurable accounts—embedded within specific times, places, and histories—that service providers will be best able to *give an account* of the ways that specific competencies and particular behaviors serve the ends, goals, or goods toward which they work. In turn, professionals who provide care can be equipped as moral agents to make decisions aligned with the ends defined by their agency.

Within the field of developmental services, this means that direct support professionals must be equipped with a robust and well-articulated under-standing of what *flourishing* looks like for people with intellectual disabilities from within their tradition, and service providers must recruit employees who are passionate about this vision.

Many service agencies, focused on the day-to-day concerns of running a business in times of transition and the practical challenges identified pre-viously, have not given significant thought to the goods toward which they work. These agencies have little to no defined framework or narrative from which people who provide care might form moral agency.[25] Without under-standing the goods inherent to their practice, caregivers are unable to situate their behavior within a higher purpose or vision. They cannot act as moral agents to determine *which* behaviors need to take precedence in any given situation. Without an anthropological vantage point, professional caregivers lack the perspective from which to critique current or past ways of providing support.

Fostering Independence and Loneliness

Over the past decade, people who receive services and support have increas-ingly self-directed those services. Their own goals and dreams have taken priority over the needs of organizations that provide care. Independence helps to reduce the risk of coercion and abuses of power by service agencies, and there is still much work to be done in the area of the core competency of *fostering independence in others*. However, increased independence does not necessarily translate into meaningful friendships. The available evidence suggests that up to half of persons with intellectual disabilities are chronically lonely, compared with around 15–30 percent of people in the general popu-lation.[26] People with intellectual disabilities still have few friends outside of family, other people who receive services, and paid professionals.[27]

Service providers desire for people to go beyond being "present" in society to build real and meaningful friendships in their community. What these providers miss, however, is intentional dialogue around how particular professional competencies might *lead to* or *detract from* this need. Again, the "goods" are received as given, rather than as questions to be wrestled with in the context of a larger anthropological picture.

Given the process of establishing core competencies, especially in light of rapidly transitioning service models, one must not rely upon an assessment of professional *effectiveness* to lead to the flourishing of people or to ethical results. Instead, service organizations must identify from their perspective the end toward which they work, *the good* as it relates to people who receive care and to society as a whole. With these driving values recognized, caregivers can be equipped as moral agents to make decisions and act ethically in response to the diverse and novel situations they encounter on a daily basis.

From Competencies to Virtues

Christian service organizations find themselves in a particular tradition with an account of goods for people that is not always going to align with that of their nonreligious contemporaries. As MacIntyre writes, "All morality is always to some degree tied to the socially local and particular."[28] In uncritically adopting professional ethical positions, these organizations merely realign with dominant cultural narratives and reinforce presuppositions that run counter to their stated beliefs.

Without an overall anthropological vision, expecting caregivers to make creative decisions and respond quickly in changing situations is to set them up for failure. Each tradition aims at some *good* embedded in the practices of the organization.[29] The question that arises is whether this good is one that is only internal to the particular focus of the organization or practice, or whether it is a good that is believed to be important for humanity as a whole.

A senior leader of the organization for which I work once told a story about a time when she was on vacation. She came across a family on the beach. The son in the family had autism and was having difficulty navigating the many environmental factors and new experiences on the beach. The mother was struggling to respond to the young man's behavior in the public eye. My colleague simply went over and, using the skills she had learned in years of direct support, helped the child and the mother regain their composure. In telling this story, she was not seeking to inspire core competencies or particular professional behaviors in her listeners. Instead, as she made clear, the priority of "fostering belonging," born out of organizational roots in the Christian faith, was one that she hoped influenced employees' lives beyond the scope of their expectations *as* employees.

Implications that the priorities of care provision go beyond the workplace are problematic from a professional standpoint. Do not these expectations or hopes for employees go beyond the scope of what can be asked? In

MacIntyrian terms, this leader was saying that the *good* of people who experience disabilities belonging to their community is one that is not only internal to the practice of professional care. Rather, from a Christian standpoint, she believes that society should *foster belonging* and that each person should adopt this as a priority in her or his own life. She is appealing to a value that transcends a particular practice.

Alasdair MacIntyre describes *virtues* as acquired human qualities, the possession and exercise of which enables us to achieve certain goods.[30] While this is true within the context of a certain practice, such as care provision, MacIntyre goes on to qualify that "no human quality is to be accounted a virtue unless it satisfies the conditions at each of the three stages."[31] These three stages include qualities necessary to achieve goods internal to practices, goods of a whole life, and the good for human beings (as defined within a particular ongoing social tradition).[32]

When a leader seeks to inspire behaviors or qualities that aspire to goods that go beyond the scope of one's work, these qualities are better understood as virtues than as competencies. These qualities contribute to the good of a whole life *and* enable the good for human beings as defined within the ongoing social tradition of Christian service, not only the goods internal to the practice of social work.

A Way Forward

If a faith-based service organization claims to be interested only in competencies as demonstrated while at work (professional ethics), this is incommensurable with an understanding of morality as found within the Christian tradition as the good for human beings. If, however, this same organization begins to monitor behaviors outside of paid employment, then it would overstep its reach as an employer.

The way to avoid incommensurability is not to abandon the Christian faith tradition or to violate employment and human rights legislation. Instead, faith-based organizations may monitor professional ethical obligations while inviting those who join the organization to investigate the underlying principles that motivate faith-based service. In other words, Christian care provision must inspire employees *qua human beings* to embrace their responsibility as moral agents who promote flourishing for all people. Precisely because care cannot be "manufactured" by service organizations, these agencies must foster an environment where caregivers are free to assess and make ethical decisions toward full human flourishing. In short, caregivers must be free to care. However, given diverse (and often unconscious or unstated) perspectives on what constitutes "human flourishing," each organization must also be clear on what it considers to be flourishing from within its tradition. It must then work to attract, equip, and inspire caregivers who resonate with this vision of flourishing.

Vocation and profession, conceived apart from "higher" moral obligations or an anthropological framework, fail to provide an adequate basis for ethical motivation or formation for Christian caregiving. The process of establishing professional core competencies reveals a lack of appreciation for the implicitly adopted value of effectiveness as a moral fiction. What is needed is an account of *the good* or human flourishing from within the Christian tradition. The doctrine of the *imago Dei* marks a theological anthropology of care that is profoundly human, deeply humble, and beautifully relational, for people of all abilities.

FROM VOCATION TO ENCOUNTER

Language of *calling* or *vocation* is inherent in the work of care provision, wherever there is a deep desire to go beyond task-oriented service. We recall Nouwen's words, "True care is mutual care. If their only reward had been the small salary, their care would soon have become little more than human maintenance."[33] When we encounter one another with care and vulnerability, our transcendent ethical obligation is inescapable. We are *called to* and *called by* one another. A delicate balance of belonging and distance of perspective is necessary to engage in resilient caregiving.

Professional ethical competency training fails to provide the foundation from which to establish human equality or a framework from which to empower moral action within ever-changing models of service. Professionalism relies on a moral fiction of managerial effectiveness and lacks a clear conception of the human *good* or *goods* toward which professional caregivers work.

In the Christian tradition, the call to care finds its basis in love for one's neighbor. Each neighbor is created profoundly equal *before God*. This "before God-ness" can be understood through the lens of what it means to be created in the *imago Dei*. As the coming pages explore, certain ways of interpreting this *imago* lend themselves to a rich and interpersonal model of Christian caregiving. Other interpretations may, instead, marginalize and exclude people—in particular, undermining the full flourishing of people with intellectual disabilities.

II

ENCOUNTERING MY NEIGHBOR

4

Traces of the Divine

The *imago Dei* and Human Ability

> So God created human beings in his own image.
>   In the image of God he created them;
>   male and female he created them.
>
> **Genesis 1:27, NLT**

These words, beginning Judeo-Christian Scripture, set the stage for Jewish, Christian, and Islamic theological anthropology. To appreciate an ethical posture in Christian caregiving, the *imago Dei* is unavoidable.

To understand the goods internal to the practice of care as discussed in the previous chapter, one must grapple with the ways in which the divine image shapes a Christian understanding of who we are as human beings. This theological anthropology frames what it means for human beings to *flourish*. Does the divine image apply equally to all people, independent of physical or intellectual ability? If people with disabilities are assumed to reflect this image to a lesser degree, this will have a significant negative impact on caregiving relationships. An interpretation of the *imago Dei* that fully includes people with disabilities is essential to ethical faith-based care provision.

It is as we encounter the divine image in one another that our love for God translates into love for people created in God's image. We begin to recognize that we have a fundamental moral responsibility to every other, and *no one* is exempt from reflecting this divine image.

THE IMAGE OF GOD AND DISABILITY

Through the millennia, Jewish and Christian theologians have sought to understand what it means for human beings to be created in the image of the divine. Several views have arisen out of their theological investigations. Here we briefly touch on the *substantive view*, the *functional view*, and the *relational view* of the *imago Dei* and their implications for people who experience disabilities.

1. The **substantive view** of the *imago Dei* claims that something within the physical, psychological, or spiritual makeup of the human being *resembles* God. Somehow, human beings have a unique capability to interact with the world in a way that no other animal can. Often, this resemblance is thought to be located in the intellect or will or the creativity that arises from these capacities. Hans Reinders refers to the substantive view when he observes that, through history, "the 'human being created in the image of God' was taken to mean that human beings are closer to God than any other living creature because of their capacity for reason and will."[1]

2. The **functional view** builds on the verse that follows the creation of humankind, "Then God blessed them and said, 'Be fruitful and multiply. Fill the earth and govern it. Reign over the fish in the sea, the birds in the sky, and all the animals that scurry along the ground.'"[2] Here, the *imago* is closely related to the context of *calling*. God's commission to Adam and Eve to "govern" and "reign over" creation is thought to be the uniquely divine mandate to human beings. The *imago Dei* is located in human dominion over and care for creation.

3. In the **relational view**, God's intimate inter-personality forms the basis of the *imago Dei*.[3] Karl Barth points to the odd Hebrew phrasing "Let *us* make man in *our image*" and the Trinitarian nature of the divine to posit that humanity is reflective of the "I-Thou" existence of God. In the Eastern Orthodox notion of *perichoresis*, between the Father and the Son, "there exists such a dynamic activity of exchange, a love which opens up through the Holy Spirit to the whole of creation."[4] The Holy Trinity serves as a model of love and belonging that defines what it means to be human beings created in the divine image.

Initially, the differences between these interpretations may appear to have little bearing on caregiving. On the contrary, perspectives on who *was* or *was not* created in God's image have had significant and occasionally catastrophic effects in human history. In *Mein Kampf*, Adolf Hitler claims the phrase "highest image of God" for Aryans. He declares, "Whoever would dare to raise a profane hand against the highest image of God among His creatures would sin against the bountiful Creator of this marvel and would collaborate in the expulsion from Paradise."[5] The Nazi ideology based in this belief of racial and able-bodied supremacy was instrumental in the Holocaust as well as Action T4, a "euthanasia program" to kill incurably ill, physically or mentally disabled, emotionally distraught, and elderly people.

At other times, the doctrine of the *imago Dei* has been an agent for positive social change. John Locke derived his principle of human equality in part from the belief that all human beings have been created—male and female—in the image of God.[6] This basis for equality became central to both the Declaration of Independence and the Universal Declaration of Human Rights. As an Enlightenment thinker, though, Locke's concept of the divine image is problematic. He maintains a substantive view, where human intellectual prowess and its resultant abilities relate people to the divine.[7] Stacy Clifford Simplican argues, "Understanding Locke's treatment of disability provides a new way to read his social contract as a *capacity contract* that bases political membership on a threshold level of capacity and excludes anyone who falls below."[8] Locke's substantive view of the *imago Dei* undercuts the very equality that he champions.

Potential dangers of the substantive view also arise in relation to the full, faithful flourishing of people with intellectual disabilities. Peter and Mary Birchenall write from the perspective of nursing. They starkly exemplify the mentality that excludes people with intellectual disabilities from meaningful spiritual engagement, writing that "people with a profound mental handicap [*sic*] possess a limited ability to reason at the complex level, and are therefore not able to work through any doubts and develop any sort of faith."[9] While many pastors or care providers would not state this principle directly, the belief that people with intellectual disabilities are not able to be faithful because of a "limited ability to reason" is one of the possible ramifications of associating the image of God with rationality.

Substantive views of the image of God open the possibility that certain people lack the substance of God's image. This is not a new challenge to full equality but one that has been handed down from Greek philosophical privileging of rationality through Christian theology. While ancient conceptions of reason do not align neatly with cognitive ability, it is difficult to avoid over-tones of intellectual ableism. Augustine writes, "Man's excellence consists in the fact that God made him to His own image by giving him an intellectual soul, which raises him above the beasts of the field."[10] Aristotle, Augustine, and Aquinas all carry forward a nuanced conception of the intellectual soul that convey full human status on those who might only have the *potential* for reason. However, their insights into what is "intellectual" have in popular understanding been reduced to modern rationality. One observes the implications of this misstep when Aquinas goes on to observe, "Therefore things without intellect are not made to God's image."[11] Because one can ultimately encounter God only by the gift of grace, and not through human intellect, the God-relation is not dependent upon human ability. Yet, because we can also obtain a kind of knowledge of God by use of the human intellect, Aquinas echoes Augustine that the image of God can be clouded "as almost to amount to nothing" in "those who have not the use of reason."[12]

Following this line of substantive thinking, pastors, community leaders, and Christian caregivers may consciously or unconsciously believe that people with intellectual disabilities cannot participate fully in a life of faith. Similarly, because full practice of virtues is presumed to require a degree of cognitive understanding—at least regarding one's intent—people with intellectual disabilities are considered to be ethical or virtuous only in a secondary or qualified way. Is it possible to work toward the full flourishing of people receiving care if they are not presumed to

a. fully reflect the image of God,
b. fully experience a life of faith or spirituality, and
c. fully engage in ethical or moral action?

While a *functional view* of the image of God can be nuanced and suggest ways of caring for the creation that do not require the same kind substantive ability, these views can also call into question the *imago Dei* of people with intellectual disabilities if they are not believed to be able to "rule" or shape the world around them in a tangible way. Disabilities that interfere with one's capacity to "have dominion" may be viewed as a distortion of the image of God.[13]

HUMILITY AND UNDERSTANDING

As someone invested in the lives of people with intellectual disabilities, I am tempted to respond with strong intellectual arguments against theological perspectives that call into question the divine image of people for whom I care. The irony of relying upon highly developed rational arguments for these purposes is not lost on me. It is for our own good, though, that the Bible does not provide solid ground from which to attack others' views on God's image polemically. Nowhere does Genesis explicitly say what it means to be created in the divine image. In the New Testament, the apostle Paul writes that Christ is the (visible) image of (the invisible) God.[14] Followers of Christ are then to be conformed into Christ's image.[15] Even in these contexts, there is little content given as to what precisely the authors mean by this "image" or whether they are using the *imago Dei* in the same sense as it was used in Genesis.[16] New Testament writers appear to be more intent on conveying the significance of this divine resemblance than in spelling out what it means.[17]

We must proceed from a posture of humility. From the outset, we are disposed to curiosity and reverence rather than confidence and conceit. The divine image is mysterious. It will be seen that this mystery forms our encounters with other human beings, ourselves, and God. Even in its biblical source, the *imago* is clothed in secrecy. Thomas Reynolds notes, "It is crucial to observe that the Genesis account never precisely defines what the image of God is. The language is elusive, perhaps deliberately so."[18] There is a way in which being made in God's image sets human beings in relation with God, and with one another as also created in God's image, without too narrowly indicating what is meant by this relation. Our hermeneutic posture when reading these accounts must be an opening toward the mystery at their heart, a mystery that calls us deeper into love for God and one another. Continuing, Reynolds suggests

> that to be created in the image of God means to be created for contributing to the world, open toward the call to love others. Three dimensions are implied: creativity with others, relation to others, and availability for others. The point to be stressed is that all people can be contributors, representing a range of both gifts and limitations.[19]

The concern to offer a response to theological views that undermine the full *imago Dei* of any people group, such as those with disabilities, is as much pastoral as theological. There is no debate as to whether God commands those created in God's image to *love one another*. Seeking to live into this love means questioning approaches or interpretations that may undermine the commitment to love one another. This is not to say that we recreate theology or biblical interpretation in order to make it easy to love one another. It does, however, mean that we must question the times that scholars have "filled in the gaps" with interpretations that lead to hierarchies of humanity. To read the image of God as a set of traits that defines certain human beings as *more* or *less* created in this image from the outset is theologically unjustifiable.

Built into the scriptural account, then, is a "check" on any application of reason that claims to have clear proof from the start. A relationality is introduced that lacks full rational clarity. Relation takes priority over reason, or, as Emil Brunner puts it, "Man's relation to God is not to be understood from the point of view of reason, but reason is to be understood from the point of view of man's relation to God."[20]

What, then, are the theological possibilities of the *imago Dei* that lead to flourishing for people with intellectual disabilities within communities of faith and in society? Both the substantive and functional views of the *imago Dei* tend toward a capacity framework: certain abilities inherent in the human being or the capacity to rule and adapt the world. While these capacities are not inherently wrong, to connect them too strongly to the *imago Dei* risks undermining Christ's command to *love one's neighbor* with a love built on a fundamental respect for human equality. There are aspects of the substantive and functional views that are also worth exploring, yet it is the relational view that carries the greatest potential as we seek full dignity and respect for people with disabilities.

THE RELATIONAL IMAGE: A HIGHER CALL TO LOVE

The language of calling and vocation continues to be haunted by transcendence, a sense of moral obligation to invest in and engage with one's work and the people whom one encounters. In most current professional caregiving environments, the moral motivation of people providing care goes unrecognized within a frame of immanence. That is, without consideration of the sacred, spiritual, or transcendent call of care provision, people providing care are not given space to explore the weight of ethical encounter in their interactions and relationships. Similarly, without a clear sense of the *telos* or good of human beings within care provision, caregivers are not equipped as reflective moral agents in making daily choices. Particularly within a context where services change rapidly, caregivers are left scrambling to respond to people's needs with ethical integrity.

In a context of Christian care, a relational view of the *imago Dei* may serve as a fruitful basis from which to articulate *the good* for people and, more specifically, for people with intellectual disabilities. Thomas Reynolds' tentative outline of what it means to be created in God's image touches upon the themes of "creativity with others, relation to others, and availability for others." Any of these aspects relates to *another*, or as he describes it, leaves us "open toward the call to love others."[21] If a sense of spiritual calling necessitates *belonging* to a place or domain, to other people, and with oneself, then discovering this belonging within a community of loving care would appear to be a good place to start.

The transcendent call to love others that flows through the caregiving experience finds its source in the divine image. The apostle John writes, "Whoever does not love does not know God, because God is love."[22] Kierkegaard reflects on this passage, "As Christianity's glad proclamation is contained in the doctrine about man's kinship with God, so its task is man's likeness to God. But God is love; therefore, *we can resemble God only in loving*."[23] Just as love flows between the Persons of the Godhead in the Christian conception of the Trinity, so this love can flow in human relationships with one another and the divine. The "task" of growing in likeness with God, then, can be understood as a "higher calling" that takes shape within a tradition of moral formation concerning how one grows to *resemble God in loving*.

Have we really come further than substantive or functional views of the *imago Dei* in this way? If people convey the divine image in relation to the degree of love they have for others, then this still may imply a hierarchy of "godlikeness." A crucial distinction is needed. In returning to the quest for moral *motivation* and *formation*, it becomes apparent that what is being considered here is the ways in which people are *formed* toward the good. It is, however, entirely possible to accept *an idea* of the good and have full knowledge of the path of moral formation without ever fully committing to it. One must also have an initial impetus to love, a motivation that causes one to commit to ethical action. The root of the motivation *to* love finds its moral significance elsewhere, outside of an intellectual framework of ethical theory or well-formed theology. Caregivers must reflect upon appropriate, ethical courses of action. They must also be motivated to act in this way. Being *called* in the sense of a fundamental ethical obligation always comes *before* understanding the moral framework from which to act. We are called to respond to the encounter with God and with one another, created in God's image.

In its commitment to an eternal equality between human beings, with all of their strengths, weaknesses, and limitations, the Christian moral framework and its view of human flourishing must draw its weight from the posture of being *before God* rather than similarities or differences between people. In other words, the weight of ethical Christian caregiving must arise from the *imago Dei*.

Emil Brunner distinguishes between the "formal" and "material" senses of the *imago Dei*.[24] Brunner's classification helps to make sense of both the Genesis account of being *created* in the image of God and the New Testament calling to be *formed* into the image of God.[25] Ethical motivation and obligation arise from the first, whereas Brunner's "material" *imago* more closely relates to what it means to be formed by love in encountering one another. Where the formal image serves as an intellectual boundary marker, describing limits on our understanding, the second inherits a *telos* that guides ethical action and moral formation, though one that still does not depend upon one's intellectual ability for its significance. Let's explore Brunner's distinctions in more detail.

The Formal Likeness (*Imago Dei*)

Emil Brunner builds on Kierkegaard's work before him when he emphasizes the posture of the human being *before God*.[26] This essential relationality is the inheritance of human beings whether they have chosen to follow the Christian God or not, whether they have chosen to follow in the way of love or not. The "formal likeness" involves a fundamental responsibility and responsiveness to one another *as* created in God's image.[27] The sense of responsibility lies at the heart of Emil Brunner's theology and anthropology:

> Thus the original nature of man [*sic*] is being in the love of God, the fulfilment of responsible being, the responsibility which comes not from a demand but from a gift, not from the law but from grace, from generous love, and itself consists in responsive love.[28]

Human responsibility to God and one another arises not because of any particular human attribute but because of God's *gift of generous love*. Jane Deland observes, "When God is imaged through the lens of disability it becomes clear that God's love and grace are not contingent on physical appearance or ability."[29] This *before God-ness* is our "original nature." It is not something that is dependent upon any particular ability or comprehension. It presents an *opportunity* to respond to a gift of love and grace rather than being a demand to "pay back" God's gift—something that no one could achieve, no matter her ability.

According to Kierkegaard, the appropriate response to this gift is to attempt to be like God not in a direct way but rather indirectly. If God is the giver of good gifts, being "like" God means to receive these gifts with gratitude and adoration. If God is the Creator, ruling over creation, then the appropriate response is not to attempt to rule oneself but to submit to God's creative reign:

> It is glorious to stand erect and have dominion, but most glorious of all is to be nothing in the act of adoration. To adore is not to exercise dominion, and yet adoration is precisely that wherein humanity is like

God. . . . Humanity and God are not to be likened in any direct way, but inversely: it is only when God has infinitely become the eternally omnipresent object of adoration, and humanity remains forever the one who adores that they are "alike."[30]

In *Receiving the Gift of Friendship*, Hans Reinders stresses that friendship and human dignity are received from God rather than based on the efforts or ability of any human person. As with Kierkegaard, one's "likeness" to God must be something that is not achieved or attained but only received. This *imago* is equally the inheritance of people with diverse characteristics, with and without disabilities. Reinders observes, "The fact that humans differ with respect to the abilities and capacities characteristic of the human species does nothing to qualify or alter this unique relationship. . . . God's love is unconditional and thus cannot be broken because of human limitations."[31] This inclusivity does not render the distinctive characteristics of human beings unimportant; rather, these distinctions do not bear on the status of being created in God's image. In speaking of the *formal* image of the divine, we find a basis for the transcendent call to respond to one another in love—the root of moral obligation. It is a responsibility that comes to bear on each one equally, as fully and completely bearing God's image. "In the loving eyes of God . . . there are no marginal cases of being 'human.'"[32]

Kierkegaard offers not only a critique of the substantive and functional views of the *imago*, which rely on inherent abilities or "dominion," but a foreshadowing of Brunner's theology of relationality and encounter. According to Brunner, the nature of the human being is "responsibility from love, in love, for love."[33] The love of God is a gift that has already been given, and this love bears the gift of *image* and *likeness*.

The nuances of this understanding of the formal *imago* from a relational perspective is perhaps best understood in contrast with that of Luther and Calvin. In Luther's view, "The essential thing about the human creature was not its rationality . . . nor its will . . . but its capacity for relatedness with God."[34] This "relatedness," though, requires active participation, or the image of God in the human being is lost. In his "Lectures on Genesis," Luther remarks, "I am afraid that since the loss of this image through sin we cannot understand it to any extent."[35]

John Calvin concurs. "At base, what is referred to is not something that we *have* or *had* but something that we *do* or *fail to do*. We *image* God if and insofar as we are oriented toward God. Rightly turned to God, we reflect the divine image, as mirrors reflect what they are turned toward." Calvin's insistence on action and response means that "the image of God is thus not a permanent endowment, any more than a given reflection in a mirror belongs to the mirror, but a quality that is dependent upon our posture vis-à-vis God."[36] Calvin writes:

> Since the image of God had been destroyed in us by the fall, we may judge from its restoration what it originally had been. Paul says that we are transformed into the image of God by the gospel. And, according to him, spiritual regeneration is nothing else than the restoration of the same image (Colossians 3:10, and Ephesians 4:23).[37]

Even certain conceptions of the relational view of the *imago Dei* can leave people outside of the divine image, or at least only questionably related to the divine. If relation to God depends, at least in part, upon the ability of the human being, then we may always question whether "this" or "that" person bears the image. There must be at least an aspect of the divine image that is received entirely as gift if all human beings are to be equal before God, fully worthy of love and respect regardless of human limitation.[38]

Moral Obligation and the Formal Likeness
Giving an Account: The Hospital

When Hiroshi was doing well, he was a joy to be with. The way he would walk, hands dancing in front of him, was lovely to witness. When he was in pain, though, we would know by the behavior we saw—the behavior we felt. The more we needed to dodge his advances to avoid being scratched or grabbed, the more pronounced we knew his pain to be. If this activity ended with him curled up on his bed, we knew it was time to go to the hospital. His gastrointestinal pain, due largely to the combination of medications he was on, was not being addressed by the other cocktail of drugs that he took to alleviate these symptoms.

I'll never forget one of my visits to the hospital where he was staying. As a new support worker with a large Christian organization serving people with intellectual disabilities, I had just arrived to spell-off a colleague. Hiroshi always required two-on-one support, in case crisis intervention was required to keep him or others safe. I learned upon stepping into the sterilized room that he had been sleeping or "knocked out" for several hours. Given the situation, my coworker thought it would be fine for her to step out to grab some food at the cafeteria.

I went to sit down in a less-than-comfortable chair in the corner of the room. Scanning the space as I had been trained to do, I recognized the danger immediately. The danger was that there were too many hazards to take in all at once. At Hiroshi's home, he had his own apartment, which balanced hospitality and his sense of identity with safety, to minimize potential harm to himself or others. Sharp objects were gone, and corners had been padded. His television was securely lodged behind plexiglass, and the speakers that played his favorite blends of classical or worship music were up high, beyond reach.

The hospital, though, was another story. While the austere decor might have conveyed a minimalist aesthetic, metallic medical instruments lay just beyond reach and sharp corners were everywhere. It was not the controlled environment in which we were used to working.

Glancing back to the hospital bed, sudden movement caught my attention. Eyes, wide with pain and confusion caught my own. Hiroshi was up and out of his hospital bed before I had time to comprehend the situation.

In that moment, the crisis intervention techniques I had learned were ineffective. They were designed for two people, to minimize the risk of injury. It immediately became a matter of personal safety, for both of us.

In hindsight, I suppose this was a decision point. Either I abandoned him to save myself and find my coworker, seeking help. Or I could do what I could to intervene, to prevent self-injury on his part. Intervening in this way, I risked serious injury to myself. Solo intervention broke policy and failed professional ethical standards for crisis support.

At the time, though, there was no real choice to make. There was no question in my mind where my obligation lay. As I caught his eyes, coming toward me, a mixture of pain and confusion haunting his expression, my own instinct to self-preservation was overridden by an encounter, by a *demand*. Before professional commitments, before learned techniques and rational calculations, I knew—if it can even be called knowing—what I had to do. As we danced in that hospital room, adrenaline coursing through our bodies, I had no idea what the outcome would be. I had no time to consider it. I was committed to preventing him from seriously injuring himself and, secondarily, to protecting myself.

The moments that followed are a blur in my mind. My colleague eventually returned, and we were able to use two-person techniques to support Hiroshi again. Miraculously, both he and I escaped unscathed. Since that day, Hiroshi has learned to use an iPad to communicate. His medications have been brought under control, and his scars on his face from self-injurious behavior have begun to disappear.

What I realize looking back on this account is that no amount of training or ethical study could have prepared me for this situation. No matter how much moral *formation* I had, the instinct to respond, to intervene, came down to moral *motivation*. Indeed, this motivation ran deeper than my instinct for self-preservation. It ran deeper than any conscious decision, any moral deliberation. Underneath an intellectual recognition that I needed to help him lay a fundamental obligation that compelled me to act in the way that I did.

It is this fundamental moral obligation to one another that we "gesture toward" when we describe other human beings as created in God's image. My obligation—my call—was to respond to Hiroshi as an image-bearer of the divine. What we hesitantly, haltingly, and imperfectly hint toward is that we experience a profound responsibility to other human beings that transcends (or undergirds) any rational calculation. In the way that we find ourselves *before God*, we likewise find ourselves *before* one another. We are "our brother's keepers."[39] We are *accountable* for the human being who stands before us before we might even begin to form an account. At any given moment, it may be demanded of us, "Where is your brother?" or, "Where is your sister?" The weight of any ethical account-ability is not established or justified within an intellectual tradition or moral framework, or by a professional organization or even a religion. This "grounding" runs deeper than comprehension to an *encounter* with another. However, it is not "another" in any quantifiable, objective, or descriptive sense. Emmanuel Levinas would describe this as an obligation to *the face of the other*.

Within what Emil Brunner describes as the "formal likeness" of the *imago Dei* lies perhaps its most significant ethical weight. In line with its mysterious references in Genesis, we speak of being created in God's image to point to—yet not articulate—the radical moral obligation that human beings have toward one another.[40] This is a responsibility that *comes before* any attempt to understand how ethical accountability works itself out in everyday life.

Emmanuel Levinas and the "Trace" of the Divine. It is Emmanuel Levinas, of Lithuanian Jewish descent, who perhaps captures the ethical weight of the *imago Dei* better than any other. However, Levinas never uses the phrase *imago Dei* or even the Jewish term, *tselem Elohim*.[41] In his essay "God and Philosophy," Levinas describes that "the God of the Bible signifies the beyond being, transcendence."[42] He goes on to say, "What the Bible puts above all comprehension would not have yet reached the threshold of intelligibility!"[43] At least to a certain extent, the *imago Dei* must remain incomprehensible because God as the infinite cannot truly be thought.[44]

Perhaps the "lack of information" about what qualities, competencies, capacities, or abilities are related to human godlikeness is precisely because even godlikeness transcends human comprehension. Levinas protests that if one were to take even the sense of "image" too literally, it would be as though human beings are a "living icon" of God.[45] Rather, the likeness and the source of our call to respond to the needs of our neighbor are found in what might be called a "trace" of the divine—something too indefinite to begin to comprehend.[46] It is for Levinas questionable as to whether our initial encounter with the divine image *in ourselves* is even conscious. It is more passive than this. Receiving the infinite is a kind of "awakening" or "wakefulness," and this receiving of the divine for Levinas is a kind of trauma.[47]

It is through this trauma that the initial demand, our initial obligation to an *other* is born. We encounter the sense of the other, the *holy*, as Levinas describes, "as desirable it is near but different."[48] I am thus awakened "to proximity," to a responsibility for the neighbor, to the point of substituting for him.[49] This encounter forms the heart of moral responsibility.

Through this trajectory, out of the initial wakefulness of the idea of the Infinite, Levinas outlines the birth of ethics from a Source that precedes even consciousness. "Ethics is not a moment of being; it is otherwise and better than being, the very possibility of the beyond."[50] God is prior to every neighbor and every encounter yet makes possible the ethical encounter *with* one's neighbor. The result is an obligation toward one's neighbor, that same obligation or "call to respond" that I encountered in the face of Hiroshi. "Before the neighbor I am summoned and do not appear,"[51] and it was this summoning to which I responded—to which I had no choice *but to* respond.

To be *before* one's neighbor as one created in God's image (in the sense of Brunner's formal likeness) is inextricably tied to what it means to be *before God*, before the One who calls from transcendence. Within the Judeo-Christian tradition, then, the ethical obligation or motivation of caregivers with those whom they serve happens before any core competency, before any ethical framework, and before any conception of moral formation.[52]

It is for this reason that I speak of *encountering* another. While "encounter" may convey a kind of informal meeting, its roots lie in the Latin *incontra*, or "in front of."[53] We find ourselves *before* each other as created in the divine image. In this encounter, we "face" one another, and the face of the other holds me accountable in a Levinasian sense. I recall that moment in the hospital, when the ethical summons (call) was received as a challenge to respond *at that moment* to the needs of my neighbor—the one who was near. "Encounter" also carries with it the connotation of being unexpected. Within the space of this encounter, then, we face an unexpected summons that we cannot quite place. Does an encounter with the other present us with a gift? With a demand? With a challenge and opposition? The mystery of these human interactions carries within it all these aspects and more. While we come to know more about some people (friends, family, loved ones) than others, this fundamental ethical posture of being *before* one another as being before an image of the divine is never lost; neither is it ever entirely subsumed or comprehended.

The primary root of moral obligation—of caregivers or in any human interaction—refers back to this mysterious aspect of the *imago Dei*, that which always precedes ethical description or calculation. Moral obligation is a *given*. Indeed, ethical accountability arises out of the *givenness* of the other before any formulated professional guidelines or legal responsibilities. This same *imago* is at the core of our own identity and relation with ourselves. We are formed in this image, formed together with others *in* this divine image. Our very awakening, our entry into consciousness, always already bears the trace of divine creation. In this way, creation in God's image is always ex nihilo, for we have no words or understanding that arises before this givenness. Similarly, the near one for whom I care is *given*, an encounter that I can never entirely explain or comprehend. My fundamental obligation, responsibility, and motivation likewise *appear* in the face of my neighbor. In Levinas' account of the face of the other and God as trace, we find a radical call to responsibility. This responsibility hints at Brunner's "formal image" of the divine, perhaps even exceeding Brunner's own initial intent to apply the *imago* to all human relations.[54]

The Material Likeness (*imitatio Dei*)

In the moment in the hospital room with Hiroshi, I was not lacking training in how to respond to his needs. While I could not use many of the crisis intervention techniques while I was alone, the necessary training for supportive posture and reducing the chance of injury to others and to me was useful. Where my initial obligation and motivation arose out of my encounter with my neighbor created in the divine image, the kinds of ethical *formation* I had received gave my motivation the tools it needed to act. Within the Christian tradition, the *imitatio Dei*, or as called by Brunner the *material* consideration of the *imago Dei*, serves as a framework by which to understand moral formation.

The distinction between the formal and the material for Brunner lies not in the relational nature of what it means to be a human being *before God* but in the way human beings respond *to* God. While all human beings bear God's image, to respond in love to this initial gift is to "live into" God's image as revealed in Christian Scripture in the person of Christ. In this way, according to Brunner, it is possible to lose the *material* sense of the *imago* by not responding to the call to love others.

The loss of the *Imago*, in the material sense, does not remove the responsibility from man [*sic*]; he still stands "before God," and he is still a human being. . . . The loss of the *Imago*, in the material sense, presupposes the *Imago* in the formal sense.[55]

Like Calvin, Brunner reflects upon the imagery of a mirror. Brunner does not relate the mirror analogy to the *imago Dei* as a whole but only to the material likeness of the *imago*. According to Brunner, while every human being retains the image of God formally, this image is perfected as the human being seeks to imitate Christ. Brunner considers 2 Corinthians 3:18, "But we all, with unveiled face reflecting as a mirror the glory of the Lord, are transformed into the same image from glory to glory." Christ is the "Primal Image" whom human beings are called to imitate. As Reynolds echoes, "The image of God both marks and fosters a human imitation of God: the *imago Dei* is an *imitatio Dei*."[56]

Rather than emphasizing the disobedience of humankind in this falling-away from the material image, Brunner restates that not responding to God is the turning away of a gift. In standing "against" God (the language of adversarial encounter is appropriate here), human responsibility to God is

not first of all a task but a gift; it is not first of all a demand but life; not law but grace. The word which—requiring an answer—calls man, is not a "Thou shalt" but a "Thou mayest be." The Primal Word is not an imperative, but it is the indicative of the Divine love; "Thou art Mine."[57]

Because "God is love," even fundamental moral obligation arises not only as a call and a demand but as an opportunity and gift. To be formed into the (material) divine image through love is God's grace to us. We recall the similarity here with Søren Kierkegaard's words in *Works of Love*: "As Christianity's glad proclamation is contained in the doctrine about man's kinship with God, so its task is man's likeness to God. But God is love; therefore *we can resemble God only in loving*."[58] One aspect of this likeness is the initial disposition of each person *before God*. Everyone is a human being in the formal sense of having been created by God and loved into existence by God. However, it is only in reflecting upon this creation (post-encounter) that we are able to put words to it, and only hesitantly and tentatively so. We find ourselves always already *responsible* to God.

To live into this formal image through the moral formation of being shaped by God's love is also open to all. Unlike substantive capacities for reason or functional abilities to rule, to love and to be loved is to live into the fullness of our humanity: "Thus, every human being can know everything about love, just as every human being can come to know that he, like every human being, is loved by God."[59]

The material *imago* finds its source only in the formal *imago*. Our response to God is only ever made possible by God. In other words, no human being can simply manufacture love in God's image. It flows from God's initial creative love:

> Just as the quiet lake originates deep down in hidden springs no eye has seen, so also does a person's love originate even more deeply in God's love. If there were no gushing spring at the bottom, if God were not love, then there would be neither the little lake, nor a human being's love.[60]

The mystery of God's love is like a hidden spring giving rise to the possibility of loving one another. It cannot be fully comprehended or understood, but we know that God is love *because* we can love one another—formed in the divine image. John writes, "We love because he first loved us."[61] Because God's love is a mystery to all, it is accessible to all. Intellectual ability will not get anyone closer to the love of God. This love is a gift freely given, a hidden spring that gives rise to love for one's neighbor.

Because Levinas and Brunner come from significantly different traditions and religious backgrounds, it is important to highlight a tension here between their projects. In Levinas, on the one hand, an encounter with the face of another human being reveals the glory of God as a kind of "first ethics." The encounter presents a summons, a demand. It is an ethical imperative that makes me response-able to the One whom I encounter. For Brunner, on the other hand, an encounter with God's love begins as a gift and not a demand. The call of neighbor-love flows from a *prior* love, a transcendent love that forms human persons to love in the way that he first loved us. According to Brunner, "[God] is the One who wills to have from me a free response to his love, a response which gives back love for love, a loving echo, a living reflection of His glory."[62]

In Kierkegaard, the human being "before God" in the *imago Dei* is both a demand *and* a gift. The "gushing spring" of God's initial love for humankind both makes possible human love and calls human beings *toward* each other in love. God's love is a gift that is always also a demand. The capacity of being response-able, however, is also made possible by this prior gift of God's love.

Where the formal *imago Dei*, as understood in light of Levinas' ethics, captures the root of human identity and moral obligation, the material image (being formed to resemble God in love) describes the path toward moral formation within the Christian tradition. In reflecting upon the life of Christ as God, it is possible to come to understand—although still only in part—a "higher calling" that we can begin to describe. Much of Christian ethical theory and discussion falls within this second category of the *imitatio Dei*: learning what it means to imitate God by seeking to understand through Scripture what it means to follow Christ. This is not to say that having a robust *understanding* of Christian moral formation is necessary to *love well*. Indeed, God's initial gift of love has made the fullness of a life of love possible. Peter puts it this way: "By his divine power, God has given us everything we need for living a godly life. We have received all of this by coming to know him, the one who called us to himself by means of his marvelous glory and excellence."[63] It is not the knowledge of Christian ethical systems that renders ethical action possible but knowing God in the sense of having encountered God and other human beings created in the divine image.

Love as the Fulfillment of the Imitatio Dei

The greatest ethical commandment, according to Christ, is to "love the Lord your God with all your heart and with all your soul and with all your mind" and to "love your neighbor as yourself."[64] John Swinton reminds us that these are not two distinct commands but belong together:

> The two are not separate linear or consecutive commands. They belong together, and in fact interpenetrate each other; we cannot truly understand one without the other. The basis of our love stems from our essential relationship with God.[65]

In the biblical account of Jesus Christ, we discover not only a human being created in the image of God but a God who became human to *love like us* and to show us the way to love one another. God's love is reflected in the ways Jesus cared for those who were considered "the least of these," sharing meals and his life with people looked upon as sinners.[66] In doing so, Jesus loved not imperfectly or hesitantly but fully and completely—perfect love.

> This is how God showed his love among us: He sent his one and only Son into the world that we might live through him. This is love: not that we loved God, but that he loved us and sent his Son as an atoning sacrifice for our sins. Dear friends, since God so loved us, we also ought to love one another.[67]

In being conformed to this image, to the likeness of Christ, human beings live out of the *imago Dei* and become fully alive.[68] The material conception of the *imago* reminds us that the *telos* or goal of humanity is not one of achievement, success, human ability, or intellectual prowess. Rather, human fulfillment of the divine image is found in the relational responsibility in which each person is her brother's keeper. The end toward which we work in human flourishing is not capital gain but faithful response to one another.[69] Brunner points to this responsibility to love one another as the "core of humanity":

> This means the discovery of a new idea of humanity, which does not find the distinctively human element, the core of humanity, in the creative or perceptive reason, but in community, as the fulfillment of responsibility.[70]

In loving one another, we discover who we are and who we are called to be. It is here, in relational responsibility, that we discover what it means to be created in the image of the divine.

BARRIERS TO RECOGNITION

The call to love and to care for others demands pastoral considerations of what it means to be created in God's image. Particularly, in acknowledging the profound mystery at the heart of the biblical text around what it "actually" means to be created in God's image, we are committed to an interpretation of the *imago Dei* that does not relegate people with disabilities to the status of second-class human beings.

Theoretical and theological analysis are limited in the exploration of ethical motivation and formation. Efforts to locate the *imago Dei* in "this" or "that" quality of being human inevitably fall short, failing to capture the fundamental moral obligation and formation that we seek. Emmanuel Levinas' *trace* of God in the face of the other provides a description that does not attempt to overarticulate a theory of ethical motivation. Rather, Levinas gestures toward the phenomenological experience of encountering one another as created in God's image. Perhaps Levinas has grasped better than Brunner what it means that "man's relation to God is not to be understood from the point of view of reason, but reason is to be understood from the point of view of man's relation to God."[71] The human-divine relation is not to be "understood" in any conventional sense of intellectual capacity. We *encounter* God's image in one another before we begin to recognize or become conscious of this divine trace.

Following his death and resurrection, Christ's interaction with his disciples on the road to Emmaus demonstrates the relation between encounter and recognition. As the two disciples were walking, "Jesus himself came up and walked along with them; but they were kept from recognizing him."[72] It is not until later, when Christ breaks bread with the disciples that their "eyes were opened and they recognized him."[73] Christ then disappears. Yet they had already *encountered* Jesus on the journey. "Were not our hearts burning within us while he talked with us on the road and opened the Scriptures to us?"[74] To recognize each other as created in God's image is a gift, a revelation that cannot be summoned by intellectual prowess. It always arrives *too late*, following our encounter with the divine image in one another.

As caregivers, either professionally or personally, the challenge is not whether we encounter one another as created in God's image. The challenge is that we face significant barriers in *recognizing* that it is God's image that we encounter in one another. The best we can do of our own accord is to confront the barriers that prevent us from recognizing these encounters.

In attempting to "think through" the *imago Dei* in our encounters with God and one another, we are confronted with mystery and revelation. Where mystery is that which we cannot describe because we cannot comprehend it, revelation is that which we understand only because we have *received* it. Neither can be conjured up by intellectual ability. Because of this, any account we can give of ethical obligation or formation in the Christian tradition only goes so far. In seeking to *give an account* of moral action and calling upon others to do the same, we tend to rely upon transparency myths that presume to know or understand more than we are able to. To leave space for the mystery of moral obligation as those created in the *imago Dei*, we must not only recognize the limited possibility of intelligible accounts of a Christian teleology of love but acknowledge the epistemic limits of our understanding. It is to these limits, to these barriers, and to these myths of transparency that we turn next.

5

Seeing You through Me

The Myth of the Transparent Other

My initial ethical responsibility to the person for whom I provide care precedes any rational strategy or intellectual conception of *the good*. With time, I may be able to put words this sense of obligation, as Emmanuel Levinas does with *the face of the other*. These words do not justify the initial posture, only give it expression. Moral obligation toward other human beings is a key function of the Judeo-Christian concept of the *imago Dei*, particularly in its "formal" sense.

The "material" *imago Dei*, on the other hand, may involve further ethical deliberation concerning what it means to imitate God, by resembling God in love. Christian moral teleology depends upon this development, yet it only becomes possible out of the source of love that originates with God and is revealed in Christ, the image of the invisible God.

Between our initial ethical encounters with one another and a developed theological anthropology of the *imitatio Dei*, we face significant challenges to loving one another fully as created in the divine image. Some of these challenges can be understood and confronted intellectually, while others require the patient practice of love with people who are different from us.

The following three chapters explore the human hubris that impulsively views others, us, and the divine as largely comprehendible or "transparent" to the intellect. This impulse undermines the very moral obligation that is the foundation to all ethical interaction. We rely on our own understanding rather than welcoming the mystery at the heart of the *imago Dei*. Our first experience of this hubris is in our interactions with one another, presuming that we "know" others in the same way we think we know ourselves. Then, we presume to know ourselves or to be able to "give an account" of our own lives from an ethical standpoint. Finally, we must confront the theological hubris that presumes that an intellectual understanding of God—the God in whose image we are created—is both possible and primary. The myth that others, myself, and the divine are somehow transparent to my understanding undermines my responsibility to every human being that I encounter.

ENCOUNTERING THE *IMAGO DEI* IN MY NEIGHBOR

> I never could understand how it's possible to love one's neighbors. In my opinion, it is precisely one's neighbors that one cannot possibly love. . . . It's still possible to love one's neighbor abstractly, and even occasionally from a distance, but hardly ever up close.
>
> **Ivan in Dostoevsky's *The Brothers Karamazov*[1]**

It's surprising how easy it is to love one another, to care for others well, and to act ethically toward human beings *in theory*. We recognize, intellectually, that all people are created in God's image. This does not necessarily mean that we treat them well in actuality. In *The Brothers Karamazov*, Ivan goes on to say, "If we're to come to love a man, the man himself should stay hidden, because as soon as he shows his face—love vanishes." It is one thing to acknowledge the need to promote flourishing by loving one's neighbor and quite another to love one's neighbor "up close" or *face to face*. If we desire to *resemble God in loving*, theologically recognizing that our neighbor is created in God's image does not go far enough. We must figure out how to love the person who is before us, encountering the divine image in *this person* who is near.

Adam and the Transparency Myth

Henri Nouwen wrote eloquently and passionately about his time with Adam. He grew to care for Adam despite his initial hesitations and fears about Adam's disability. In many respects, Nouwen's reflection about this time is a beautiful picture of the value and dignity of people with disabilities. Nouwen learned a great deal through his time with Adam. Adam became Nouwen's "trusted listener."[2] Because Adam could not articulate who he was in contrast to Nouwen's beliefs about him, however, Nouwen presumed that his views on Adam were correct. When people do not verbally oppose our views regarding who they are, it becomes easy to believe that our opinion is accurate. We are quick to assume that the other person has become "transparent" to us—that we can *see through* who they are and that our interpretation of their life story is valid. In intimate connections with another human beings, we can be tempted to stifle the mystery of their unique complexity by replacing it with the stories we tell about who they are. Rather than being opportunities for further discovery and exploration, we fill in gaps in knowledge with an account that we create.

Throughout the book, Henri Nouwen is quick to present Adam as "an image of the living Christ."[3] Any time someone's life story is defined in terms of what their life means *for someone else*, we have good reason to pause. In this instance, Adam becomes "an image of the living Christ" *for Nouwen*. Our assumptions can easily define others in terms of the role they play in our own lives. A striking example of this is when Nouwen observes, "A few times when I was so pushy he responded by having a grand mal seizure, and I realized that it was his way of saying, 'Slow down, Henri! Slow down.'"[4] Perhaps Adam's seizures *were* a clear indication that Nouwen needed to slow down. However, the significance of these seizures in Adam's life went far beyond being learning opportunities for Nouwen.

It is not that Nouwen failed to recognize our propensity to project assumptions onto the lives of others. Once, one of his friends came to visit and met Adam. Nouwen's friend had a very different perception of Adam and let Nouwen know in no uncertain terms that Nouwen was wasting his time with Adam and others with disabilities. His friend said things like, "Why should such people be allowed to take time and energy which should be given to solving the real problems humanity is facing?"[5] Nouwen reflects, "I quickly realized that he was not seeing the same Adam I was seeing. What my friend was saying made sense to him because he didn't really 'see' Adam."[6] Rather than allowing this experience to challenge his own assumption of "seeing" Adam, the implication here is that Nouwen *did* see the authentic Adam while his friend did not.

Perhaps Nouwen presumed that since his view could be considered favorable and complimentary to Adam it was satisfactory. While it is true that people with disabilities face degradation, stigma, and discrimination on a regular basis, an opposite but closely related tendency is to present disabled people as inspirational or exemplary. People with intellectual disabilities may be assigned only the best feelings or intentions in their lives and actions. They are denied the complexity of a full range of human emotions, and it is assumed that their intentions and interpretation of the world are readily *transparent* to the onlooker.

Giving an Account: Widening the Welcome

We met in the basement of a local Anglican church, a small group of church leaders and community organizers considering what it might look like to "widen the welcome" with people with intellectual disabilities and their families. Several people with lived experience had joined the conversation. Each person was unique and introduced important considerations and perspectives. One of the well-meaning church ladies turned to a seemingly confident woman with Down syndrome, "I'm just so inspired by you. Everything you do is so filled with joy." The response came without a second thought, "Actually, I hate my life." Appearances to the contrary, this was a woman who struggled with depression and had great difficulty finding joy in the life that she was living. Her prompt and truthful response disrupted the stereotype of people with Down syndrome living happy-go-lucky lives no matter what happens to them.

Witnessing this interaction challenged some of my own assumptions held to that point about people with intellectual disabilities. I never want to be in the seat of judgment that colors someone else's life with a single brushstroke. In the awkward silence that followed, I'm sure that the woman from the Anglican church learned the importance of always stopping to listen and learn how life is experienced by another.

When I read Nouwen's account of Adam, I see parallels with this interaction. Reading Adam's story, there is little to make us believe that he was capable of doing wrong in Nouwen's eyes. Actions that might have been called "sin" for others are is written off as "little vices" for Adam.[7] Nouwen's failure to complexify the account or acknowledge the mystery of Adam's life and experience is striking. In fact, Nouwen goes so far as to claim that when writing Adam's story, "I didn't embellish it. I didn't soften or sweeten it. I tried to write it as simply and directly as I could. I am a witness of Adam's truth."[8] In another place, "I am convinced that Adam was chosen to witness to God's love through his brokenness. To say this is not to romanticize him or to be sentimental. . . . He became a revelation of Christ among us."[9]

As we get to know others, we face the danger of thinking that we have arrived at a clear or transparent understanding of who they are. It is tempting to reduce someone else's life to their impact on us. Nouwen exclaims, "[Adam] simply lived and by his life invited me to receive his unique gift, wrapped in weakness but given for my transformation."[10] We can all too easily interpret the person in light of our own transformation, instead of remaining open to ongoing revelation about who the person is or how they experience the world. That Nouwen was changed by his encounter with Adam is beyond question. That Adam was *given for* Nouwen's transformation risks perpetuating the myth that people with disabilities are objects for inspiration and edification rather than complex, mysterious, and unique human beings created in the image of God. Nouwen has fallen prey to a transparency myth: that Adam could be "seen" for his "real self."

> As I grew closer to Adam, I came to experience his most beautiful heart as the gateway to his real self, to his person, his soul, and his spirit. His heart, so transparent, reflected for me not only his person but also the heart of the universe and, indeed, the heart of God.[11]

Hans Reinders concurs that Nouwen oversteps in this passage: "It appears that Nouwen's claim to the transparency of Adam's heart is simply saying too much. God's unconditional love means that he is with Adam, but how the relationship between them affects Adam's soul is something I don't think we should pretend to know."[12]

Nouwen's relationship with Adam left a lasting impact on his life and ministry. His books, shaped by this relationship, have gone on to affect thousands of readers around the world. One wonders how Adam might have told the story of his own life had he been able to do so. Nouwen's account leaves little room for the complexity of a full human life. As Reinders rightly observes, "Adam's heart is a mystery that only God knows."[13] Nouwen denies his readers the opportunity to appreciate the opacity of Adam's life and the dignity of Adam's secret story, one as mysterious as it is revelatory. Instead, we are asked to accept the story of Nouwen's transformation projected onto Adam's "heart."

The temptation to *give an account* of and for others is not Nouwen's challenge alone. As human beings, we search for answers to our questions and stories to make sense of our own lives and the lives of others. However, not everyone has the opportunity or the ability to speak out on their own behalf or has the audience to do so. In caregiving relationships, care providers often have greater mobility, access, capacity, and ability to provide these accounts than the people for whom they care. In the case of Nouwen, thousands have heard his account of Adam's life, and many readers will accept this account as unproblematic. Unfortunately, many of these readers will not have or embrace—for one reason or another—similar opportunities to get to know someone with an intellectual disability. Their primary interpretation of not only Adam but others with intellectual disabilities will be determined by Nouwen's retelling of Adam's story.

Life stories are inevitably reductionistic. Whether these accounts are given by others or are stories we tell about ourselves, they never fully capture the mysterious complexity of people created in the *imago Dei*. Often, as in the case of Adam, these narratives fail to depict the person as a moral agent demonstrating the full range of sin and virtue. Stories in general tend to portray people as villains or saviors, hardly ever as opaque and ambiguous compositions of the two. Tragically, people with intellectual disabilities in particular may be perceived as "amoral," incapable of ethical action and responsibility. This denial of fundamental ethical capacity presumes a great deal not only about someone's intellectual ability but about the relation between reason and morality. Myths of transparency, and the implicit assumption that intellectual clarity is a key component of moral action, wield a tyrannical hold over the stories that we tell. They expect accounts to be given in black and white rather than grappling with the opacity and ambiguity inherent in the human experience. The result is often a watered-down depiction of a human being instead of stories that reflect the complex mystery of the divine image.

It is the temptation to reduce the lives of others to simple stories that often prevents us from getting to know others in the first place. Once we believe we have successfully understood or even categorized another human being, she may not be perceived as worth the effort to get to know. The accounts we give can limit the possibilities of getting to know and be known by others.

Myths of transparency, reflected in the accounts we give, shape not only our stories but our experience of others. Presuppositions that we *know* or *understand* people can reinforce instinctual rejection of people who experience the world differently.

If we are to encounter one another as people created mysteriously in the image of God, it is crucial to question these myths of transparency in order to be open to the experience of others. The journey of learning to *resemble God in loving* means putting preconceptions aside. The Christian doctrine of the incarnation, God's *enfleshment* in the vulnerable person of Jesus Christ, is a powerful witness that people are not always as they first appear. The "Word became flesh" so that embodied human beings might come not only to love the divine but to love human beings created in the divine image.

WORD BECOME FLESH: EMBODIMENT AND ITS DISCONTENTS

> Seeing is the most astonishing of our natural powers. It receives the light, the first of all that is created, and as the light does it conquers darkness and chaos. It creates for us an ordered world, things distinguished from each other and from us. Seeing shows us their unique countenance and the larger whole to which they belong. Wherever we see, a piece of the original chaos is transformed into creation. We distinguish, we recognize, we give a name, we know. "I have seen"—that means in Greek "I know."
>
> **Paul Tillich**[14]

Writers often use sight as a metaphor for understanding and light for revelation or truth. These metaphors permeate Western thought, particularly through the Enlightenment but tracing back through ancient Greek philosophy. We think, for instance, of the allegory of the cave where Plato equates the light of the sun with the revelation of truth, in contrast to the shadows on the wall. It is important to note the problematic nature of metaphors of sight from a disability perspective. They generally do a disservice to people who are blind or visually impaired, subconsciously associating loss of sight with a lack of intelligence. These metaphors are so ingrained in common speech, however, that we must address the ways that they are used in order to address perceptions of cognition.

Vision and light mirror cognitive processes in various ways. As our understanding of the mechanism of sight has evolved, then, so has our perception of how we relate to truth. Gavin Frances writes in *Adventures in Human Being*, "Ancient Greek opinion was that vision was possible because of a divine fire in the eye—the lens was a kind of transmitter that beamed energy into the world."[15] Plato held this theory, yet Aristotle began to question it. Why, then, could we not see in the dark? English philosopher Roger Bacon attempted a compromise between the ancient and modern understandings: "The soul reaches out from the lens in a projection which 'ennobles' our environment, but that environment projects itself back into the eyes."[16]

Through the work of astronomers and scientists such as Johannes Kepler and Isaac Newton, we came "to see" objects of sight primarily as the work of light and physical objects outside of ourselves. While this classical understanding was considered scientifically accurate, it remained to be determined whether this understanding was helpful when transferred to metaphors of cognition and consciousness. Recent theories of consciousness lead us to believe that human beings are "prediction machines": our projections, more than our physical environment, determine how we experience our world. Anil K. Seth, professor of cognitive and computational neuroscience at the University of Sussex, writes, "People consciously see what they expect, rather than what violates their expectations."[17] In other words, signals that we receive from the outside world consist primarily of mistakes in our predictions, rather than what is actually there. Most conscious experience follows a predictive path, accepting visual cues as confirmation of that which has been cognitively projected or anticipated. Seth continues, "A number of experiments are now indicating that consciousness depends more on *perceptual predictions*, than on *prediction errors*."[18]

Why are the metaphors we use and their relation to scientific understanding important? Because as we encounter one another, the temptation is to believe that the stories we develop and the accounts we give are primarily *received* from outside of ourselves. However, the way we present our encounters with one another is actually more closely related to ancient understandings of sight and contemporary research on consciousness than to classical theories of perception. Our knowledge of others involves more *projection* than it does *observation*. Our already established predictions of *who* and *what* people are or are not outweigh our openness and ability to listen to and learn from others. Put differently: we regularly fail to recognize that we encounter the image of God in one another because of our own cognitive presuppositions.

The Power of Projection

> The beginning of this love is the will to let those we love be perfectly themselves, the resolution not to twist them to fit our own image. If in loving them we do not love what they are, but only their potential likeness to ourselves, then we do not love them: we only love the reflection of ourselves we find in them.
>
> **Thomas Merton**[19]

Embodied encounters involve a strange crossover of both sides of the metaphor of sight. As researchers of political campaigns have discovered, our beliefs about a person's character are closely tied to our initial visual impression of them. It only takes a tenth of a second to form a first impression about a stranger's character from their face. Longer exposures do not significantly change these initial impressions, though longer exposures may boost confidence in our first judgment.[20] How often, then, might our embodied reactions to others dismiss meaningful encounters before they have even begun—based on a glance as brief as a tenth of a second?

Flannery O'Connor was an American writer who delved deep into the subconscious prejudices of the society that surrounded her. She brought these prejudices "to light" and illustrated them in her work, painting caricatures of people as they were seen and then subverting the often racist, sexist, or ableist projections of her day. O'Connor was once invited to write an introduction to a story about a real girl named Mary Ann Long, whose face had been disfigured by cancer. The growth of a tumor led to "blood transfusions, radium, X-rays, and the removal to one of her eyes, but the tumor continued to grow."[21] Driven by an instinctual repulsion to a photograph of the girl, O'Connor initially rejected a request to write about Mary Ann. O'Connor later changed her mind after an extended time with the photo, wrestling through her initial response and preconceptions. This encounter with Mary

Ann, who only lived until the age of twelve, profoundly influenced O'Connor's writing. She later remarks that "the Mary Ann piece" is something that future readers would need to understand to comment on her work.[22] Timothy Basselin reflects:

> To accept what we perceive as good to be from God is a simple matter. To be able to look into the face of Mary Ann and see a face "full of promise," a face that is fully given and not half-taken or half-full of promise, is entirely different.[23]

Throughout the stories that follow, O'Connor wrestles with the tension of "the grotesque."[24] She writes in reflection, "Few have stared at [the good] long enough to accept the fact that its face too is grotesque, that in us the good is something under construction."[25] Where human beings instinctively fear or reject that which appears grotesque, O'Connor found deep meaning in wrestling through her tendency to dismiss others based on appearance. In each one of us, the good is "under construction," no matter how hard we might work to disguise our vulnerabilities and limitations.[26]

O'Connor effectively problematizes the myth of the transparent other. Her characters are anything but transparent to themselves or others: they are mysterious and complex. In a world where the reason for learning was presumed to be to *eliminate* mystery, O'Connor worked to make mystery real and present in her writing.[27] In the short story "Revelation," for instance, Mrs. Turpin's perception of who would enter heaven first is called into question. It is not the "God-lovin' country folk" who rise to heaven first but "battalions of freaks and lunatics shouting and clapping and leaping like frogs."[28] The world is much more mysterious than Mrs. Turpin's prejudice makes space for, and those Mrs. Turpin perceives as *grotesque* are those from whom she has the most to learn. O'Connor's project is profoundly theological. According to Basselin, "O'Connor wants us to look into the face of the grotesque and recognize Christ on the cross as the ultimate good."[29] In the mystery of Christ's suffering on the cross, we begin to encounter the captivating mystery at the heart of the human experience. His suffering was grotesque, just as it was grotesque that the Son of God would suffer in the first place, and yet God choosing to work in the world in this way gives meaning and significance to those experiences and embodied realities that might otherwise be deemed "grotesque."

O'Connor's stories carry richness and depth born out of a life wrestling with disability and suffering. Our own projections onto the embodiment of others are stories, too. Too often we tell ourselves stories about others based upon initial perceptions of who they are, based on first impressions. We give accounts of others not out of long-suffering relationships of knowing and loving but based on momentary glances or brief encounters. We spin a fictional tale out of a reaction of fear—be it fear of what it might be like to be similarly embodied, fear of not being able to connect through difference, or fear of encountering our own vulnerabilities. Just as Flannery O'Connor problematizes easy transparency in her literature, so must we problematize this easy transparency in the stories we tell ourselves about those whom we meet. In doing so, we begin *to see* that the grotesque lies not in the embodiment of another but in our fear. It is by confronting the grotesque fears and reactions *in ourselves* that we may begin to see the beauty in those around us and perhaps even experience the beauty of friendship.

Entering into the experience of caregiving, working in direct support with people with intellectual disabilities, I was confronted with my own perceptions of people based on my initial encounters with them. Their stories may not be "grotesque" in the same way Flannery O'Connor experienced the photo of Mary Ann Long, yet each person has their peculiarities and unique qualities that I could be quick to judge as "other." The ethical approach challenges these assumptions—the stories I tell myself about others. I must embrace the good, in me, as a work in progress as well. Even my tendency to reduce others to my perception of them is a work in progress.

Research bears out that an ugly trail of isolation and loneliness follows in the wake of a society unable to recognize its grotesque presuppositions. Available evidence suggests that up to half of persons with an intellectual disability are chronically lonely, compared with 15–30 percent of people in the general population.[30] We have come a long way in people with intellectual disabilities being present in the community. Unfortunately, while presence is a good start, it does not necessarily mean deep social connection or friendship. Research has found "that people with intellectual and developmental disabilities have few friends and mostly they name other disability service users, staff, and family members as their friends."[31] Friendship is an invaluable aspect of our embodied experience as human beings, yet people with intellectual disabilities are at increased risk of being marginalized and excluded. Tragically, the opportunities for people with intellectual disabilities to form deep and meaningful connections are often abandoned before the person has the opportunity to be known, simply based on misperception and mis-projection. When working direct support, I experienced this firsthand as I saw gawking onlookers gaze at people I support as we walked together. Little did these onlookers know that the possibility of meaningful friendship existed if only they were to start with "Hello!"

The Divine Grotesque

> He had no form or majesty that we should look at him,
>   and no beauty that we should desire him.
> He was despised and rejected by men . . .
> As one from whom men hide their faces
>   he was despised, and we esteemed him not.

Isaiah 53:2-3, ESV

"The Real Face of Jesus" appeared in *Popular Mechanics* in January 2015. In this article, Mike Fillion reports from the field of forensic anthropology how British scientists, assisted by Israeli archaeologists, roughly reconstructed what Jesus' physical appearance may have been.[32] The face that gazes out from the page is not like many, if any, depictions of the Son of God found in Western art. It is somewhat unremarkable, although decidedly Jewish and Middle Eastern. The eyes are perhaps curious or astonished more than stately and wise. The mouth neither smiles with profound and endless love nor is pursed as though set to take on the world. It is a face that has no beauty that we should desire it, no form or majesty that would cause us to take a second look. It is grotesque not in the sense of being remarkable but in its very *unremarkability*.

Studies in first impressions reveal that that people's initial, instinctual reaction to someone else's physical appearance dramatically shapes their judgment of that person from then on. In "The Look of a Winner" in *Scientific American*, the authors highlight a growing body of research indicating that "voters seem to be heavily influenced by a candidate's appearance, and in particular the kinds of personality traits that a politician's face projects."[33] Even children, to a remarkable extent, can predict the outcome of significant political competitions based merely on the physical appearance of the candidates.

Judging by the height of his contemporaries, there is a high probability that Jesus Christ was close to 5 feet 1—by no means a tall and stately figure by modern Western standards.[34] An article in the *Leadership Quarterly* indicates that height also helps political candidates to succeed. "Candidates that were taller than their opponents received more popular votes, although they were not significantly more likely to win the actual election. Taller presidents were also more likely to be reelected. Also, presidents were, on average, much taller than men from the same birth cohort."[35]

We cannot predict with certainty the appearance of Jesus Christ of Nazareth. However, based on the prophecy of Isaiah, together with forensic anthropology and archaeology, we can be confident that Christ would not have resembled a leader that the modern Western world would follow based on instinctual impressions alone. It would not be the first time that God has subverted notions of normalcy when choosing an earthly representative. Consider David's unremarkable beginnings as the youngest son of Jesse, a shepherd. Upon surveying Jesse's eldest son, the Lord says to Samuel:

> "Do not look on his appearance or on the height of his stature, because I have rejected him. For the LORD sees not as man sees: man looks on the outward appearance, but the LORD looks on the heart."[36]

Samuel comes face to face with the complex interplay between heart and height, between spirit and spectacle, between human eyes and divine perception.

Jesus Christ is the image of God in Brunner's "material" sense. He is the "second Adam," in whom Christians find the pattern of true humanity, the example of loving God and loving one's neighbor. Despite being the model for humanity, John the apostle writes succinctly, "He was in the world and though the world was made through him, the world did not recognize him."[37] In paying attention to the particular ways in which we fail to recognize the image of God in Christ, we may begin to understand the reasons why we similarly fail to recognize that we have encountered the image of God in people for whom we care, including people with intellectual disabilities.

Søren Kierkegaard pays attention to the unrecognizability of Christ on earth. In Christ, Kierkegaard observes, God has gone *incognito*: "And thus it is unrecognizability, the absolute unrecognizability, when one is God, then to become an individual human being."[38] There is a way in which being an individual human being is the "greatest possible distance, the infinitely qualitative distance, from being God, and therefore it is the most profound incognito."[39]

The unrecognizability of Christ plays a particular role in Kierkegaard's theology. This "God-man" is a "sign of contradiction," and, as such, is not comprehensible by the intellect. "Immediately, [the God-man] is an individual human being, just like others, a lowly, unimpressive human being, but now comes the contradiction—that *he* is God."[40] In being an "offense" to the intellect, the incarnation as a critical tenet of Christianity can only be an object of faith.[41] Just as intellectual humility is necessary in appreciating the *imago Dei*, so intellectual humility for Kierkegaard is essential to encounter Christ through faith. To believe that we have transparently comprehended Christ by our intellectual prowess is simultaneously to reject faith in Christ as the God-man.

How might that which is beautiful, spiritually, be bound up in that which might be considered "ugly" or "grotesque" physically? How might our prejudiced reactions to other peoples' experiences of embodiment hinder or prevent an encounter with the divine? Perhaps in the example of Christ—from whom we "hide our faces"—we learn that at times our instinctual responses, and our unquestioned acceptance of those first impressions, keep us from those relationships wherein we might find the greatest revelation and transformation.

The Command to Love

Christ experienced firsthand the tragic impact of instinctual prejudice based on physical appearance and public ridicule through his suffering on the cross. When human beings merely perceive, judge, and move on, first impressions and the encounters that follow serve only to reinforce existing prejudice. This "prejudging" will at times work in favor of the person encountered, as when their leadership qualities are upheld simply based on their height or gender. More often, prejudice condemns those with bodies that fall outside of the "norm" to isolation and, at times, ridicule.

We return to Kierkegaard's questioning of *preferential love*. When love is based on one's similarity to the one who is loved it seems effortless and natural. However, for Kierkegaard, it does not yet qualify as Christian love. Preferential love is an extension of self-love: "Self-love and passionate preferential love are essentially the same."[42] In this way, following first impressions of those with whom one has an immediate affinity only reinforces one's initial opinion.

To embody true Christian love, Kierkegaard maintains that there must be something that pushes us beyond an initial love based on preference. There must be a divine command to love those from whom we are different. This command is found in the Great Commandment, to *love our neighbor as ourselves*.[43] Whereas preferential love chooses the one to love, Christian love "teaches us to love all people, unconditionally all."[44]

Outside-in: Toward the Inward Grotesque

> Approved attributes and their relation to face make every man his own jailer; this is a fundamental social constraint even though each man may like his cell.
>
> **Erving Goffman**[45]

Christ does not command that each person present themselves as "lovable" to be loved by God and others. Instead, the command is to love God and one's neighbor, with no indication that the one who is loved must change into one who is considered to be beautiful or lovable. Our outward appearances, including "approved attributes and their relation to face," are (for the most part) fundamental social constraints. It is difficult, or at least expensive, to alter the way we are interpreted upon a first impression.

Following the command to love God and to love one's neighbor, Christ is asked, "Who is my neighbor?"[46] In other words, "Am I to love those who live in my immediate community, those who resemble me or think like me, those whom I prefer?" The example Christ gives of neighborly love "comes across with disorienting clarity."[47] Unexpectedly, Jesus turns the question around to demonstrate what it means to *be* a neighbor to others. Not only this, but it is "the half-breed heretic, the Samaritan, who offers himself and shows mercy."[48] The example of Christ subverts the cult of normalcy rather than working within it. Thomas Reynolds argues that Jesus has

> turned the question around. It is not who our neighbor is that matters—that is, who has prestige, who believes the right things, who has the body capital and thus deserves love and care. It is who we are as neighbors that matters, that is, how we act toward others set before us in their vulnerability as human beings.[49]

The love of Christ, the love that defines what it means to live into the *imitatio Dei*, transforms relations of preference and prejudice into devoted neighborliness. Indeed, in this parable it is the one who has been stigmatized and marginalized who extends the hand of friendship across the lines of "fundamental social constraint." The kingdom of Christ presents an alternate way to live, to love, and to be together in society. Jesus offers a model for community life founded upon the command to love people who appear to be on the margins because they may, in fact, be at the center of what God is doing in the world.

The history of stigma conveys more about the ways our communities and society operate than it does about those who have been stigmatized.[50] In the same way that beauty is described to be "in the eye of the beholder," so is all that the eye finds abhorrent and strange. We need the two-part Great Commandment because, as "beholders," we need to be commanded not only love God but to love our neighbors with new vision. Reflecting on metaphors of sight, it is a vision that has more in common with ancient conceptions of sight than with classical views. The way "we see" is determined more by projections and assumptions than it is by the person or object of sight. Theologian Amos Yong considers the history of freakery and stigma when he writes,

> The "monsters" of the Western culture have represented its internal crises and vulnerabilities, its deepest fears, its enemies, the strangers in the midst, and the borders demarcating the unfamiliar, unknown and incomprehensible that have lurked within.[51]

Not only do stigma and projection represent the internal crises, vulnerabilities, and deepest fears of Western culture, but they bring us face to face with these internal crises within *ourselves*. As I encounter a neighbor who calls into question my presumption of what is "normal," I am forced to respond to my own incomprehensibility as a self formed by culture and yet responding within culture. Friedrich Nietzsche warns, "He who fights with monsters should look to it that he himself does not become a monster."[52] Perhaps it has always been the monsters within ourselves that we have been fighting.

Christian theology professes that human beings are created in the image of God, yet our actions all too quickly deny others the fullness of this image. Mystery confronts us on all sides: the mystery of what it means to be created in the *imago Dei*, the secret of the formation of the self and why we respond the way we do to others, and the opacity of the neighbor whom we reject because they are unfamiliar, unknown, and incomprehensible to us. Mystery can lead us to appreciate and love one another, but it can also drive us apart. Facing our own initial presumptions and preconceptions opens us to the possibility that we do not know ourselves as thoroughly as we first imagined. There is a profound mystery at the heart of what it means to be a human being, and that mystery is encountered both in my neighbor and within me.

Ethical encounters involve a mysterious interplay between our fundamental ethical obligation to respond to the human other as created in God's image and the call to *imitatio Dei*, following Christ's command to love our neighbors as ourselves. The command to neighbor-love is a "higher call" than our instinctual response to those who are different than us. It *must* be commanded to confront the intellectual preconceptions and presuppositions that prevent us from recognizing that we encounter the image of God in one another. This does not mean that everyone must know and understand Christ's command in order to act ethically. Rather, those who presume that the accounts they give of others are accurate require the commandment to neighbor-love. Christ's command breaks down myths of transparency and opens us to love our neighbors as they are.

If we genuinely believe that human beings are created in the image of the divine, it should not come as a surprise that we approach mystery and opacity in our encounters with one another. Throughout Scripture, God is both revelatory and mysterious, at once transparent in immanence and opaque in transcendence.

The humility that was called for in our understanding of God's image in one another is the same humility that must guide our caregiving practices. We must come to terms with our limited *epistemology* in the same way that we grapple with the limits of our theology.

COMPLEX DEPENDENCY AND NARRATIVE LIMITS

> The care I offer, and the care I receive, springs forth from . . . partial and sometimes misguided narratives.
>
> **Stacy Clifford Simplican**[53]

Philosopher Eva Feder Kittay, in her caregiving relationship with her daughter Sesha, privileges the ideal of transparency while acknowledging that it is never entirely attainable.[54] She seeks a caregiving relationship in which "the perception of and response to another's needs are neither blocked by nor refracted through our own needs and desires."[55] This is, in a sense, the opposite of Henri Nouwen's *Adam*, where Nouwen reads his own story into Adam's life. Kittay strives toward an ideal that Nouwen seems to neglect, an account where the person receiving care is understood independently from one's own interests.

Understanding the needs and desires of people who receive care, without privileging one's own interests as a care provider, is an often communicated and regularly reinforced aspect of caregiving ethics. It is closely related to what might be called "person-centered" or "self-directed" service provision. Indeed, caregiving would be less than caring if a person providing support fails to listen or to attempt to discern to the needs of the person receiving care.[56] At the same time, someone else's needs will never be completely transparent to us, nor will our own interests be entirely removed from the equation. Stacy Clifford Simplican goes further in asking whether it is even healthy for caregivers to abandon their own needs and desires to "adopt" the perspective of the person receiving support.

Eva Feder Kittay knows her daughter well. "It is because I see Sesha close up, because I have a deep and intimate relationship with her, that I am able to see what is hidden from those who are not privileged enough to see her when she opens up to another."[57] Even then, there are aspects that Kittay admits she doesn't know. For instance, "What cognitive capacities Sesha possesses I do not know, nor do others. And it is hubris to presume to know."[58]

In Kittay's writing, we discover a tension between professions of intimate transparency with her daughter and the recognition that "no self is ever truly transparent in this sense."[59] Simplican maintains that holding an ideal that caregivers forfeit their own desires in caregiving relationship, seeking an unattainable transparency with the needs and desires of the care receiver, is a dangerous and untenable position.

To explore this question further, Simplican offers a stirring account of Sky Walker and his mother, Trudy. Sky had autism and was prone to acts of violence. Trudy was worn down from lack of support and was unable to take the steps needed to release her son into more intensive care. She died after being severely beaten by Sky in 2010. Sky acknowledged what had happened with the simple yet heartbreaking words, "Sky sorry hit Momma."

As a devoted mother, Trudy subscribed to a kind of transparency myth that her needs and interests were to be entirely subordinated to the needs of her son; in other words, that she was to become transparent or invisible as a care provider in meeting Sky's needs. Trudy's perspective, partnered with a lack of outside support and caregiving fatigue, led to an overinvestment in Sky's life and psyche. Trudy experienced an oppressive belonging without the support that could have helped to provide perspective. A year before her death, Trudy wrote the following letter:

> If this letter has been opened and is being read, it is because I have been seriously injured or killed by my son, Sky Walker. I love Sky with my whole heart and soul and do not believe he has intentionally injured me.[60]

Simplican describes the mother-son relationship here as one of *complex dependency*. Understood one way, Sky was reliant on Trudy and other caregivers and professionals. He was vulnerable and dependent. However, his caregivers were at risk of being seriously injured by Sky. He was vulnerable to Trudy, but Trudy was also vulnerable to Sky. It was a relationship of complex dependency, one not easily grasped or quickly transparent in terms of needs and power dynamics.

Parents have shared the difficulty of describing their caregiving relationships. They want to be honest about their experiences. They know that forthright conversations about their needs and potentially the dangers or discomfort they face as part of the caregiving journey are the way to preserve their own health and to get the support that they need. Conversely, they do not wish to stigmatize disability further or perpetuate stereotypes of their children by describing their negative interactions. If they seek additional assistance by acknowledging the challenges inherent in their care, they might even be perceived as contributing to ableist perceptions of disability in society. Many parents err on the side of downplaying their difficulties rather than accurately describing what life looks like for them. As in the case of Trudy and Sky, it is possible to internalize a hope and longing for a better relationship as one's perception of reality. When one's own needs and desires are put completely on hold, it becomes difficult to see the actual state of affairs and the potential dangers and complex dependency of the caregiving relationship.

Trudy Walker's letter portrays a mother who is determined and fearfully committed to saving her son from the perception that he acted maliciously and the resultant consequences that might occur. She attempts to release Sky from any account of wrongdoing through her writing. Together with Simplican, I cannot help but wonder how the situation with Sky may have resolved differently if Trudy had not been so fearful of the ethical implications of the stories that she tells of life with her son. We need an alternate approach to care ethics, one where ethical encounters do not rely upon transparency myths or intellectual hubris to ground moral action.

Simplican suggests that Kittay's own emphasis on interdependence in her writing should have left more room for opacity and mutuality in caregiving relationships. Kittay questions an Enlightenment emphasis on the primacy of reason, yet, "in this regard, Kittay's transparent self closely resembles the liberal self from which her theory means to depart. Both selves idealize cognitive capacities."[61] Following Judith Butler, Simplican notes:

> In attempting to have mastery over knowledge of another, we foreclose the ways in which identities are never closed but always in flux. In contrast, when opacity grounds our relationship with another we make room for each other—room to flourish, regress, hurt, and surprise.[62]

In examining the myth of the transparent other, the goal is not to minimize or discredit the possibility of knowing others in profound and meaningful ways. Rather, as we leave room for the mysterious and opaque in relationship of care, we open the possibility of encountering one another in complex and authentic ways. Every person I encounter, created in God's image, eclipses the limits of my understanding and my capacity to interpret her actions transparently. It is not that I need to manufacture a kind of "distance" from other human beings in response to the call to care, because every person is already an *other*, unique and distant in their very difference from me. Instead, in honoring the distance between us, I open myself to the discovery of who the other is—to the possibility of *revelation*. We must not assume our initial accounts of others' experiences do justice to the world that they inhabit or the bodies in which they dwell.

YOUR STORY, MY STORY

We must unsettle the presumption of cognitive mastery that appeals to the ego, whether in theological ethics or in direct interactions with the people whom we encounter. As humility is required in interpreting the *imago Dei*, so it is needed in our interpersonal relationships.

In Nouwen's account, Adam's story is subsumed within the revelation of Christ to Nouwen rather than being afforded the mystery of a complex encounter. It is too easy to assume the stories of others based upon their impact on our own lives. Adam's relationship with Nouwen was profound and transformative and, therefore, so was Nouwen's interpretation of Adam's life. A kind of transparency is presumed that does not permit the rich mystery of what it means for someone to be created in God's image, in all of his or her uniqueness and opacity.

The Person of Jesus challenges preconceived notions. In coming as one "from whom we hide our faces," Christ overturns easy associations of the good with surface beauty or normalcy. In all of us, goodness is something "under construction," as we are reminded by Flannery O'Connor. Stigma reveals the ugliness not in the one who is stigmatized but in the perceiver. It is our perceptions that need transformation. In fact, we need to *unsee* the "ugliness" of our neighbor. As we question our own assumptions, the beauty of our neighbors is revealed.

God's incarnation in Jesus Christ and the command to love our neighbors subverts our immediate associations of preference with love, beauty with goodness, sight with knowledge. We realize that our instincts and inclinations arise out of our own disordered desires, and our failure to embrace one another as created in God's image traces back to the ways in which we tell our own stories. We will never become "transparent" to ourselves in the caregiving experience, and failing to appreciate our interior mystery can have tragic consequences. It is to these partially opaque autobiographies and the myth of the transparent self that we now turn.

6

The Stories I Tell
The Myth of the Transparent Self

TELLING STORIES, GIVING AN ACCOUNT

The truth about stories is, that's all we are.

Thomas King[1]

As human beings, we process our understanding of ourselves and others primarily through stories. By "stories" I mean the *accounts that we give* of ourselves and one another. This is an expansive definition, one that could go so far as to include the numerical. A human life included in a statistic in a ledger is also a kind of accounting. The numerical offers a drastically reductive story, to be sure, but a story, nonetheless.

Stories—the accounts we give and receive—help us to make sense of the world around us. Autobiographical accounts frame our consideration of what it means to be *called to* others in caregiving. It was noted that every great philosophy, and perhaps every great theology, is "a confession of faith on the part of its author, and a type of involuntary and unself-conscious memoir."[2] No project, no matter how logically argued, is exempt from the conscious or unconscious intentions and direction of its author.

The stories told by Western, post-Enlightenment philosophy and theology do not do justice to the myriad voices and accounts given by the disabled community. Marginalization and stigma are a result of practices of normalcy that tell stories about who human beings *need to be* to be happy and healthy contributors in society. People whose accounts fall outside of these standards experience the negative effects of prejudice and rejection. In churches and faith communities, beliefs on healing and how one is "supposed to behave" become problematic for similar reasons. People who interpret their disability as an integral part of their identity might still receive prayer for "healing." Those whose behavior falls outside of the expected community norm may be relegated to a segregated space or asked to leave. Shared stories demand that one "give an account" according to a specific framework. These norms often fail to leave room for mystery or experiences that fall outside of community expectations.

Our understanding of the *imago Dei*, then, must be shaped by an encounter with disability—either our own or others'. Just as the human experience does not depend upon intellectual ability or the capacity to perform certain functions, so the divine image must encompass the beautiful diversity of human ability and relationships. We find ourselves *before God* and *before one another* in profound humility, called to respond ethically out of a love first received.

The accounts and stories we give of one another are remarkably limited and deeply entwined with our own story and qualified understanding. As observed in Stacy Clifford Simplican's work, caregiving entails complex relationships of dependency. Our narratives about ourselves and others are always partially opaque and in flux.

Just as our accounts of the *imago Dei* often overreach and leave little room for an ethics of responsibility amid mystery, our self-narratives do the same. We presume the "intelligibility" of our own stories and look to the accounts that we give of ourselves as the litmus test for ethical accountability.

The Intelligibility of Our Stories

Alasdair MacIntyre is a forerunner in the field of narrative ethics. He writes, "Narrative history of a certain kind turns out to be the basic and essential genre for the characterization of human actions,"[3] and "any specific account of the virtues presupposes an equally specific account of the narrative structure and unity of a human life and *vice versa*."[4] Human beings are understood to be *storytelling animals*, and one's ability to situate oneself ethically in the world depends on the story one tells about oneself and the stories one has been told.[5]

The question that is important to ask related to an ethical account of caregiving is not primarily *whether* we are storytelling animals. Rather, recognizing our intellectual limits, "What role do mystery and opacity play in our ethical accounting?" MacIntyre admits that we find ourselves "in the middle" of stories. Our narratives will never be simple or easy to interpret.

We are always only coauthors, never the sole author of our story.[6] "We enter upon a stage which we did not design and we find ourselves part of an action that was not of our making."[7] Even as actors, we cannot proceed exactly as we would see fit: "Each character is constrained by the actions of others and by the social settings presupposed in his and their actions."[8] In the course of our lives, we constantly encounter unpredictability, never knowing precisely what will happen next.[9]

Despite these concessions to the human limits of storytelling, MacIntyre's primary emphasis remains on the *intelligibility* of our actions. Ethical accountability depends upon our ability to know our own intentions, and "where intentions are concerned, we need to know which intention or intentions were primary."[10] Moral credibility is determined largely by the transparency of our intentions.

This criterion presents great difficulty to people with intellectual disabilities. As a direct support worker, I often had difficulty understanding exactly what the people I supported were trying to communicate, even related to basic human needs. Were they in pain? Hungry? Bored and needing a new environment or activity? At times it was a process of trial and error to find out what each person needed. Now, imagine that I attempted to discover someone's *primary intent* behind a specific action. Leaving aside for a moment the question of whether the person consciously recognized their own primary motivation, even the process of *communicating* this intention—without words, at times—would have been highly problematic.

If human ethical accountability depends upon our ability to intelligibly communicate the primary intention behind our actions, people with intellectual disabilities will consistently be perceived as second-class moral agents. The burden of proof, then, lies with MacIntyre to demonstrate that this intent is intelligible (transparent) and that this intelligibility should be the core determinant of our morality.

To illustrate his position, MacIntyre provides the example of a man gardening. To characterize his actions, one must know whether the man is gardening primarily because it is a healthy activity or because it pleases his wife. To do so, we would need to

> know the answer to such questions as whether he would continue gardening if he continued to believe that gardening was a healthful exercise, but discovered that his gardening no longer pleased his wife, *and* whether he would continue gardening, if he ceased to believe that gardening was healthful exercise, but continued to believe that it pleased his

wife, *and* whether he would continue gardening if he changed his beliefs on both points.[11]

Until we can answer such questions, MacIntyre asserts, "we shall not know how to characterize correctly what the agent is doing."[12]

I can imagine few situations in which our gardening friend would ever come under such scrutiny that he would have to answer these questions. Perhaps if said gardening activity resulted in a court conviction? Most of the time we are unconscious of our intentions in carrying out activities to the extent that we could determine precisely our *primary* motivation.[13]

The stories of our lives can be told, understood, and retold in countless ways. Some of these stories will have greater or lesser degrees of internal coherence. They reveal clues to our intent while simultaneously concealing much of our conscious or unconscious motivation.

In the caregiving experience, the stories we hear may not always match what we understand to be "the facts." If intelligibility is the ultimate priority, then the process of separating fact from fiction could be an all-consuming task.

As social psychology and MacIntyre's gardener demonstrate, it is difficult to interpret *anyone's* story, not just the stories of people with intellectual disabilities. Everyone has a propensity to look favorably on their own actions and less charitably upon the actions of others.[14] We interpret others' intent by the effect of their action on us, rather than by any genuine indicator as to their motivation. In conflict mediation, it often takes hours of hard emotional labor to get close to a believable intent behind any given situation. Mediators know that even then there are likely countless unexplored encounters and experiences with family, friends, and others that have led up to a particular response or interpretation of someone else's action. The lack of transparency in these processes is not simply due to participant dishonesty, though this may be a factor. Often people going through conflict mediation are only just beginning to understand the reasons they acted or behaved in the way that they did or the deep needs and interests that drive their positions.

As we look to the Christian tradition of moral formation, Jesus references this propensity to view ourselves differently than others in Matthew 7:

> And why worry about a speck in your friend's eye when you have a log in your own? How can you think of saying to your friend, "Let me help you get rid of that speck in your eye," when you can't see past the log in your own eye? Hypocrite! First get rid of the log in your own eye; then you will see well enough to deal with the speck in your friend's eye.[15]

We have a natural tendency to see the world through the rose-tinted glasses of self-interest rather than in light of our moral failings. We are quick to judge the intent, the intelligibility, and the ethical shortcomings of others and slow to reflect on our own moral failings. We each confess and hope with the apostle Paul that "we see in a mirror dimly, but then face to face; now I know in part, but then I will know fully just as I also have been fully known."[16]

The Strangeness of Our Selves

Our encounters with one another carry an incomprehensible, unexplainable transcendence. Emmanuel Levinas describes this as the trace of the infinite, an impression left by the divine. In Christian theology, this is the mark of the *imago Dei*, the grounding for ethical accountability, responsibility, and possibility. László Tengelyi seems to be gesturing at something similar in *The Wild Region in Life-History*. He builds on Maurice Merleau-Ponty's observation that in meeting the embodied other, we encounter something that is "beyond the objective body as the sense of the painting is beyond the canvas."[17] There is a "strangeness" in each meeting similar to the strangeness of a painting we have not seen before. We may try to domesticate this peculiarity within our framework of understanding. Ultimately, we will be unable to do so. On Tengelyi's account, this "wild region" is beyond all culture and cannot be comprehended within an intelligible story. Tengelyi argues that "the ground of selfhood is to be sought not in the unity of a narrated life story, or in life as a complex of told stories, but in life as a totality of lived experiences."[18] There will always be aspects of these lived experiences that escape narrativity. These elements may be ignored, dismissed, or repressed in our stories, "but they leave significant traces in our lives and may reemerge in striking ways."[19] For Tengelyi, "to understand life in narrative terms is to confer upon it a coherence that it does not possess and to disguise that which belongs to the wild."[20]

Tengelyi's "wild region" is a way of getting at the mystery at the heart of the human experience that goes beyond our ability to tell a coherent, intelligible story about it. This mystery is present in our self-awareness, and it is present when we attempt to make precise judgments about the intentionality of others.

In *Ethics in the Conflicts of Modernity*, Alasdair MacIntyre responds to Tengelyi's critique by again acknowledging that there will always be aspects of the human experience of which one is not the "author," but he stresses that regardless of these opaque experiences,

> there is always a story to be told about it. We can acknowledge the incoherence and unintelligibility of this or that aspect of our lives in a

coherent and intelligible narrative without disguising or misrepresenting the incoherence and unintelligibility. Indeed, there is no other way of acknowledging them adequately.[21]

Within MacIntyre's framework, the only way to address the lack of transparency in our own stories is to be transparent about their incoherence or unintelligibility. What *can be told* continues to be the primary value of MacIntyre's ethical accountability. He is not saying that we need to understand these areas of mystery, only that "giving an account" of incoherence is enough to render our stories intelligible again. We must "acknowledge" this incoherence, and this acknowledgment is adequate in the quest for a coherent account.

It is entirely possible to believe that human beings are storytelling animals, and that the primary way we communicate and learn about one another is through the power of story, without insisting that narrative accountability must carry the weight of ethical responsibility. The stories and accounts contained within the Old and New Testaments are the primary sources for all of Christian theology. We must, however, confront the epistemic hubris that presumes that the weight of our moral actions and interactions can be captured in words and that ethical responsibility can be contained in the account that we give of ourselves.

The root of moral obligation and motivation arises from our initial *givenness*, not from our ability to describe our actions in an intelligible way. It is our encounter with the *imago Dei* in one another that grounds ethical action, not our ability to intellectually comprehend this *imago*. This being said, intellectual investigation and the accounts that we give can help to confront myths of transparency. These myths, whether in relation to one another, ourselves, or the divine, cloud our recognition that it is our encounter with the mysterious *imago* in one another that grounds ethical action and response.

The tyranny of ethical transparency plays out in a myriad of ways in the lives of people with intellectual disabilities. Unable to meet the demand of intelligibility, their stories and lives are overlooked as incomprehensible or reduced to one-dimensional caricatures. Rather than being looked to as representative of the profound and mysterious dignity of the human experience, narrative ethics that prioritizes *intelligibility* relegates people with ambiguous or opaque stories to second-class humanity. The formal conception of the *imago Dei* confronts this account with the dignity of our shared, incomprehensible "before God-ness."

Making space for the incoherence and unverifiability of the accounts that we give is not only necessary for people with intellectual disabilities, however. Our stories simply cannot bear the weight of ethical accountability. Human beings are not only storytelling animals but in many ways *irrational* story-telling animals. The function of our stories is seldom to reveal a transparent or logical chain of actions or events. Studies on game theory, performative contradictions, cognitive biases, and even the research referenced previously on first impressions, prejudice, and consciousness make this abundantly clear.[22] Robert Wright notes in *The Moral Animal*, "Human beings are a species splendid in their array of moral equipment, tragic in their propensity to misuse it, and pathetic in their constitutional ignorance of the misuse."[23] Stories help us to relate to one another, to convey emotion and seek to establish trust, to restore relational connection, and to build a qualified understanding in order to work and move forward together. They entertain us, move us, infuriate us, and compel us to action. In certain contexts, stories *can* help us to understand our rationality and empower moral reasoning. Thanks to our built-in cognitive biases, limits, and propensities, however, stories should not be expected to carry the weight of our moral responsibility to one another.[24]

A Rational Account?

> The universe is an immense allusion, and our inner life an anonymous quotation; only the italics are our own. Is it within our power to verify the quotation, to identify the source, to learn what all things stand for?
>
> **Abraham Joshua Heschel**[25]

MacIntyre's criteria for providing an intelligible account of action and motivation include "understanding [one's] animal identity through time from conception to death."[26] However, what if human beings have difficulty fulfilling even this basic ethical request? What would it mean for the self to be unable to provide a coherent self-identifying story through time in this way? What are the ethical implications of failing to *recognize* oneself? Or, as philosopher and gender theorist Judith Butler asks in *Giving an Account of Oneself*, "Does the postulation of a subject who is not self-grounding, that is, whose conditions of emergence can never fully be accounted for, undermine the possibility of responsibility and, in particular, of giving an account of oneself?"[27]

In Butler's question we recall our consideration of the *imago Dei*. What it "means" to be made in the *imago* is profoundly mysterious. We must then ask whether it is the *intelligibility* of the divine image that grounds ethical action. Perhaps our theological conjectures simply gesture toward what Levinas calls the "trace," an ultimately incomprehensible transcendent response-ability of encountering one another *as* created in God's image. While the "material" *imago Dei* in the pages of Scripture offers us the example of Christ as a model of what it means to live *into* the loving image of the invisible God, it never gives an account of precisely what is meant *by* human beings being created in this image. Our fundamental human ethical motivation or obligation toward one another must find its basis outside of the "story" we tell about moral action. It is not transparent to intellect and therefore lies in the mysterious and hidden space outside of the text—in the *wild region* of human encounter.

Responsibility in caregiving or otherwise must not and *cannot* depend only upon our ability to provide an account of our actions and motivation. Moral accountability always arises before our ability to give an account—either of God's prior action toward us or of our encounter with one another. Judith Butler's work, from a nontheological standpoint, captures the dynamics of this accountability with one another amid the partial opacity of the stories we tell about ourselves and one another.

Practical reasoning of the type MacIntyre calls us to has a valuable place in moral reasoning when kept within humble epistemological limits. We can become *more* transparent and intelligible to ourselves through social relationships and the stories we tell. Yet the fullness of who we are as people created in the *imago Dei* will always exceed, overwhelm, and mystify attempts to render the self fully transparent. The mystery and opacity at the heart of human responsibility are not merely elements to acknowledge as incoherent. In ways that are impossible to make entirely intelligible, we are *radically relationally constituted*. The tragedy of broken relationships is not primarily that we may lose access to social capital. Neither is it that we lose another vital perspective in understanding who we are as human beings, though both of these may well be painful losses. To undermine or sabotage our relational responsibility to one another is to chip away at the ethical foundation of our very identity, an identity held as much in "between" ourselves and others as it is held in our own consciousness. The mysterious opacity that MacIntyre relegates to a minor subplot in the story of the self may, in fact, be the space, the pause, and the silence that holds the whole story together.

ENCOUNTERING THE *IMAGO DEI* IN MY SELF

> All autobiography is storytelling; all writing is autobiography.
>
> **J. M. Coetzee**[28]

The Self as Relationally Composed: Social Emergence

MacIntyre begins in the direction of a relationally composed self in his emphasis on human interdependence: "There is no point then in our development towards and in our exercise of independent practical reasoning at which we cease altogether to be dependent on particular others."[29] Here MacIntyre acknowledges the impact and range of human social dependency. However, he stops before this theme of dependency might challenge the premises behind his emphasis on intelligibility as a whole. Judith Butler takes dependency further. If the grounding of ethical accountability cannot be captured within the accounts that we give, our dependency upon others has greater importance than MacIntyre recognizes. To find oneself unable to *give an account* means "the very meaning of responsibility must be rethought on the basis of this limitation, it cannot be tied to the conceit of a self fully transparent to itself."[30]

Butler begins her argument with an observation similar to MacIntyre's that "there is no 'I' that can fully stand apart from the social conditions of its emergence." Where the two diverge, though, is when Butler goes on to say that "this self is already implicated in a social temporality that exceeds its own capacities for narration."[31] It is not simply that we lack or have lost the words or language we need to communicate our experience. Rather, we do not even have the knowledge or understanding of our own social reality that we would need to communicate it. This is not to discount the difficulties of ethical language, which MacIntyre also acknowledges. The terms that we use are "given" to us, just as the norms and expectations we are surrounded with are not of our own making.[32] We always already find ourselves within a social matrix that "decide[s] in advance who will and will not become a subject."[33] The *very being* of the self is dependent "on the social dimension of normativity that governs the scene of recognition."[34]

Through Butler we continue to appreciate our significant limits in *recognition* and *intelligibility*. While her primary concern is not barriers to recognition of the divine image, she appreciates the crisis that these limits present to dominant ethical theories that rely on intelligibility and articulation. If narrative ethics cannot capture our responsibility to one another in an intelligible manner, does this mean that ethical obligation is dead?

Butler argues that if we ground ethical inquiry in intellectual transparency then we undermine the relationality of our moral obligation to one another. Because the self (or subject) is opaque to itself,

> not fully translucent and knowable to itself, it is not thereby licenced to do what it wants or to ignore its obligations to others. The contrary is surely true. The opacity of the subject may be a consequence of its being conceived as a relational being, one whose early and primary relations are not always available to conscious knowledge.[35]

Where for MacIntyre ethical responsibility is grounded in the *account that is given*, for Butler it is grounded precisely when we are *unable to give an account*. Relationships for MacIntyre are what help us to develop independent practical reasoning, which forms the basis for ethical discourse. It is through independent practical reasoning that we can give an ethical account of ourselves. Butler proceeds in an entirely different direction. Relationships may help us to learn more about ourselves on a conscious level, yet our fundamental constitution as relational beings "unsettles" us in a way that makes it impossible ever to be fully transparent and knowable to ourselves. We are not transparent to ourselves precisely because our "early and primary relations" are not always available to conscious knowledge. Our opacity places us at the mercy of relational connections that we can never fully articulate, just as it demonstrates our fundamental responsibility toward one another at a subconscious level. Through these opaque primary relations, we are always "before" one another. We encounter our neighbor in the very depths of selfhood.[36]

In his work, MacIntyre argues that confronting other moral traditions presents opportunities to recognize incommensurable ethical claims and strengthen or revise one's own tradition.[37] In a similar way, Butler highlights inconsistencies, interruptions, and challenges to recognition that occur through accounts given at an interpersonal level. She sees these disruptions as an opportunity not simply to come to greater self-awareness but to appreciate how the human other can confront the norms that we might take for granted. "Sometimes the very unrecognizability of the other brings about a crisis in the norms that govern recognition."[38] The exceptions, the freaks, and the misfits are those who remind us that Reynolds' "cult of normalcy" makes recognition possible for some and not for others.[39] Butler observes that our desire to be recognized by others and to recognize others in ways not acknowledged by this cult call its norms into question.

Our encounters with others who are not "recognized" by the cult of normalcy prompt us to question the norms that may previously have gone unquestioned. In the practice of caregiving, we regularly meet people whose stories are not the dominant stories told by media and news journalism. Assumptions that disability or ill health necessarily lead to unhappiness or a lack of contribution are quickly challenged when we get to know people living lives of flourishing not only in spite of but sometimes *because of* their limitations. Encountering people with intellectual disability and confronting our own intellectual limits challenge the assumption of the human ability of independent practical reasoning. We are all interdependent not simply on a practical level but on a profoundly existential and ethical level. Grasping that our ultimate moral obligation to one another is not fully comprehendible frees us to enter into one another's journeys as companions rather than as guides on the road to human flourishing.

We Are (Fictional?) Storytelling Animals

> It is quite true what philosophy says: that life must be understood backwards. But then one forgets the other principle: that it must be lived forwards. Which principle, the more one thinks it through, ends exactly with the thought that temporal life can never properly be understood precisely because I can at no instant find complete rest in which to adopt the position: backwards.
>
> **Søren Kierkegaard**[40]

Life must be understood backward, as we reflect upon it. However, life must also be lived forward in such a way that we are always changing, growing, and adapting to the situation in which we find ourselves. So much so, Kierkegaard concludes, that we never find ourselves in such a state of rest or reflection that we might truly understand life. We are always *in medias res* or beginning in the midst of a play or a story that has been partially written and determined.[41] We find ourselves partway through the narrative, being asked to author an account of ourselves *to* ourselves and others, having already been given the language, framework, and terms of recognition with which to do so. The situation that we find ourselves in has determined us, and our origins and the reasons behind why we ended up where we are always are at least partially opaque. As Butler describes, "I am always recuperating, reconstructing, and I am left to fictionalize and fabulate origins I cannot know. . . . My account of myself is partial, haunted by that for which I can devise no definitive story."[42]

What might it mean to "author" our accounts in media res? To what extent or degree can we claim authorship of our stories? We are constrained by the actions of others and our social situations.[43] We can discover aspects of the stories of which we are already a part. However, we do not find ourselves on a level playing field in this regard. Whether due to intellectual ability, the ways we are "marked" or perceived in relation to the cult of normalcy, socioeconomic status, or simply the time we have available to us to consider these stories, insightful self-reflection is a luxury not everyone can afford. Not one of us comes to "rest" in a Kierkegaardian sense to the extent that we will fully understand ourselves or become *transparent* to ourselves or one another.

In this light, the discrepancy between Butler and MacIntyre comes down to the extent to which *narrative accountability* should serve as the basis for ethical obligation and responsibility. For Butler, "precisely my own opacity to myself occasions my capacity to confer a certain kind of recognition on others. It would be, perhaps, an ethics based on our shared, invariable, and partial blindness about ourselves."[44]

The demand to give a continuous account of oneself and to present a coherent self-identity is a kind of ethical violence. Norms always determine the space within which these practices of account-giving take place. Imbalances of power determine the weight of each account given. The stories we tell may be deemed more or less reliable because of someone's status or ability to align with the cult of normalcy. In fact, the one who has sufficient body capital and social capital may seldom be asked to defend their actions or behavior, while another who is prejudged by their ability, skin color, ethnicity, gender, etc. finds themselves constantly called to account for their actions.[45] These norms allow for all too quick judgments of a person's intent and disposition. Someone in a position of power might be immediately assumed to "know what they're doing," while those who are vulnerable are constantly questioned and presumed to be making poor decisions.

In each of these scenarios of prejudice, power, and the cult of normalcy, "recognition sometimes obligates us to suspend judgment in order to apprehend the other."[46] What we need, rather than an ethic of critical narrative accountability, is an ethic of mercy on a journey of mutual discovery. Knowing that we are limited and partially opaque does not transform this mystery to transparency. The extent of our epistemic limits is a revelation for many of us, but this revelation must go on to transform our posture and our practice with one another. Acknowledging our shared opacity, for Butler, calls for a disposition of humility and generosity alike: "I will need to be forgiven for what I cannot have fully known, and I will be under a similar obligation to offer forgiveness to others, who are also constituted in partial opacity to themselves."[47] The *significance* of what hides in the mystery of selfhood forms the basis of profound humility and generosity, a posture of forgiveness toward both ourselves and one another for all that we cannot know or for which we cannot be held accountable.

Giving an Account: Joe Arridy

The man you kill tonight is six years old,
He has no idea why he dies,
Yet he must die in the room the state has walled
Transparent to its glassy eyes.

Marguerite Young[48]

In 1937, Joe Arridy was convicted of murdering fifteen-year-old Dorothy Drain. He had an IQ in the 40s and had been born to Syrian immigrants. He was convicted because he confessed to the murder. The many discrepancies in his account should have alerted authorities to the reality that he had not committed the act. Frank Aguilar had previously been convicted, as he had concealed the axe used in the attack in his apartment. Dorothy's sister, who was brutalized during the attack but survived, testified that Arridy had not been present. Despite all evidence to the contrary, Arridy was executed on January 6, 1939. Prison warden Roy Best called Arridy "the happiest prisoner on death row." He requested ice cream for his last three meals and seemed unaware of his imminent death, spending most of his time playing with a toy train. Arridy was posthumously pardoned in 2011.

Joe Arridy had given an account of himself. It was a flawed account, but it was an account. To those who interrogated him, it had enough indicators of "authorship" to hold Arridy accountable. He found himself at the mercy of prejudice and a significant power differential. We will never know exactly why Arridy confessed to a murder he did not commit. We do know, however, that suggestions and prompting can be a powerful primer for people who are in a vulnerable position. If it seems that a captor or person in a position of power is *looking for* a certain answer, especially if the person answering does not have a clear sense of the potential outcome of their answer, they may comply simply to please their interrogator. People with intellectual disabilities, for example, may attempt to provide the "account" that they think a support worker is requesting. Perhaps Arridy's way of saying that he did not want to cause trouble was to respond with the words he thought were expected of him. Whatever the reason, Arridy gave an account of himself that got him killed despite having the intellectual capability of a young child.

In today's legal system, Arridy may not have been convicted because of a diagnosis of intellectual disability. However, the principles of power, prejudice, and the demand to provide a narrative account continue to dominate Western law.[49] The demand to give an account, or in this case a confession, carries with it a kind of ethical violence for people like Arridy or others who find themselves vulnerable and at the mercy of the legal system.

Our intent here is not to overturn centuries of law practice to introduce principles that might be better found in Indigenous community processes or conflict mediation approaches. Alternate approaches demand more time and investment but take into greater consideration cultural, systemic, and relational factors that may be at play in any given situation. As it relates to caregiving, we must acknowledge that the demand for transparent accountability present in legal proceedings can be the same hidden principles operative in caregiving relationships. If our identities and actions are bound up in relational dynamics for which we cannot give an account, our primary posture toward one another must not be that of a judge and the accused or vice versa. Rather, in this space of loss and opacity, we are met with an *opportunity*, "a chance—to be addressed, claimed, bound to what is not me, but also to be moved, to be prompted to act, to address myself elsewhere, and so to vacate the self-sufficient 'I' as a kind of possession."[50] It is not from a coherent command of my own authorship that I act or find respond to an ethical call but precisely in those moments when I feel unable to call myself "author." "My very formation implicates the other in me . . . my foreignness to myself is, paradoxically, the source of my ethical connection with others."[51] It is in our *inability* to express ourselves and in the moments where we *fail* to recognize one another or ourselves in the stories we tell that our true humanity is revealed—a deep relationality formed by and sustained by our connections with others.[52]

Virtues do not need to be discarded as we question an overemphasis on narrative accountability. On the contrary, virtues are all the more needed in times when we lack the resources, information, or ability to understand precisely where we stand. The virtues that are needed in these times must be shaped by the experience of human limitation and loss, rather than seeking to go beyond these limits. We are called to the virtues of *being with*, of being comfortable with one another amid confusion and our inability to give accounts of ourselves. Perhaps if Joe Arridy or others like him were invited into spaces of mutuality, places where they were not called to "give an account" within systems of power and coercion, then they would be heard and understood in different and more meaningful ways.

Stories like Arridy's provide the disruptive opportunity to recognize the failure of transparency myths and to look for a better way. Indeed, the gentle and interdependent relationality of Arridy's subversive confession may itself point to a new way of being human together, one that is patiently open to journeying with others in mutual discovery rather than condemning others based on first impressions or hasty generalizations. In Arridy's confession to a crime he did not commit and subsequent execution, we recall Christ's own refusal to comply with illegitimate demands that he "give an account" before Pilate. It is to verses from Isaiah that Philip turns in Acts to explain the good news of Jesus, as he travels with the Ethiopian eunuch:

> "Like a sheep he was led to the slaughter
>   and like a lamb before its shearer is silent,
>   so he opens not his mouth.
> In his humiliation justice was denied him.
>   Who can describe his generation?
> For his life is taken away from the earth."[53]

Christ's vulnerable incarnation and gruesome crucifixion challenged humanly constructed systems of condemnation and punishment, exposing their failure to recognize legitimate authority and the ethical way of love. In his refusal to comply with the "cult of normalcy" that had been established by the Romans and religious leaders, Jesus opened the possibility that another way was possible. Both Arridy and Christ, in their respective circumstances, were examples of how the "unrecognizability of the other brings about a crisis in the norms that govern recognition."[54]

In our encounters with one another, as beings who can never be relied upon to give a transparent account, we must learn to hold forgiveness at the ready. This is a forgiveness both for us—for all we cannot know or remember—and for one another, with whom we share this partial opacity. "Above all," the apostle Peter instructs, "love each other deeply, because love covers over a multitude of sins."[55] Or, as Paul puts it, love "keeps no record of wrongs."[56] This is not to say that no records should ever be kept or no memory retained. There are times and places and situations for accountability and the pursuit of justice. Precisely because of the profound experience of human limitation and vulnerability, however, our default approach as we encounter one another must not be driven by law but by love. And love does not demand a transparent account, because now we see only partially, a reflection as in a mirror.[57] Perhaps one day we will be fully known and know one another fully, encountering each other face to face. Until that time, though, we must stumble forward together, always ready to extend an arm to support one another through the mysterious fog of our unknowing.

The Self as Relationally Composed: Established by God

> Is it possible to evade the ultimate issue by withdrawing within the confines of the self? The awareness of wonder is often overtaken by the mind's tendency to dichotomize, which makes us look at the ineffable as if it were a thing or an aspect of things apart from our own selves; as if only the stars were surrounded with a halo of enigma and not our own existence. The truth is that the self, our "lord," is an unknown thing, inconceivable in itself. In penetrating the self, we discover the paradox of not knowing what we presume to know so well.
>
> **Abraham Joshua Heschel**[58]

In and through the stories we tell, the limits of our narrative readily become apparent. Judith Butler and others demonstrate the ways in which our account giving is always bound together with the accounts and experiences of others. We find ourselves a part of worlds that are not of our own making, plots of which we are not the author. Perhaps, then, the key to transparency is to turn inward, to seek to know and understand oneself.

In the Christian tradition, even the interior of the self is to be understood only as within the God-relation. In *The Sickness unto Death*, Kierkegaard explores this relation under the pseudonym Anti-Climacus.[59] After beginning by describing human beings as *spirit*, Anti-Climacus expounds:

> Spirit is the self. But what is the self? The self is a relation that relates itself to itself or is the relation's relating itself to itself in the relation; the self is not the relation but is the relation's relating itself to itself.[60]

Anti-Climacus' words are not easy to decipher. We must begin with what he means by "the self is a relation that relates itself to itself." A human being is understood as a kind of synthesis between tensions, tensions such as the infinite and the finite, the temporal and the eternal, and freedom and necessity. At this point, the human being is still not considered to be a *self*. The self is not in these syntheses but in that which relates these syntheses *to* itself.[61] We still have a self-contained relation. No extrinsic force guides or constrains *how* the self might relate itself *to* itself.

There are two possibilities here. Either the self established itself or was established by another. Anti-Climacus concludes that the self did not create itself but is a derived, established relation.[62] Because of this, the self "is yet again a relation and relates itself to that which established the entire relation."[63] In relating itself to the One who established it, the self is dependent and is unable "to arrive at or to be in equilibrium and rest by itself" but must also relate to the one who established it.[64]

Søren Kierkegaard is adamant that his readers not conflate his own views with the views of his pseudonyms. Each pseudonym must be considered for its distinct role in the authorship. This being said, there is evidence that on this depiction of the self, Anti-Climacus and Kierkegaard agree. A similar passage can be found in Kierkegaard's non-pseudonymous *Journals* of 1848, a year before *Sickness unto Death* was published:

> In the composite of the eternal and the temporal, man is a relationship, in this relationship itself and relating itself to itself. God made man a relationship; to be a human being is to be a relationship. But a relationship which, by the very fact that God, as it were, releases it from his hand, or the same moment God, as it were, releases it, is itself, relates itself to itself.[65]

Human beings relate to one another. Human beings relate to themselves *qua self*. Human beings also relate to God, as the One who creates human beings in relationship, in God's own image as a relational being. The self, as "released from [God's] hand" may also *misrelate* to God as the One who established it. Denying one's radical dependency and relationality results in a state of unrest known as "despair" in *Sickness unto Death*.

The arrogance that I am an autonomous or self-established being may help to loosen my ethical bonds with my neighbor and with God, but Anti-Climacus describes this position as being a king without a country, building castles in the air.[66] The presumption that I have established my self is to claim an authority that I do not have. In the language of story or narrative, it is to claim an authorship I have not earned. To be an author is to be an originator, the *one who establishes* the plot or narrative. It is to have *authority*, providing the "true" account of (in this case) the self.[67] According to Anti-Climacus, the remedy for despair is not to wrestle control from one's divine maker but to have faith, to rest in one's establishing relation with God.[68]

In Kierkegaard's journal, he goes outside the language of *Sickness unto Death* to put the dependence forward as an anthropological principle: "To need God is man's highest perfection. . . . Man's highest achievement is to let God be able to help him."[69] According to Kierkegaard, human beings are radically dependent upon God. To live into this dependence and to embrace these established limits is the human being's greatest act. If we were self-established beings who set our own limits, dependence would be a concession. Rather, as *established* beings, dependence upon the One who established us is our highest perfection.[70] Encountering the self as radically dependent is not a theoretical principle that helps one achieve independent rationality. Instead, embracing our profound mystery and only partial authorship lies at the core of what it means to flourish as a self created in the image of the divine.

DISPOSSESSED IN THE *IMAGO DEI*

"You are not your own; you were bought at a price," writes the apostle Paul.[71] We are always already "unsettled" or dispossessed in our own bodies and in the accounts that we give of ourselves. To claim transparent authorship for our lives is at best ignorance and at worst hubris. To reject our fundamental dependency upon God (Kierkegaard) and upon one another (Butler) is to deny our own constitution, the fabric of who we are and who we are becoming.[72] Whenever we provide narrative accounts of our lives, these narratives are "disoriented by what is not mine, or not mine alone."[73]

In Judith Butler's work, the self is unable to give a complete account of itself because it is radically relationally constituted by human others and conditions prior to narrativity. For Kierkegaard, the God-relation constitutes the self as its establishing Power. We recall that for Kierkegaard, the fundamental posture of the self is "before God," and it is this posture that establishes *every human other* in eternal equality before God. To tie these threads together, the language of encountering one another as created in the *imago Dei* connects our radical relational constitution with human others to the divine relation. We are *formed together* as human beings created in God's image, never as isolated individuals but always in relation to one another and to God.

The "trace" of God (Levinas) in others through the formal *imago Dei* also postures us *before* our neighbor, responsible to God and responding to God's call to love our neighbor. This is an ethical obligation grounded not in intellectual recognition but in the encounter with God *through* the *imago Dei* in human others and as the establishing Power of our selves.[74]

Calling has come full circle. In being called *to* others in relationships of care as a "higher calling" we respond to the same voice that calls to us *through* the person who needs support. To encounter our neighbor in need is to encounter the divine power who calls, summons, and compels us toward ethical action. To be called *to* another is bound up in being called *by* another. In the relational circle of the community of God, we are pushed *toward* our calling as caregivers as, simultaneously, we are *drawn by* the trace of God in those to whom we are called. The divine image in me is called to respond to the divine image in you, and together we are equal before the mysterious God who formed us both.

Faith in God, particularly in the language of *Sickness unto Death*, is to rest in and depend upon the God-relation. There is a kind of trust present in this faith that is reminiscent of Butler's ethics of mercy, "a disposition of humility and generosity alike."[75] To be *dispossessed* by God and by one another calls for profound humility without negating the gift of selfhood and our responseability to those around us.

In the coming chapter we will explore the poignant beauty of being created and sustained in the image of a God of revelation and mystery. Embracing dependence allows us to take ourselves less seriously, stepping back from our own causes and concerns. This dispossession opens us to enter more readily into the causes and concerns of others. Resting in our constitutive relations, we will not be so quick to impose the criteria of ethical accountability on the stories of our neighbors. Rather than constantly demanding intelligible accounts, we will be free to enter into others' lives, open to discovering the revelation and mystery of our shared stories.

7

A Mysterious Revelation

The Myth of a Transparent God

MYSTERY AND THE DIVINE

> So what are we to say, brothers, about God? For if you have fully
> grasped what you want to say, it isn't God. If you have been able to
> comprehend it, you have comprehended something else instead of God.
> If you think you have been able to comprehend, your thoughts have
> deceived you. So he isn't this, if this is what you have understood; but if
> he is this, then you haven't understood it. So what is it you want to say,
> seeing you haven't been able to understand it?
>
> **Augustine**[1]

If you can think "God," it is not God whom you have thought. Because of
this, if we attempt to say something *about* God we are never able to fully
capture who God is in our speech or our writing. Biblical narrative exhibits
a complex interplay between mystery and revelation, in part because of the
reality that God transcends human understanding or language. However, in
downplaying the role of mystery in theological investigation, contemporary
Western Christianity has granted revelation primacy. It is tempting to *say* too
much about God, to profess a transparency with the divine that is unattainable. Associating the *imago Dei* with particular aspects of human functioning
is one example of this theological hubris. In the pages that follow, we find
that this same inclination carries the myth of transparency into our understanding of other aspects of *who God is*.

In Mark 4:11-12 and similar passages in Matthew and Luke, Jesus' followers ask him why he speaks in parables. He answers:

> "To you has been given the mystery of the kingdom of God, but those who are outside get everything in parables, so that while seeing, they may see and not perceive, and while hearing, they may hear and not understand, otherwise they might return and be forgiven."

The paradox of this passage is that even those who are "insiders," those who follow Christ as Lord, may very well continue to wrestle with *why* these parables hide their truth from those who do not follow Christ. Why would a God "who wants all people to be saved and come to a knowledge of the truth" simultaneously reveal and hide this truth through parables?[2] A response given to clarify Christ's mysterious storytelling practice raises further questions. *At the heart of revelation lies mystery.*

Exodus similarly depicts a dance of revelation and mystery for those who walk closely with the divine. God says to Moses:

> "I will cause all my goodness to pass in front of you, and I will proclaim my name, the LORD, in your presence. I will have mercy on whom I will have mercy, and I will have compassion on whom I will have compassion. But," he said, "you cannot see my face, for no one may see me and live."
>
> Then the LORD said, "There is a place near me where you may stand on a rock. When my glory passes by, I will put you in a cleft in the rock and cover you with my hand until I have passed by. Then I will remove my hand and you will see my back; but my face must not be seen."[3]

It is this sense of God "having passed by" Moses that Levinas carries into his discussion of the *trace* of God. This passage in Exodus demonstrates a God who desires to be known and to be revealed to human beings and yet knows that full divine revelation is beyond human capacity. No one can see God's face and live. To come face to face with God exceeds our capacity for reception and for recognition. We can never profess mastery over the God whom we serve, because God always exceeds our capacity for narration or comprehension.[4]

No matter how open human beings are to God's presence in the biblical account, revelation is always partially concealed, partially opaque. When the prophet Elijah's encounters God,

> the LORD said, "Go out and stand on the mountain in the presence of the LORD, for the LORD is about to pass by."

Then a great and powerful wind tore the mountains apart and shattered the rocks before the LORD, but the LORD was not in the wind. After the wind there was an earthquake, but the LORD was not in the earthquake. After the earthquake came a fire, but the LORD was not in the fire. And after the fire came a gentle whisper. When Elijah heard it, he pulled his cloak over his face and went out and stood at the mouth of the cave.

Then a voice said to him, "What are you doing here, Elijah?"[5]

The NRSV translates "gentle whisper" or *qol dmamah* in this passage as "a sound of sheer silence." Abraham Joshua Heschel similarly interprets it as "a voice of silence."[6] It is as though the silence itself reveals God, as though the voice of God is not quite audible as a voice at all. It is a silence in which God speaks and a voice that cannot even quite classify as a whisper. We are reminded of Job's exclamation: "How small a whisper do we hear of [God]! But the thunder of his power who can understand?"[7] The image of a thundering, demanding deity is perhaps the picture many people have of the God of the Old Testament. In these and other passages, even when God reveals, God conceals. "The secret things belong to the LORD our God."[8] Were God to become transparent, to "thunder," we would be incapable of understanding or comprehension. No one can see God and live.

The suggestion here is not that God is *only* mysterious and incomprehensible. It is rather that God is never confined to the comprehension of our intellectual faculties or the capacity of our physical senses. In its very nature, theological discourse privileges that which can be comprehended, written, or spoken. Proverbs reminds us, "When there are many words, sin is unavoidable, but the one who controls his lips is wise."[9] Any discourse runs the risk of exceeding comprehension, but this is unavoidable when speaking about God. As theologians, we are tempted to receive Job's question as a challenge to overcome rather than the rhetorical device it is: "Can you discover the depths of God? Can you discover the limits of the Almighty?"[10]

Via Negativa and Theopoetics: Modes of Telling the Story of God

Via negativa is one way philosophers and theologians have attempted to uphold the mystery of the divine while considering *what can be known* about God. Theologians of the "negative way" build on the work of Plotinus and Neoplatonist philosophy. Some of the first theological work along these lines came from Pseudo-Dionysius the Areopagite of the late fifth to early sixth century. In contrast to cataphatic theology that affirms certain attributes of God to gain understanding, apophatic theology seeks to describe God by means of negation. It acknowledges that any language that attempts to comprehend God's nature will always miss the mark. Dionysius, for example, professes that God is not any *thing* or *attribute* according to the way of human understanding:

> We maintain that [God] is neither soul nor intellect; nor has he imagination, opinion, speech, or understanding; nor can he be expressed or conceived, since he is neither number nor order; nor greatness nor smallness; nor equality nor inequality; nor similarity nor dissimilarity; . . . neither one nor oneness, nor godhead nor goodness; nor is he spirit according to our understanding.[11]

The negative way typically begins by denying those qualities that are considered antonyms of God (e.g., "God is not evil"). It then works through descriptors until it denies even those qualities that are regularly attributed to God (e.g., "nor is he spirit according to our understanding"). This is a philosophical reality as much as it is a theological one. That which exceeds sensory perception cannot be received by it. The infinite or that which is beyond description cannot be contained within limited speech or understanding.

Early Christian writer Tertullian observes:

> That which is infinite is known only to itself. This it is which gives some notion of God, while yet beyond all our conceptions—our very incapacity of fully grasping Him affords us the idea of what He really is. He is presented to our minds in His transcendent greatness, as at once known and unknown.[12]

Should theologians, pastors, and laypeople simply stop talking or writing about God? After all, would not silence be the speech closest to the divine? Certainly, in a time of constant communication and unending content distribution, the world needs more silence to hear the "still small voice" of God. Philosopher Ludwig Wittgenstein once wrote, "What can be said at all can be said clearly, and what we cannot talk about we must pass over in silence."[13] For Dionysius and other mystics, silence is considered the highest form of divine contemplation:

> The higher we soar in contemplation, the more limited become our expressions of that which is purely intelligible; even as now, when plunging into the Darkness which is above the intellect, we pass not merely into brevity of speech, but even into absolute silence.[14]

When transparency is privileged, silence becomes a rare commodity. When we encounter the mystery of God, silence is sometimes the only appropriate response. We will return to focus specifically on the virtue of silence and "quiet attentiveness" later in this book. The practice of quiet attentiveness is appropriate not only before God but as we respond to those who are created in God's mysterious image. After Job's suffering and lamentation, God finally responds to him out of a whirlwind, "Who is this that obscures my plans with words without knowledge?"[15] Too many of our words are without knowledge, whether knowledge of the divine or knowledge of one another. In these moments, we are called to silence. We again confront the tension of speaking the unspeakable. How might one provide a narrative of that which is beyond narrativity?

With the Judeo-Christian belief that God is also revealed through the pages of Scripture, mystery cannot be "all there is." Even the *via negativa says something* about God, if only to deny that God's attributes fall within our comprehension. Instead, when gesturing toward God in speech and language, we beg a grace that is best expressed in C. S. Lewis' *Footnote to All Prayers*,

> He whom I bow to only knows to whom I bow
> When I attempt the ineffable name, murmuring Thou,
> And dream of Pheidian fancies and embrace in heart
> Meanings, I know, which cannot be the thing thou art.
> All prayers always, taken at their word, blaspheme
> Invoking frail imageries a folk-lore dream;
> And all men are idolaters, crying unheard
> To senseless idols, if thou take them at their word,
> And all men in their praying, self-deceived, address
> One that is not (so saith that old rebuke) unless
> Thou, of mere grace, appropriate, and to thee divert
> Men's arrows, all at hazard aim, beyond desert,
> Take not, oh Lord, our literal sense, but in thy great,
> Unbroken speech our halting metaphor translate.[16]

Words written or uttered about God are unskillful arrows that miss their mark. All prayers are in the spirit of Pheidias, the Greek sculptor who crafted the great statue of Zeus at Olympia. Any outline of God we might sculpt bears little resemblance to God's image. We might recall here Levinas' objection to understanding human beings as *living icons*. There is no icon or statue, only a *trace* of the divine.

To speak of (or to) God, we must cling to confession and forgiveness, moving *toward* God in courageous humility—virtues that will be explored later in the context of caregiving. We beg pardon for our faltering prayers and in humility speak only with the courage that we will be forgiven for our inappropriate and bumbling phrases.[17]

In recent postmodern approaches to theology and literary theory, one finds examples of how language has been employed with humility to gesture toward the divine. *Theopoetics* shares principles with negative theology as it disputes the ability of language to carry the fullness of divine truth. Rather than simply being poetry *about* God, it questions the ways in which the *logos* of theology (logic, order, rationality, etc.) tends to dominate discourse. Theopoetics seeks to challenge fixed meanings and ultimate realities and "has a heavy emphasis on the importance of aesthetic, sensual, and experiential knowing," without concluding that nothing *can* be known or merely descending into skepticism.[18] Behind recent theopoetic writing lies the understanding that words about God contain a gesturing toward God. Talking or writing about God changes our understanding *of* God, and each person will relate to this work differently, based on their own experiences.

It is important to note that theopoetics does not so much replace theology as it provides a different way of *doing* theology, one that bears the "accent of someone whose first tongue is not academic but sensual, whose dialect betrays an origin of flesh."[19] Put differently, theopoetics is theology that attempts to take mystery and embodiment seriously in not only its outcomes but also its methods.

Walking the path of *via negativa* or exploring theopoetics serves as a reminder that mystery lies at the heart of divine revelation. However, these practices alone may lead one to emphasize mystery or opacity *without* leaving room for God's revelation. Jesus Christ, the Word made flesh, serves as the Christian model for *imitatio Dei* or the "image of the invisible God."[20] We now turn to examine some of the biblical texts that best display God's self-revelation in the pages of the New Testament.

THE HIDDEN REVELATION OF CHRIST

Within the Christian tradition lies a rich moral teleology of *imitatio Dei*. Theologians have grappled for millennia with what it means to grow to imitate Christ and to "resemble God in loving."[21] However, this moral tradition cannot simply be captured in a rulebook or a code of conduct. Within even this "material" image of God, we find a rich complexity of revelation and mystery. Intellectual capacity or ability, while it might grasp revealed precepts of the Christian faith, is not privileged in receiving either mystery or revelation. Mystery confounds the intellect while revelation must be received from *outside* the intellect. To be *revelation*, it cannot arise from the powers of cognition. Since there is no easily intelligible rulebook to follow, those of us who seek to follow Christ cannot calculate our way into resembling him. To imitate Christ requires ongoing practice and discernment as we step forward in faith. We do so in fear and trembling, unable to fully comprehend the neighbor whom we are called to love.

The apostle Paul writes that Jesus is the "image of the invisible God, the firstborn over all creation."[22] In Romans, Paul refers to Christ as the "revelation of the mystery which has been kept secret for long ages past,"[23] and it is through Christ that God has "made known to us the mystery of His will."[24] The writer of Hebrews begins by describing how Christ is greater than the prophets who came before him. Whereas God previously spoke through prophets in various ways, God has now spoken through his Son, "the radiance of God's glory and the exact representation of his being, sustaining all things by his powerful word."[25]

However, there are important differences between the revelation of Christ and the myths of transparency that presume to know the truth by way of intellectual ability. In 1 Corinthians 1, Paul observes:

> The message of the cross is foolishness to those who are perishing, but to us who are being saved it is the power of God. For it is written:
>
> > "I will destroy the wisdom of the wise;
> > the intelligence of the intelligent I will frustrate."
>
> Where is the wise person? Where is the teacher of the law? Where is the philosopher of this age? Has not God made foolish the wisdom of the world? For since in the wisdom of God the world through its wisdom did not know him, God was pleased through the foolishness of what was preached to save those who believe.[26]

The good news of Jesus' birth, ministry, death, and is not complicated; it is *difficult*. To believe the message of the cross is not to grasp a sophisticated algorithm; it is to receive God as the suffering Christ: to encounter the God *hidden in suffering*.[27] To receive the message of the cross is to acknowledge our fundamental dependence and the absence of self-mastery. This is a message that seems like foolishness to those who prefer the acclaim and sense of competence that intellectual mastery provides.

Paul goes on to proclaim that he did not come to the Corinthians "with eloquence or human wisdom," but rather, "resolved to know nothing . . . except Jesus Christ and him crucified."[28] Through the remainder of the passage, Paul contrasts the world's wisdom with God's wisdom, "a mystery that has been hidden and that God destined for our glory before time began."[29]

Paul is clear that the revelation of God comes through the person of Jesus Christ. In having *the mind of Christ*, the Holy Spirit searches out the deep and mysterious wisdom of God and makes it known to those who love God. Those things which "no human mind has conceived . . . are the things God has revealed to us by his Spirit."[30] Human knowledge cannot manufacture the wisdom of God. Even within God's revelation lies the mystery of the ways in which the Holy Spirit works to communicate with God's people, with words taught not by human wisdom but by the Spirit.[31]

Faith: Christ as Paradox

Chapter 5 identified Kierkegaard's insistence on the *incognito* of the God-man. Precisely because the concept of God is so foreign to the limits of a lived human life, there is an incomprehensibility in the united dichotomy of the God-man that makes Christ the *Paradox*. To consider God dying on the cross as a human being is a profound foolishness. That the Infinite would become finite, that Perfection would take on limits, or that the One would become one of the many confounds human wisdom. As paradox, the mystery of God in Christ is not only "an objective uncertainty" for Kierkegaard's pseudonymous Johannes Climacus but a *necessarily* objective uncertainty. There is no way to arrive at this kind of truth apart from a leap of faith, "An objective uncertainty, held fast through appropriation with the most passionate inwardness."[32]

Kierkegaard does not rule out the possibility of evidence that makes Christianity more palatable to the intellect. The work of apologists may be effective to a certain point. Fundamentally, however, the offense of Christ lies purposefully at the heart of the Gospel message so that no one may enter the kingdom of heaven by intellect alone. Kierkegaard has harsh words for those who mislead others into thinking they attain heavenly truth by worldly measures:

> Woe to him, therefore, who preaches Christianity without the possibility of offense. Woe to the person who smoothly, flirtatiously, commandingly, convincingly preaches some soft, sweet something which is supposed to be Christianity! Woe to the person who makes miracles reasonable. Woe to the person who betrays and breaks the mystery of faith, distorts it into public wisdom, because he takes away the possibility of offense![33]

Karl Barth follows Luther's theology of the cross and Kierkegaard's writing above, insisting upon the failure of reason to grasp faith in Christ. "There is no such thing as a mature and assured possession of faith: regarded psychologically, it is always a leap into the darkness of the unknown, a flight into empty air."[34] Barth emphasizes that Christ is the revelation and the Word of God, yet he is also clear that we encounter Christ only by faith and not by a logical or rational "way" to God.

> The revelation which is in Jesus, because it is the revelation of the righteousness of God, must be the most complete veiling of His incomprehensibility. In Jesus, God becomes veritably a secret: He is made known as the Unknown, speaking in eternal silence; He protects Himself from every intimate companionship and from all the impertinence of religion. He becomes a scandal to the Jews and to the Greeks foolishness.[35]

The beauty of this scandal is that Christ is accessible to all. It is not those with greater wisdom or intelligence who are primed to follow Christ. Indeed the call to "trust" may find greater resistance among those who seek intelligibility and transparency in all matters. Similarly, Christ is not only accessible to those who understand themselves, those who believe they are able to *account* for their actions. Those who understand their life as moral and upright may more fully resist the call of Christ to "follow me." Jesus is the basis for a morality and spirituality that in no way relies upon intellect or education. Being a disciple of Christ is a journey of moral formation that requires trust and commitment without hubristic aspirations to knowledge and competency.

Love: Christ as Pattern

Faith is a key aspect of the Christian life that goes beyond intellectual transparency. "Now faith is the reality (or assurance) of what is hoped for, the proof (or conviction) of what is not seen."[36] Love, the heart of the relational *imago Dei*, similarly transcends intellectual accounting. The "blindness" of love moves into territory unattainable by sight. In Judith Butler's *Giving an Account of Oneself*, partial blindness as a metaphor is the basis for her ethics of responsibility. There are ways the presumption that "one sees" actually prevents one from encountering revelation. Where justice may be said to be objectively "blind," love is blind in its passionate subjectivity.[37] As N. T. Wright has observed:

> The point about love . . . is that it transcends the object/subject distinction. Of course it does: when I truly love, whether the object of my love is a planet or a person, a symphony or a sunset, I am celebrating the otherness of the beloved, wanting the beloved to be what it really is, greater than my imagining or perception, stranger, more mysterious. Love celebrates that mystery: in that sense, it is truly "objective"; but it is also of course delightedly "subjective."[38]

For Kierkegaard, there is always a risk or an investment in faith, because it is not assured in its intellectual powers of its object. Faith requires a *leap*, and the God-man can be an object only of faith, not of intellect. Love is a similarly a risk, for what is loved may cause suffering. Where faith takes a leap toward that which lies beyond the subject/object divide, love *falls* toward the object of its desire. Where the intellect seeks revelation that lies higher than itself, love passionately plunges toward the one it loves. Where loss of faith may entail an intellectual and existential crisis, a lost love causes deep suffering, and one often suffers on behalf of one's beloved. Love reaches for what is best in the other, believes in the other, hopes in the other, and in doing so frees the beloved to live into their potential even when that person does not see the potential in themselves.

GOD WITH US: THE MYSTERY OF SUFFERING LOVE

> The striking thing about the Precious Blood is the bond it establishes between love and suffering in our experience, a bond that has become so close that we have come to think of suffering accepted with joy as the most authentic sign of love with any depth at all.
>
> **Gabriel Marcel**[39]

There is a form of mystery in the story of Christ that is distinct from the philosophical question of Kierkegaard's leap of faith. Looking beyond the intellectual paradox provided by the question of "how" the Word became flesh, the question arises as to "why" the Word would become flesh. The answer seems to lie in the well-known verse spoken to Nicodemus, "For [because] God so loved the world that he gave his one and only Son, that whoever believes in him shall not perish but have eternal life."[40] At first glance, this appears to be a comprehensive rationale. As one continues to read John's account of the life of Jesus, however, this answer may provoke more questions than answers. Why did Christ have to go through the pain and suffering that he did so that people might be saved? *Why* would God love the world if human beings cause so much pain? Here, intellectual answers fail. In Paul's words, we are struck by *fear and trembling* before a God who would die for humanity. This is love that we cannot grasp, a love that can never be fully responded to. It can only be received.

The mystery of Christ's death and resurrection and the power of sacrificial love *draws* us more than it answers our questions. Thomas Reynolds reflects on Christ's death:

> In the lowly destitution of the cross we find what we are looking for—a God who comes to us, welcoming us into the divine presence in and through direct solidarity with us, both as temporarily non-disabled

persons and persons with disabilities. God's power is loving, vulnerably present in the depths of the tragic, both in terms of being victimized by instruments of dominion as well as in terms of identifying with death itself. This is why Moltmann calls Christ crucified humanity's "true theology and knowledge of God."[41]

In the aftermath of Christ's death and resurrection, Paul's exhortation to the Corinthians begins to take shape: "No eye has seen, no ear has heard, and no mind has imagined what God has prepared for those who love him."[42] The width, length, height, and depths of God's mysterious love have been revealed in Jesus' death on the cross and in the miraculous resurrection that followed.

There is a qualitative difference between intellectual understanding and relational knowledge, two types of "knowing." Moltmann writes, "To know God in the cross of Christ is a crucifying form of knowledge, because it shatters everything to which a man can hold and which he can build . . . and precisely in so doing sets him free."[43] To believe in Christ's death and resurrection is to receive meaning that transcends human rationality. To believe the message of the cross is to be convinced that the height of human accomplishment lies not in intellectual prowess but in sacrificial love. The cross does not seek to convince by incontrovertible arguments but by lived example, a demonstration of the resurrection power of divine love.[44] We cannot fully comprehend or articulate this love in human words. It is a love that we find we have always already received, a love that has "come before" us and in which we are radically constituted. *We love because he has first loved us.*[45]

Hans Urs Balthasar in *Love Alone Is Credible* writes, "The totally-other, the ever-greater appears and seizes hold of us in the very act of overwhelming us through the ultimately incomprehensible character of that love."[46] According to Barth and Balthasar, there is no *via negativa* by which one may reach God. One must be reached *by* God. It is through God's prior love that we encounter the person of Jesus Christ, the Word become flesh. The way through which we receive God's love, however, will always remain mysterious, both because of the paradox of the God-man and because of the mystery of the "ultimately incomprehensible character" of God's love.

LOVE BEFORE US, LOVE BEHIND US

Part 2, "Encountering My Neighbor" began with the premise that the *imago Dei* is critical to any account of ethical motivation or formation within the Christian narrative. The relational *imago Dei* can be approached in two ways. A "formal" understanding takes the creation of human beings in God's image at face value: each human being has already *received* this divine image. This is not something that can be articulated or grasped as a particular aspect or attribute of the human being. It is the trace of the divine we encounter in our neighbor, the basis for ethical obligation and responsibility. The material *imago* describes Christ as the *imitatio Dei*. We seek to follow the example of Jesus as the image of the invisible God.

The chapters that followed investigated the barriers human beings face in recognizing this *imago Dei* in one another. Transparency myths regarding the people we encounter, self-knowledge, and our knowledge of the divine prevent us from recognizing that we encounter God's image in our neighbor. Following Butler, we discover that responsibility must be grounded in our shared partial opacity rather than in transparent accountability. The weight of our moral obligation and motivation lies in a fundamental responsibility to God (Kierkegaard) and one another (Butler) that comes before our ability to articulate what this responsibility "looks like." We are *formed together* in the divine image, and yet we are unable to describe precisely how we have come to be who we are or why we act in the ways that we do.

Even within the *imitatio Dei*, as we learn to "resemble God in loving" by following the example of Christ, revelation is shrouded in mystery. Only through the mysterious gifts of faith and love might we embrace Christ as paradox and receive God's sacrificial love.

The Christian tradition subverts any easy association of education, knowledge, or intellectual ability with moral uprightness. It is a story that calls, draws, and attracts those whose stories remain mysterious to themselves and others. The relational *imago Dei*, on the one hand, is the basis for the weight of all moral obligation, the root of ethical motivation. Christ's mysterious suffering love, on the other hand, serves as the basis for moral formation that is just as accessible to those with intellectual disabilities or to children as it is to caregivers. Any Christian theological anthropology must leave room for this mysterious love. Any virtues or practices of Christian caregiving must be grounded in humble recognition of Christ's sacrifice and our inability to grasp what is received only through faith.

III

RESPONDING TO THE CALL

8

Formed Together in Love
Toward an Ethic of Christian Care

> What it is to be human is not a bundle of capacities. It's a way that you
> are, a way that you are in the world, a way that you are with another.

Eva Feder Kittay[1]

As human beings, our identities are shrouded in mystery, radically relationally composed in concert with one another by God. We are always already
responsible to one another. We are called *to* one another and *by* one another
and are part of each other's stories in often-inexpressible ways. This primal
ethics precedes even our comprehension of ethical forms and systems, comes
before any ability to discern moral teleology.

To suggest that the root of responsibility and the instinct for ethical motivation and obligation precedes conscious thought does not, therefore, mean
that thought is purposeless in moral *formation* as we care for and serve others.
It does indicate, however, that intellectual capacity is not privileged in deter-
mining the moral weight of human action. We may cautiously begin to rein-
terpret moral reasoning not on the basis of transparency myths but in humble
acknowledgment of our shared and partial opacity to others and ourselves.
Alasdair MacIntyre was right to begin to think through virtues of acknowledged dependence in *Dependent Rational Animals*; however, here we do so
recognizing that our dependence goes far deeper than MacIntyre admitted.

In this way, we return to the language of virtues. We pick up not only
on MacIntyre's initial definition of an "acquired human quality," possession
and exercise of which enables "us to achieve those goods which are internal

to practices,"[2] but also on his later clarification that no human quality is to be accounted a virtue unless it satisfies the conditions at three stages:[3]

a. Qualities necessary to achieve the goods internal to practices
b. Qualities contributing to the good of a whole life
c. Qualities that enable the good for human beings, "the conception of which can only be elaborated and possessed within an ongoing social tradition"[4]

In fact, building on this final point, it was an investigation of the good for human beings within the ongoing social tradition of Christianity and *imago Dei* theology that facilitated the critique of MacIntyre and the presuppositions of transparency contained in this book.

The way we tell our stories, and the way that we listen to the accounts given by others, is a litmus test of our willingness to acknowledge not only our own dependence but also the interdependence of humanity. Do we attempt to construct a narrative history from birth to death, making every detail fit along the way? Or do we approach one another with a sincere appreciation for the mystery of these stories we tell? There will be times when I (or the person whom I encounter) am unable to give an answer to the questions demanded of me. This is not, in itself, an ethical failing or lack of the fullness of human morality. It may, instead, provide an opportunity for ongoing discovery and deeper relational trust. Our narratives are more poetry than factual autobiography, gesturing toward the deeper realities of our experiences and our establishment.[5] Love and gratitude, grief and despair, hope and peace often leave us struggling to make sense of ourselves or to articulate our experiences.

The beauty of this mystery is that moments of discovery—moments of revelation—will occur along the way as we journey with others. These revelations occur not only as we discover the lived reality of others but as we experience *ourselves* in new ways. If we understood ourselves or one another to the extent that the myths of transparency would have us believe, there would be little room left for genuine discovery.

We begin to glimpse the importance of virtues that depend not only upon what we know about our history, our traditions, and one another, but virtues that take delight in those aspects of our selves that lie in silence.

THE SECRET OF DISCOVERY

In Kierkegaard's *Fear and Trembling*, the pseudonymous Johannes de Silentio attempts to write the story of faith—a faith that cannot be adequately expressed or articulated. This faith seems absurd to those like Johannes de Silentio who do not share it. Abraham is caught between the temptation to speak, to try to explain, to "give an account" for his choice to sacrifice his son Isaac at God's command. "Abraham *cannot* speak, because he cannot say that which would explain everything . . . that it is an ordeal such that, please note, the ethical is the temptation."[6] It was not possible for Abraham to put into words his faith, or the reasons for his commitment to his faith, that led to his decision. There is a sense in which each of our actions, identities, and relations to one another are "secret." We each carry with us histories and stories that we are not conscious of, let alone able to put into words.

Jean Vanier recounts the story of Claudia:

> She lived in our community in Honduras, in Suyapa, near Tegucigalpa. She was autistic and blind. She rarely spoke any word. . . . I recall that one day, when I was sitting across from her at table, I asked her in Spanish, "Claudia, why are you so happy?" She replied after quite a long pause, "God." When Claudia says one word, there is no need to ask another question! One word from Claudia is verbose! Afterward, I went to see Nadine, who had founded the community, and I said, "Did you hear what Claudia said?" Nadine said she had. "How do you interpret her response?" I asked. She said, "It's her secret." We each have a secret in the depth of our beings, in union with God and with others.[7]

Caught up in an existence that is so dependent upon the relationships that have made us who we are, every person is an extraordinary singularity. We cannot capture this singularity, this secret, in language. Jacques Derrida writes, "As soon as one speaks, as soon as one enters the medium of language, one loses that very singularity."[8] Any account that we give of ourselves is immediately reduced to the language in which it finds its expression. It attempts to give an expression of the singularity, the "authorship" of the life of which it speaks but is unable to do so. There are times when attempting to give an account of ourselves betrays the very givenness of our identity. In these moments, all we can do is respond as Claudia did. After reflecting on her answer, Vanier observes, "The good shepherd is called to respect that secret within each one and help that secret to grow and to deepen."[9]

Looking back on Vanier's account of Claudia, we realize that Vanier was the one putting words to Claudia's secret. Claudia's secret remains a secret even through Vanier's account of her, even though he is the one with the power and the audience to be able to tell of her secret. It may be true that everyone has a secret in the depths of a being that is known only to God or others, but this also means that others can never adequately convey this secret on our behalf.

As we walk alongside people in caregiving relationships, we become a part of their secret and they, ours. We must resist ethical pride that does violence to this secret, breaking it apart to stand as judge and juror over the story of another, or using our own power to tell the story of another. Any "account" of virtue and moral practice must integrate a profound respect for this secret at the heart of the lives of others and the secret at the heart of our own life. In this secret place resides "God," the *imago Dei*, beyond comprehension and narrativity. In this inexpressible secret place lies, hidden, the root and weight of all ethical action and discourse.

There is another kind of secret that must also be acknowledged here. This is the secret darkness that we know of ourselves yet refuse to bring to the light. There is a hiddenness that comes from incomprehensibility of the *imago Dei*, and there are those things that we know yet hide—the secrets that actually tear apart the fabric of our relationships with one another, secrets that come not from a place of love but from a place of power, control, and selfish ambition. Vanier spoke freely of Claudia's secret, the kind of secret that cannot be articulated or confessed. He refused, though, to confess his own secrets—an account that demanded he reveal the evil that lay in his own heart.

This is why, among the virtues of care to come, the *virtue of confession* must not be overlooked. We must confess not only those things that we cannot give an account of but even more those aspects of our lives that we *know* are wrong yet conceal from one another. These kinds of secrets can inflict incalculable pain on others.

Let us return to the secret identity that is not concealed from others because of sin but because it is inexpressible. Within the Christian tradition, we believe that through Christ's death we have each died and our lives are "now hidden with Christ in God."[10] There is a mysterious way our identities are not fully revealed until Christ, who forms our identities, appears in glory.

Rather than attempting to establish an ethical system, I suggest that in our places of dependency and vulnerability, in our contemplation of the related rootedness of what it means to be created in the image of God, we are always already *toward* one another. In being formed together, we are always already accountable *to* one another and to God even though we are unable to give this account transparently. While what MacIntyre calls "independent practical reasoning" continues to be helpful to work through our choices and responses in particular situations, the motivation and openness to ethical formation is already *here*. Reason or intelligence do not ground this fundamental relationality. If we ask with Cain, "Am I my brother's keeper?" we stand condemned already: it is in our shared, radical relational constitution that we "keep" one another. We are always already *keeping* our brothers and sisters, family formed in the *imago Dei*.

What has been demonstrated in the preceding chapters is that *myths of transparency* distance us from the very virtues that open us to rest in the ethical responsibility at the heart of what it means to be human. It is not in scrupulous ethical accounting that we find the motivation to act rightly with and toward others. Rather, we are called to act in profound humility and love in response to this mysterious life that we have received, an identity that is entwined with the lives of those around us. In this recognition of how much remains *unknown* we discover that we have no moral advantage over those who process information in different ways or who experience the world in bodies with different abilities and limitations. We are freed to encounter one another as equals, deeply relationally rooted in the *imago Dei*.

In this final section, we explore what it means to build upon ethical motivation as we are formed in virtue with one another, whether in professional caregiving relationships or as we care for our friends and loved ones. According to MacIntyre, these virtues must be acquired qualities that are necessary to achieve the goods internal to practice of caregiving, contribute to the good of a whole life, and enable the good for human beings as understood in the Christian tradition and social practice. This good for human beings, in light of Christian tradition, cannot be separated from the need to give and receive love. As this love troubles and complexifies any rationalistic account of the good, the virtues we seek are those that display a profound respect for the hidden "secret" of the other and, as such, are open to humbly discovering good in the lives of people of all abilities.

LOVE, THE UNSPOKEN WELLSPRING OF VIRTUE

> Your roots will grow down into God's love and keep you strong. And
> may you have the power to understand, as all God's people should,
> how wide, how long, how high, and how deep his love is. May you
> experience the love of Christ, though it is too great to understand fully.
> Then you will be made complete with all the fullness of life and power
> that comes from God.
>
> **Ephesians 3:17-19, NLT**

Love has wound through the threads of this book in ways often present but seldom explicit. This is how love works. The story of the divine through the Christian tradition is that of an unrelenting, mysterious, sacrificial love.

Love for one another is at the center of *responding* to people created in God's image. We now turn to discovering the forms of love that are "called for" in recognizing the *imago Dei* in our neighbors for whom we care. We do so not in light of the tyranny of transparency but in appreciation for the mysterious gift of divine love. We will explore virtues that are shaped by acknowledging divine relationality and shared, partial opacity—virtues of care.

These virtues of care are a gesture toward the possibilities that open up once we embody humility in our shared stories, in the recognition that we are *formed together* at a fundamental level. "Virtues of care" has a twofold meaning, then.

1. It is hoped that this book, in some small way, extols the virtues of caregiving. I believe that the call to care lies at the heart of our beautiful and broken humanity. To care with and for others—to be caregiving partners personally or professionally is a high calling.

2. The practices, postures, or virtues explored in this book flow from care in its etymological sense of *grief* or *lament*. We approach one another humbly, with grace and patience, out of an awareness of all that we cannot know and that for which we cannot give an account. We grieve the ability to transparently articulate the world to one another—an ability we once thought we possessed. We grieve the injustices that we have committed and that have been committed against us, injustices for which we will never fully account. Yet it is out of this sense of loss that we learn to depend upon one another, to forgive each other, and to act in humble courage toward one another. Grounded humility springs from a well of deep grief, just as divine mercy flows downstream from the river of love already received.

Love is an undercurrent running beneath the surface of even professional caregiving. To *speak* of love—to put it into words as such—risks defying professional codes of conduct, yet if it were not present there would be no moral substance to caregiving in the first place. Love is the heart of the profession, yet it must not be professed.

In the Christian tradition, there is a reason that love for God must supersede all other loves. The source of love is God, for "God is love."[11] We recall Kierkegaard's articulation of this in *Works of Love*:

> Just as the quiet lake originates deep down in hidden springs no eye has seen, so also does a person's love originate even more deeply in God's

love. If there were no gushing spring at the bottom, if God were not love, then there would be neither the little lake, nor a human being's love.[12]

Those who follow Christ are called to respond to Christ's command to love one's neighbor as oneself, even the neighbor who is not seen as lovable whether owing to prejudice or societal conditioning in the cult of normalcy. Kierkegaard builds on John's words in 1 John 4 in *The Duty to Love the People We See*:

A person should begin with loving the unseen, God, because then he himself will learn what it is to love. But that he actually loves the unseen will be known by his loving the brother he sees; the more he loves the unseen, the more he will love the people he sees.[13]

In their emphasis on the importance of receiving divine love *first*, Kierkegaard and Hans Urs von Balthasar agree. Balthasar calls God's love *"absolute love"* throughout the pages of his *Love Alone Is Credible*. There is a qualitative difference between human love and divine love. The suffering love of God is revealed in its mysterious fullness in the death of Christ on the cross. Through this sacrificial death, "the totally-other, the ever-greater appears and seizes hold of us in the very act of overwhelming us through the ultimately incomprehensible character of that love."[14] The love of God is ultimately incomprehensible and unexpected. To be seized by this love means that the follower of Christ loves her neighbors in ways that might also appear incomprehensible or illogical. While constrained by bodily limitation, human beings acting out of this love might demonstrate qualities of the divine *agape*: love without conditions. This is a love that does not need to first understand one's neighbor before extending love. It is a love that enfolds one's enemies and persecutors as well as one's friends and family.[15] To express this love, however, Balthasar maintains that one must first experience it. It is a love that reveals that, "in the light of this love one has never loved" and convinces each person that he or she must "start from the beginning to re-learn what love really is."[16] To love One who is "totally other" means that the human being cannot be the one to initiate this love. Rather, each person must first *receive* love.[17]

In being incomprehensible and "foreign," the love of God must be *revealed*. It must come from outside of oneself and in this sense is a discovery, though not discovered through our own powers. Indeed, this speaks to our own inadequacy of ability to grasp God's love by intellect or emotional effort. It cannot be thought or manufactured, only received. The love of God defies all expectations of what one has previously known as love. Robert Miner describes that for Balthasar,

> God's love will strike people as a "shock," a *scandalum* that cannot be assimilated to our notions of love. A person must first be scandalized; he must first experience a "pitfall" that God has prepared for the rational creature. Only then can he possibly see that he lacks any real foothold, any center in his own being.[18]

We discover that we are *dispossessed* by this love. It is only through this unsettling scandal that we are reoriented to love others in a new way. *We are not our own.* Whereas we may have previously viewed all others through the perspective of our own priorities and desires, this scandalous reorientation points us to a new kind of love that lays down its life, its cares, and its concerns in the service of others. Indeed, it is only when one's own priorities are displaced that one is truly fulfilled in loving service. This is not to say that our own perspectives and passions no longer matter, rather that they are recalibrated to include the needs and desires of our neighbors. Insofar as our identities are formed together with others, it should not come as a surprise that personal flourishing takes place only in the context of this dispossessed community care.

The givenness of our existence through the love of God, formed in the divine image, is foundational to ethical obligation and motivation within the Christian tradition. Traced back to the formal *imago Dei*, this constitutive relation and responsibility arises pre-consciousness. However, we are also called toward the ethical formation of the incomprehensible love of Christ in *imitatio Dei*. Thus, the mysterious revelation of divine love provides both the moral *motivation* and the impetus for the moral *formation* of caregiving within the Christian tradition.

Before further exploration of the virtues that arise out of this pattern for moral formation, however, we must first understand how preference and proximity shape and structure our love for others. Is it possible to love everyone equally, as seems to be the demand of neighbor-love? How do strangers, neighbors, friends, and family fit into this picture of relational responsibility? Are we called to respond differently to some than others?

Loving Every Other

According to Kierkegaard, Christian love "teaches us to love all people, unconditionally all."[19] This is demonstrated in the equality of each person "before God" and in light of Christ's command to love. Where love for family and friends is *preferential love*, Christ commands *neighbor love*, which relates to the "un-lovable object." The "ugly . . . is the neighbor, whom one shall love."[20] This is a harsh way to describe those to whom we are not initially attracted, those whom we do not prefer. Here Kierkegaard acknowledges an often-unnamed truth. In projecting onto others our own prejudices, stereotypes, and baser instincts, there are many in this world whom we fear or avoid, although we may not even admit this to ourselves. The "ugliness" we see in others is often a product of our fears and unacknowledged vulnerability. It is a by-product of the cult of normalcy and the myths of transparency. We feel as though we have good reason to avoid others but are not willing to question the myth of transparency that presumes we know why.

Henri Nouwen's relationship with Adam exemplifies that when we spend time with people and get to know them it becomes increasingly difficult to maintain our prejudices. Eventually, we open ourselves to the experience of care. "Falling in love" is a common expression, yet we can also inexplicably find ourselves "falling in care" for people with whom we thought we would never learn to relate to. As our preconceptions disappear, we come to recognize each person's gifts and discover that they have made a difference in our lives. Nouwen describes this change as Adam became his confidant: "I began to talk to Adam. . . . It didn't seem to matter to me anymore that he could not respond in words. We were together, growing in friendship, and I was glad to be there. Before long Adam became my much trusted listener."[21]

There are those whom we "naturally" prefer. This may be because of similarities in interests and passions, shared history, or any number of reasons related to the ways we *are like someone else*. Friendships and romantic relationships are often born out of these preferences. Kierkegaard describes that there are also people we need to be commanded to love. By responding to Christ's command and demonstrating care and presence with people whom we do not initially prefer, we often grow to care for them as well. This is not a magical formula. There will always be people with whom we are not comfortable, those who require a continued effort. In these cases, we are still commanded to love. Preference may grow and fade, which is precisely why love must be commanded.

As evident in the writing of Judith Butler, we are mutually and profoundly responsible to and dependent upon one another. Following Christ's command to love our neighbor opens us up to the possibility of change on a subconscious level as well. Butler's contribution is the recognition that we are already bound together in mutual responsibility on a preconscious level. We may not be able to "give an account" of these deep ties yet. Is the command to love our neighbors as ourselves a responsibility that we can ever hope to live up to? The task seems too great.

The Paradox of Absolute Duty

In *Fear and Trembling*, Johannes de Silentio wrestles with Abraham's troubling willingness to sacrifice Isaac based on Abraham's professed faith. How might one choose between God's demand for sacrifice and saving the life of one's son? How is an ethical choice possible in such a scenario? There are no easy answers, yet Abraham's willingness to sacrifice Isaac through a "teleological suspension of the ethical" is praised as Abraham "having come as the single individual into an absolute relation to the absolute."[22]

In *The Gift of Death*, Jacques Derrida deconstructs this "absolute relation." Abraham's sacrifice of Isaac would not actually have been a sacrifice unless Abraham loved his son deeply. "It is indeed this love for Isaac that makes his act a sacrifice by its paradoxical contrast to his love for God."[23] There is a sense in which, though, Isaac as a single individual is also an "absolute other" and demands ultimate accountability. "Duty or responsibility binds me to the other, to the other as other, and ties me in my absolute singularity to the other as other."[24] Ultimately, for Derrida,

> I cannot respond to the call, the request, the obligation, or even the love of another without sacrificing the other other, the other others. Every other (one) is every (bit) other [*tout autre est tout autre*], every one else is completely or wholly other. The simple concepts of alterity and of singularity constitute the concept of duty as much as that of responsibility. As a result, the concepts of responsibility, of decision, or of duty, are condemned a priori to paradox, scandal, and aporia.[25]

Every time we respond to *a particular other* in ethical responsibility, Derrida is saying, we sacrifice every other "other." The time, money, energy, and devotion we pour into one person (whether a family member, friend, or a complete stranger) are time, money, energy, and devotion that are not being invested into others.[26]

The violence of the demand of a transparently coherent ethical narrative lies in its unfulfillable demands. The dilemma that Derrida leads us to concerns calculation of the "most ethical course of action." How might we give an account for those we have sacrificed when "every other is absolute other?" When one is responsible to or accountable for every other, all others, all of the time, there is no possibility of living up to or even giving an account of one's choices.

How might we consider our obligation to love "every other" in a way that is not paralyzing? Is it possible to acknowledge our profound responsibility and respond to *an other* without becoming guilt ridden and overwhelmed with our obligation to *every other other*? With Derrida's critique in mind, it would seem that anything we do requires sacrificing all other responsibilities and duties.

Neighbor love is an approach with the potential to move us beyond the scope of preferential love to respond to "every other." We are challenged to act with a greater understanding of equality and commitment to loving even those we do not prefer. Even here, perhaps especially here, in a posture of generous hospitality, we face Derrida's paradox. To give to one *other* seems to be to sacrifice every *other* other on the altar of preference or choice, even if that choice is toward loving one's neighbor.

Giving an Account: Divided Loyalties

In my work, I provide training on resiliency, compassion fatigue, and self-care to direct support professionals. One point that often hits home is the reminder that compassion fatigue impacts those whom we care most about—our family and friends—first. We believe that they can continue to absorb the emotional impact because of their commitment to us. Meanwhile, we continue to be drained in our efforts to sustain work relationships or professional caregiving relationships.

I'm also involved in conflict resolution support. Two women had acknowledged that their conflict at work was impacting their home lives and relationships. During a mediation session, it became clear there was one incident that had severely fractured their relationship. Julie primarily worked in administrative support, and Pam provided direct care. While Pam was providing support, Julie approached her about bringing a jacket to another woman who was at home with her family. Due to staffing pressures and ultimately due to lack of sector funding, there was not another support worker around that day. Pam thought that she should handle both responsibilities as the direct support professional but also knew that the woman she was currently with was the priority at the time. Julie knew that the family of the woman who was missing her jacket already had a fraught relationship with the support team and believed that getting the jacket to her needed to be the priority. She was willing to take the jacket herself but thought that she needed permission from Pam, who was working direct support. Poor communication followed, and, building on previous negative encounters between the two team members, a harassment report was filed between the two parties.

While multiple issues impacted Pam and Julie's relationships, this particular scenario—one that led to stress and anxiety at home for both parties—was built on the sense of duty Pam felt toward two people simultaneously. She was unable to "let go" of what she considered a profound obligation to meet the needs of everyone around her, which resulted in inadequate care for people she supported and broken relationships with her colleagues. The impact on Pam's home life included her own caregiving relationship with her autistic daughter.

Direct support professionals would likely not instinctively classify staffing shortages and tough decisions around caregiving responsibilities as a tension of divided moral obligation or express that "the concepts of responsibility, of decision, or of duty, are condemned *a priori* to paradox, scandal, and aporia."[27] However, in this example we observe Derrida's critique in action. Pam faced paralysis at the thought that it was her moral obligation to meet the needs of both people that she was responsible to, and this led to interpersonal conflict with her colleague.

The paradox of Pam's felt obligation to "every other other" is evident here on a small scale. In choosing to focus her attention on the person she was with, without communicating her limits or priorities to Julie, adverse effects were felt by everyone involved and even those who were indirectly affected, such as Pam's daughter or me being brought in to facilitate mediation. However, on a macro level one might observe that even Pam's decision to work at *this particular* nonprofit organization prevented her from caring for those supported by any other nonprofit organization. Working at that residential support location meant that she was "abandoning" every other support location. Or perhaps Pam would have had a greater impact by forgoing direct caregiving altogether and becoming a wealthy philanthropist who could fund caregiving endeavors nationally or around the world.

A Debt Too Great or a Gift Already Given?

To begin to address the dread that our ethical debt to love our neighbor as ourselves might always already be too great a demand, we recall the words of Emil Brunner:

> Thus the original nature of man is being in the love of God, the fulfilment of responsible being, the responsibility which comes not from a demand but from a gift, not from the law but from grace, from generous love, and itself consists in responsive love.[28]

Brunner reminds us that the call to *respond* to the other is always in response to a gift that has been given. This is true whether viewed through the lens of the divine gift of life (God) or the giftedness of a life formed together in deep relational dependency with others (our neighbors). The call to live into human flourishing is first of all a response not to law but to grace. All that we have, we have been given. In turn, we are called to give this *grace-gift* to others.[29] This gift is outside of a system of exchange. To borrow an observation from Alasdair MacIntyre, what we have received from others is incalculable, and so, too, our ethical response defies measure. Instead, it is our *telos* to give to others in love, out of the love that we have already received. Relational reciprocity is central to human flourishing. To exercise our givenness is to celebrate the gift, to *give back* only out of a sense of obligation is to nullify it. At the core of *response-ability* lies not only a summons but also the received ability to give, to respond, and to meet the needs of another whom we encounter.[30] It is this gift that we "face" in our neighbor; in the call of the person who experiences disabilities or who requires care, in the call *to* love and serve one another.

An unobtainable demand on every side leads to paralysis or abstraction and utilitarianism. Caught between the options, paralysis sets in because we cannot fulfill our duty to love *every other*. Alternately, we distance ourselves from the situation we find ourselves in and begin to calculate how to do the most good for the greatest number of people in the shortest amount of time. To do so, we must betray the singularity of each other and ourselves in the abstraction of utilitarian calculus.

Kierkegaard's writing on the importance of subjectivity in the experience of the truth reminds us that objective abstraction does not adequately reflect the human condition—the condition of being in a position to respond to another. Yes, there are times to calculate. Throughout our lives, we encounter complex dilemmas—situations for practical reasoning and consultation with our loved ones and community to make the best decisions we can, given the information we have at hand. However, acknowledging our *givenness* also means that we find ourselves in a particular place, with specific resources, surrounded by particular people. Indeed, we would not have the same degree of ethical responsibility if we were not uniquely situated in this way. In my particular place, time, history, and ability, I have physical limitations and limited knowledge about others and myself. *In my particularity*, there will be times when I will be the only one who is "in a place" to respond to another's need, and in other times I will not be in a place to meet the needs of another. "I" have a unique ability to respond—a *responsibility* that speaks to the gift and opportunity of this encounter. This is an ability available to all, an ability carried in the very nature of the gift and the encounter with the neighbor created in the *imago Dei*.

On the contrary, if we recognize that to give back out of obligation is to nullify the pure grace of our *givenness*, then we are opened to act toward others to express our gifts rather than to repay an ethical debt. The gift is entrusted to us and comes with responsibility, but that responsibility is not to repay the gift. If we comprehend our limits, then we know that it would be futile to think that we have infinite resources to give to others, and in our dependency, we work to give what we can out of gratitude, not debt. Judith Butler describes how Derrida's position presupposes what I have previously called the myth of transparency:

> What is striking about such extremes of self-beratement is the grandiose notion of the transparent "I" that is presupposed as the ethical ideal. This is hardly a belief in which self-acceptance (a humility about one's constitutive limitations) or generosity (a disposition towards the limits of others) might find room to flourish.[31]

Generosity recognizes that others have needs and, without presumption, approaches to listen to how these needs may be met. At times meeting these needs will involve our contribution and agency; at other times it may not. Recognizing my limits, including the limits of my self-understanding, is the kind of self-acceptance that opens me to give not out of demand but out of gift. It is this unassuming generosity that postures us toward the virtues of care.

9

The Virtues of Care

Discovering Who We Are

THE VIRTUE OF COURAGEOUS HUMILITY

> The moment you have a self at all, there is a possibility of putting
> yourself first—wanting to be the centre—wanting to be God, in
> fact. . . . What Satan put into the heads of our remote ancestors was
> the idea that they could "be like gods"—could set up on their own as if
> they had created themselves—be their own masters.
>
> **C. S. Lewis**[1]

Humility was arguably the first virtue lost in the biblical creation story. After
the serpent questions God's account of the situation, it is the desire to "be like
God, knowing good and evil" that propels Adam and Eve to disobedience.[2]
They seek to "have their eyes opened" to see transparently that which was
beyond their limits. It is our sense of givenness and limitation that helps us
to remain objective to ourselves and subjective to others, humbly willing to
question our own accounts and to be open to the stories of others. This same
posture recognizes that we will not be able to respond to everyone equally.
When we answer the call to serve another, we are turning down the call to
serve *another* other, or *every other* other. Whereas pride seeks to meet the
needs of everyone on its own, humility accepts the limits of embodiment.
The experience of human limitation makes the gifts we give that much more
significant.[3] The call to love others brings us to the realization that everyone
is equally worthy of love, yet we will never be able to love everyone equally

or unconditionally. In giving to others, we also recognize that there are *other others* giving as well, and we are not alone in meeting the needs of the world.

The person of Christ, as the mysterious revelation of God, is the *imitatio Dei* of the Christian tradition and the *telos* of what it means to be created in the divine image. Christ is therefore the example who displays the virtue of courageous humility in loving the people that he encountered throughout his life and ministry.

Encountering Christ: Loving Those We See

> It is a paradox indeed that those who want to be for "everyone" often
> find themselves unable to be close to anyone. When everybody becomes
> my "neighbor," it is worth wondering whether anybody can really
> become my "proximus," that is, the one who is most close to me.
>
> ### Henri Nouwen[4]

Kierkegaard reflects on the human need for love in *The Duty to Love the People We See*. He begins by proclaiming, "How *deeply* the need of love is rooted in human nature!"[5] This drive to love and to be loved requires a profound and courageous humility as we encounter one another. Even Jesus Christ, he reminds us, "humanly felt this need to love and be loved by an individual human being."[6] Kierkegaard points to the story of Christ asking Peter whether Peter loves him—three times. There is a certain paradox in Christ's approach, "What an appalling contradiction that the one who is God loves humanly, since to love humanly is to love an individual human being and to wish to be that individual human being's best beloved."[7]

Kierkegaard is saying that to love humanly, even as the God-man, is to experience the need to be loved by particular human others and to love particular human others. We need humility to accept that we are in need of human love, and we must be courageous to approach others for this love. We need humility to admit that we will never love others perfectly and courage to love one another anyway. When Jesus was on earth, even he failed the duty of "unconditional love," if this is to be understood as an obligation to love each and every human being in the same way, all of the time. This does not mean that Christ saw some people as worthy of love and others as unworthy, but, while he walked the earth, he invested more time in some disciples than others and expressed his love to each person in different ways. The duty to love the people that we see, as John instructs in 1 John 4:20, is "the duty to find in the world of actuality the people we can love in particular and in loving them to love the people we see."[8] Repeatedly, Kierkegaard calls his readers back to actuality. Love as an ideal, calculation, or even desire is not love until it acts *toward the people we see*. We are called to love *humanly*, which is always to love the particular other.

Herein lies the importance of *the neighbor*. The neighbor is someone whom I encounter. She and I have "crossed paths," yet she is not someone I naturally love. She is a near one, sometimes even as close as a spouse or partner, yet someone whom I may have difficulty loving. Indeed, it can at times be most difficult to love our neighbor when that person is a spouse or family member from whom we have grown apart. The category of the neighbor always draws us courageously beyond our comfort zone yet never with the hubris that we will be able to love another perfectly or completely. Christ acted in courageous humility in loving *the people he saw*, which included tax collectors and sinners, Pharisees and teachers of the law, and even his own disciples when they betrayed him. Kierkegaard notes:

> Christianly to descend from heaven is boundlessly to love the person you
> see just as you see him. Therefore if you want to be perfect in love, strive
> to fulfill this duty, in loving to love the person one sees, to love him just
> as you see him, with all his imperfections and weaknesses.[9]

To love the people we see is to retain our epistemic humility, not overlooking their faults in order to love but having the courage to love them just as they are—without ever fully knowing or understanding who they are! Courageous humility means that we embrace each other knowing that we will continue to discover each other's gifts and limitations. It is to commit to courageously care for one another *in* and *through* the limits of embodied humanity.

The Reciprocity and Simplicity of Courageous Humility

Humility also admits that there are times when I need to receive from others. Sometimes it is when we feel the most grateful that we deny others the opportunity to give. We fail to see that opening ourselves to *receive* the gift of another is perhaps the greatest gift we could give. Being conscious of my own limits allows me to recognize that at times I, too, need to rest in the care of others. It takes courage to ask for help, though, and so this humility must partner with courage to accept the help that is offered or to ask for the help that is needed. On its own, humility may keep me from asking for support from others, or it may prevent me from stepping *toward* others in the faith that I have something to offer. We need a courageous humility that is willing to reach out in faith and love despite recognizing our own profound limitations.

Responding to others in love is seldom found in grandiose, self-fulfilling acts of valor. Neither is it realized in the self-deprecating sacrifice of one's own passions and interests. Instead, responsive love is profoundly human, remarkably simple, and surprisingly difficult. It calls us to rest humbly with another, becoming attentive to his needs, hopes, and fears before taking action. At times the only action that is called for is simply *being with* each other. At other times, acting looks like putting one's own safety or reputation at risk to support others. Most of the time, it looks like not much at all. As Mother Teresa is reported to have said, "Don't look for big things, just do small things with great love. . . . The smaller the thing, the greater must be our love."[10] We need to be formed together in the virtue of courageous humility in order to act in small ways with profound love. Humility on its own may be tempted to fade into the background as we come up against our limits in knowledge, strength, and ability. Courage on its own may charge ahead without recognizing these limits and so wound the one it intends to heal. This is why courage and humility must go hand in hand. Embracing our limits, we nevertheless press on in caring for one another, open to discovering each other's needs and responding accordingly.

Giving an Account: Courageous Humility in Direct Support

Many people entering into direct support with people with intellectual disabilities are unsure of what they are getting into. It was no different for me. On my first shift I was paired with another new employee who was much bigger and stronger than I. He soon decided that he could not handle working with people with significant behavioral challenges and requested a transfer. I did not. It was not because I was confident in my ability to respond to the needs of the people I had met. However, I also was not sure that I could *not* meet those needs. Going forward required an act of courage, yet it was made easier by the humility that I did not know whether I would be able to work with these gentlemen. Indeed, at that point I did not yet know whether I would be able to work with people with intellectual disabilities at all. How many similar stories are there of people who step forward with an act that was courageous for them, simply responding to a need that they did not yet know whether they could meet? It is not until we take a courageous step that we discover our limits, but this takes the humility of knowing we could fail, we could be embarrassed, we could be wrong yet stepping forward anyway.

As it turns out, it does not take a lot of courage to work with people. The courage that is required is to move beyond our own comfort zones and implicit prejudice. I am struck by the number of times I have been told what a good or special person I am for working with "those people." It is a common experience of those of us who work with people with intellectual disabilities. What is masquerading as a gesture of humility here ("I could never do that . . .") is often an expression of pride and fear. Pride, because there is a misguided perception that it is undesirable to journey with people "like that," and this is not something with which this person would be associated. Fear, because they are not willing to take the first step to discover whether this is actually something they might be able to do or enjoy doing. Their statements are a way of "delegating the call" to others out of the fear that they may find themselves in a position to respond themselves. It is a kind of humility without courage that views the work only in light of their own perceived limitations. The tragic reality here is that, because so many people abdicate the opportunity to become caregivers, the work does become difficult because of short staffing or lack of volunteers. "I could never do that" becomes a self-fulfilling prophecy with significant implications in the lives of people with intellectual disabilities. Perhaps an even greater tragedy here is that so many people *without* intellectual disabilities miss out on the human flourishing that can come with getting to know people who experience the world differently.

Working several years in recruitment, I discovered an interesting phenomenon when hiring people into the field. We had people who applied with us who had just completed their developmental services worker diploma and others who had no formal training whatsoever. Many people came through the local training program who were excellent employees. However, far too many young people applied with the sense that they already knew what they were doing. I would regularly hire people without the diploma over and above those *with* the credentials, because getting to know the people we support requires a profound humility and openness to discovering who each person is and what they need. Too often I found that trained direct support professionals had just enough training to believe that they knew what they were doing but not enough wisdom or experience to know that the call to serve cannot be answered based on textbooks and classroom study alone.

THE VIRTUE OF LOVING MERCY

Courageous humility means that, in acknowledging our own limits, we are open to receive not only the gifts but the limitations of others without compromising our equality in God's image. It sets us up to respond to the significant needs of people for whom we provide care without believing that we are in any way better than they are. In other words, it leads to the virtue of mercy born out of loving-kindness.

In writing on what he calls the virtues of acknowledged dependence, Alasdair MacIntyre expounds on how one goes beyond familial relations with one's close community to show "just generosity" to those outside of these relations. He relies on Thomas Aquinas' perspective on *misericordia*. *Misericordia* is a kind of mercy that "has regard to urgent and extreme need without respect of persons. It is the kind and scale of the need that dictates what has to be done, not whose need it is."[11]

One possible translation of *misericordia* is "pity." However, given contemporary pejorative connotations of pity, *misericordia* can more accurately thought of as a kind of mercy that encompasses both compassion *toward* another and action *on behalf* of another.[12] It is not simply a compassionate feeling but concrete action that makes a difference in someone's life. Whereas envy "sorrows over our neighbor's good," mercy "sorrows over our neighbor's evil."[13]

Here MacIntyre and Aquinas build on Aristotle. To have mercy for someone else, I must have either a "union of affection, which arises by love" or a perception of a "real union" (*unio realis*) between me and another person.[14] We grieve and suffer with those with whom we relate. Yet *unio realis* opens us to mercy that goes beyond our natural community to feel the pain of "outsiders." There still must be a perceived unity or similarity with the one who suffers, and Aquinas observes that this comes more readily to some than others:

> So it is that the old and the wise, who consider themselves able to fall upon evil things, are more merciful—as are the weak and the fearful. On the other hand, those who regard themselves as happy and so powerful that they suppose themselves able to suffer nothing evil, are not so merciful (30.2 co).[15]

It is not surprising that MacIntyre, an Aristotelian and a Thomist scholar, draws upon *misericordia* in his search for virtues of acknowledged dependence. Acknowledged dependence leads to compassionate action on behalf of or toward others. Aquinas claims that those who are old or wise, weak or fearful are more likely to have empathy for people in need because they can imagine themselves being in that same place. Those who are prideful do not recognize the need to reach beyond their own community or familial relations because they have difficulty connecting with the person in need. This also demonstrates why courageous humility leads to loving mercy—compassionate action on behalf of another. It requires humility to recognize our shared commonality as people who experience bodily limitation and suffering. It requires courage to enter into the lives of others to meet their needs. We must here acknowledge two qualifications. First, suffering does not necessarily accompany disability and suffering can occur in anyone's life, whether a person is disabled or not. It would be a mistake to equate disability with suffering. Second, embracing personal limits does not mean that able-bodied people understand the experience of disability in its complex physical or societal implications. The shared human experience is not of disability, it is of limitation. We can relate to one another's limits, not necessarily to someone else's experience of disability.

The experience of disability is one, however, that may impact any of us at any time. In popularizing the term "temporarily able-bodied" in theological circles, Nancy Eiesland reminds her readers that interdependence does not take place only on a psychological or existential level but also on a practical level.[16] Disability is the demographic that anyone can join at any time, and most of us will at some point in our lives. In exercising *misericordia* toward others, one is not only making the world a better place for those with urgent needs but working toward a world that is better for oneself. Any compassionate action here must, however, seek to understand how disabling conditions are interpreted or experienced by people who identify as disabled. Too much harm has already been done by "allies" who take action before seeking to understand impact.

According to Aquinas, *misericordia* is one of the effects of charity (*caritas*), which is a theological virtue. "Charity can be in us neither naturally, nor by natural powers that are acquired, but only by an infusion of the Holy Spirit, who is the love of the Father and the Son, whose participation in us is created by charity."[17] This mercy *flows out of* the love of God through an infusion of the Holy Spirit. Theological virtues are received as divine gift.[18] One must not attempt to predict the scope of these divine gifts, however. Thomas "does not restrict *caritas* to the set of self-described Christian believers."[19] God's mercy can flow through those who do not necessarily profess the Christian faith. One does not need to understand the *concepts* of grace or love to act in grace or love.[20]

In this way, expression of these theological virtues is not constrained to those who intellectually can "give an account" *of* the virtues or of divine charity. People with profound intellectual disabilities can exercise these Christian virtues just as well as the theologian can. "The spirit blows where it will," and God is actively at work in the lives of people who may not fully understand how God is working. Who among us can claim to be fully aware of the work of the Holy Spirit in and through our own lives?

What does this mean, then, for Christian caregivers? It means that one does not need to fully understand the concepts of love and grace to act with compassion toward another. Indeed, pride in one's own understanding of the work of love might prevent one from entering into it. Those who embrace human interdependence and are grateful for the love and support they have received themselves will more naturally express this loving mercy. Experiences of *receiving* care can help us to appreciate the "real union" that connects human beings in care partnership.

Building on previous chapters, we might expand upon this reciprocity to understand *unio realis* in a new way. No longer grounded in transparent accounts of *givers* and *receivers* of care, loving mercy is rooted in humble recognition of our shared opacity and mutual responsibility to one another. We are each in need of care. We are each radically dependent upon God in establishing the self, and we are each relationally dependent upon one another in vulnerable reciprocity. *Misericordia*, reconsidered with an appreciation for the mystery of the human condition, finds its shared *unio realis* not primarily in contingent circumstances but in the fundamental recognition of our interdependence as human beings.

Encountering Christ: Mercy and Grace in Our Time of Need

> For we do not have a high priest who is unable to empathize with our weaknesses, but we have one who has been tempted in every way, just as we are—yet he did not sin. Let us then approach God's throne of grace with confidence, so that we may receive mercy and find grace to help us in our time of need.

Hebrews 4:15-16

The pattern of Christ (*imitatio Dei*) demonstrates that we can approach God with confidence knowing that Christ can relate in *unio realis* to the human experience of weakness. The mercy and grace we receive is not simply from One who is "on high" but from one who experienced the fullness of what it means to be a human being. Christian caregivers are called to then extend this loving mercy *to* others and to seek this loving mercy *from* others. Just as we have received love, so receiving mercy opens us to be merciful with others without the false perception that we have more to give. We act in compassionate mercy not because we are complete and competent but because we, too, have sought and received mercy in our time of need.

In Christ's actions on earth, we see ongoing evidence of *misericordia* toward those around him. In Luke 7, he feels compassion for a widow whose son had died, raising him from the dead and "giving him back" to his mother. In the miraculous loaves and fishes account of Matthew 15, Jesus says, "I feel compassion for the people because they have remained with me now three days and have nothing to eat; and I do not want to send them away hungry, for they might faint on the way."[21] He teaches the crowd because he "felt compassion for them because they were like sheep without a shepherd."[22] He heals two blind men who request healing because he is "moved with compassion."[23] These are only a few of many examples where Christ demonstrates loving mercy, a kind of mercy that embodies both empathetic compassion and practical action. Isaiah prophesies about the coming Messiah that in bringing justice, "A bruised reed He will not break and a smoldering wick He will not extinguish."[24] This is the loving mercy of Jesus, that even in delivering justice he seeks to sustain the weak and broken in care.

Giving an Account: Loving Mercy in Direct Support

Being a direct support professional in times of crisis can be a thankless job. So Lisa discovered as she supported Charles through his final days.

Charles had been well known and loved within his community and his circle of friends, yet his sister had little contact with him. She was the one who ended up making decisions on his behalf as his health rapidly deteriorated and he was transferred to the hospital.

Lisa was new to direct support yet believed it was her calling. She was a devout Catholic with a sincere appreciation for the sanctity of life, yet she also respected the boundaries of her role in communicating with Charles' family. She would advocate for his value without imposing her values on Charles' sister.

The decision was made by Charles' sister, rather hastily Lisa thought, to stop providing Charles with food. He lived for another five days before passing away. Through that time, Lisa spent countless hours with him—paid and unpaid. She recognized his distress, and there were times when her presence was his only source of sustenance and encouragement.

While she maintained professional boundaries with the family, never challenging Charles' sister directly on the choices she made around his care, Lisa was wrecked by the thought that someone who hardly knew Charles could make such a rash decision about his value as a person who experiences disability.

Ultimately, the pain of this experience became too much for her, and as the weeks progressed she took fewer and fewer shifts until she stopped working altogether and resigned.

Lisa's story is a tragic example of embodying loving mercy without a balance of courageous humility. Courageous humility demands that we recognize our own limits and needs and work within them toward resilient, ongoing care. In the language of calling, Lisa experienced a deep sense of belonging without cultivating the distance she needed to sustain her work. Sharing in the suffering of Charles and taking compassionate action to accompany him through his final days exemplifies loving mercy. Some would question her decisions to care for Charles beyond her paid hours from the perspective of establishing professional boundaries. However, the needs of another human being and the call Lisa's faith rightly transcended her obligations to professional standards. What Lisa needed was not instruction to remain within her professional obligations but a faithful or theological perspective from which these limitations might make sense to her. Lisa believed that she had a vocation or a responsibility to change the situation in which Charles found himself. Humility requires, at times, that we dare to just *be* with people in and throughout circumstances that we do not have the power to change. It means that we recognize that we do not have all of the answers and that we do not know Charles' sister's story either. Courageous humility enables us to display loving mercy not only to Charles but also to his sister. It means entrusting the final act of loving mercy to God, and in this humility we may find peace. Who knows the impact Lisa might have had over the course of a lengthy career, a career marked by resilient care born out of the virtues of courageous humility combined with loving mercy.

Receiving the Scandalous Gift of Friendship

> Friends need no justification. Friendship is a gift and, like most significant gifts, it is surrounded by mystery.
>
> **Stanley Hauerwas**[25]

The loving mercy of God finds its ultimate expression in suffering love on the cross of Christ. Whether this mercy is born out of a "union of affection," which arises by "love" or a perception of a "real union" (*unio realis*) is shrouded in mystery.[26] It is a mercy that calls into question any such distinction of the relationship. Robert Miner writes that the revolutionary effect of *caritas* (charity) out of which this mercy arises is to subvert the inequality between God and humanity, making love possible with God "as equals."[27] We recall

Christ's words, "I no longer call you slaves, because a master doesn't confide in his slaves. Now you are my friends since I have told you everything the Father told me."[28] God's charity subverts models of the "more able" giving to the "less able" as it establishes the fundamental gift of equality. If Christ has called us friends, who am I to draw distinctions with another human being? Friendship is a radical equalizer.

In *Receiving the Gift of Friendship*, Hans Reinders reframes the conversation on disability and personhood in such a way that the humanity of people with profound intellectual disabilities is no longer looked at as a "moral quandary."[29] From the perspective of Christian theology, our identity as human beings rests not in specific traits or biological capabilities but rather in belonging to God. We have ecstatic personhood as we *receive the gift* of God's friendship with us. This has profound implications for the *imago Dei*, as "in an important sense, my being as *imago Dei* is not to be taken ontologically as a subsistent entity, but as a relationship that is ecstatically grounded in God's loving kindness toward me."[30]

The scandal of God's friendship with human beings means that no one falls outside of its purview. "Whatever there is to the fullness of life, it must be God's gift from beginning to end, unless one is willing to accept that there are human beings who are excluded from it."[31] Reinders here acknowledges that the gift of friendship always begins with God. God *first* loved. Because we are loved, virtue is a response to this scandalous gift of friendship.[32] It follows, then, that the *distance* God has come to call us friends makes any difference between us and other human beings fade in comparison. "To know how to receive the gift of God's friendship is to know how to receive the gift of God's friends."[33]

Just as Lisa's obligation to her faith transcended her obligation to her profession, so the radical equality of Christ and the friendship of God transcends our professional labels and discourse. In some incomprehensible way, there can be a real unity between God and human beings within which God has called us "friends." Might this mean that even within the professional-client relationship we experience real friendship?

Professional training on reducing risk and vulnerability would view as anathema the description of "friendship" with someone receiving support. It is an understandable protest. There are significant power differentials at play, perhaps the greatest of which is the not-so-simple fact that one person is being paid to be with another person. One should not use the words "care," "friendship," or "love" lightly in any relationship where such imbalances occur. Even while recognizing our shared radical dependency and vulnerability, we must not discount the power differentials at play as we encounter one another in systems and norms that define us differently.

For a caregiver to be the one who "gives an account" of the relationship as a friendship may, in fact, betray the friendship. It may confuse why the caregiver is present or the expectations of the caregiving relationship. However, who are we to presume to define who we are to another? To impose our understanding of a professional-client relationship on all of our interactions with another is to impose a pseudo—value system on the life of a person receiving care. It is to assert not only our power but also the power of the professional system. It may even do a disservice to the recognition of our fundamental equality of being human beings created in God's image.

All this being acknowledged, with profound humility and recognition of ourselves as interdependent and relationally constituted human beings, it is possible that friendship develops even if we do not use the word "friend" to describe this relationship. That God would call us friends means that *no one* on earth is too different from me, too vulnerable, or too powerful to exclude the possibility of friendship and mutual hospitality. There is no one with whom I am foreclosed from experiencing *unio realis*, from extending mercy toward, from "feeling with" their experiences. To ignore power differentials or pretend that they do not exist is to betray one's relationship with another. However, to claim that these differences are more constitutive of our identity than our fundamental equality as people created in God's image is to betray our relationship with the divine and with the divine image encountered in one another.

THE VIRTUES OF CONFESSION AND FORGIVENESS

> Forgiveness is the name of love practiced among people who love poorly. And the hard truth is, all people love poorly. We need to forgive and be forgiven every day, every hour increasingly. That is the great work of love among the fellowship of the weak that is the human family.

Henri Nouwen[34]

The virtue of loving mercy entails compassionate action. When we recognize our shared partial opacity and approach one another in courageous humility, this compassionate action *should not* be based upon the myth that the other person is transparent to us. In the example of Lisa, loving mercy meant simply being present with Charles through his final days. However, wherever there is action there will be mis-action. We are fallible and mysterious human beings, driven by forces that are beyond us and that escape adequate comprehension. These hidden forces are cause for humility, but they can also lead to actions that cause pain. Recognizing that we are our brother and sister's keeper means taking each other's pain seriously. This is the *compassion* in our action, feeling "with" each other. Our relationships matter. They shape us, and we shape others through them.

In the rush and haste of the day, people who receive care are often misunderstood. This happens particularly with people with intellectual disabilities or those who experience difficulty in communicating, but it can happen with anyone. Even with much training, it is tempting for caregivers to interpret the needs of the people they support through preconceptions of what is needed rather than being open to new interpretations or possibilities. Alternately, support staff may seek coherent stories within which to find practical ways to develop independence and life skills. In the field of intellectual disability, person-centered planning approaches can focus on "figuring out" a person without taking the time to celebrate their life as a gift and rejoice in the mystery of who the person is. We must confess the sin of presuming a transparent other. Sometimes this means saying "I'm sorry" to someone when we have run roughshod over their attempt to communicate with us, or just be with us, in the rush of any given day.

In the mindset of professionalism, the temptation can be to brush off these hurried interactions as, "Well, it just needed to get done." Behind this belief, however, often lies a sense that we know better what a person needs than they do. There are times when we need to confess and when we need to be forgiven. It does not mean the interaction goes differently. There are times when we need to take care of other responsibilities. However, admitting that we have let another down in this prioritization of tasks helps to restore the humanity of professional interactions, honoring the value of the contribution of the person receiving care. Confession cultivates humility in our decision making and relinquishes the power of the interaction, leaving it with the other person to extend or deny forgiveness. In this way, the moral complexity of the encounter does not remain in the domain of the caregiver. Instead, the relational dynamic is held *between* two unique and mysterious persons created in the image of the divine.

The dance of confession and forgiveness is the lifeblood of human interactions. Judith Butler claims that in our shared, partial opacity with one another, "I will need to be forgiven for what I cannot have fully known, and I will be under a similar obligation to offer forgiveness to others who are also constituted in partial opacity to themselves."[35] As with the understanding of *caritas*, it is of secondary importance whether we understand the theological nature of "confession" or "forgiveness" or even use these words to describe the exchanges. The posture of opening ourselves to another, of communicating, "I'm sorry" in words or actions, or intentionally letting another know that "we're okay," are healing movements born of the Spirit of God.

Jean Vanier, in his reflection on the Gospel of John, observes that Jesus calls his disciples to be "signs of forgiveness" in the world:

> The unique role of the disciple of Jesus is to forgive. But forgiveness is not a grandiose act; it is to enter into relationship with the poor and to raise each one up, saying, "You are you, and you are important."[36]

While it is true that forgiveness is characteristic of Christ's disciples, one must be very careful not to define what that forgiveness looks like or how it might look on behalf of others. Indeed, what is striking in Vanier's example is that forgiveness is offered from those in seats of power or wealth to those who are poor or vulnerable, raising "each one up." Instead, is not those who are in positions of power who must first confess? We must begin with the act that is called for from *me*, and more often than not this must begin with confession rather than forgiveness. It is not up to me to demand forgiveness of another—it is up to me to recognize that for which I need forgiveness and to confess.

It is peculiar to say that entering into relationship with "the poor" or those who have been ostracized and marginalized is an act of forgiveness. These acts are as much, or more, about confessing our own misuse of power and seeking forgiveness ourselves, whether or not it is given or is deserved. Forgiving relationships must first acknowledge the mysterious and often troubling forces that shape our lives. They call into question the tyranny of the systems of power and the biased perceptions that separate us from one another, that silence some and not others. Confession is the act that opens up the possibility of a path to forgiveness, that starts to express the ways in which we have wronged one another and are in need of forgiveness.

Encountering Christ: Communal Healing through Forgiveness

In Mark 2, a man's friends lower him through the roof for Jesus to heal him. The primary healing that takes place here is not the physical curing of the man's inability to walk; rather, it is Christ extending forgiveness for the man's sins. In this act of mercy, Christ restores the paralyzed man to his community and his faith. The physical healing that occurs takes place *to demonstrate* that Christ had the power to forgive the man's sins. Similarly, we must be open to the healing of relationships and communities that takes place through the dance of confession and forgiveness. These relational strands are woven together in the fabric of our lives in such a way that, once cut, our sense of selfhood begins to fray.

It is our formation together in the practices of confession and forgiveness rather than, primarily, the veracity of our accounts that constitutes our moral integrity. We must be willing to confess that our stories are broken and incomplete and that the way we tell our stories may be damaging to others. We must be willing to hold our accounts lightly to repair the relational fabric of our lives; then we will have overcome the most significant barriers to "speaking the truth in love."[37] On the cross, Jesus demonstrates this loving truth. As his executioners gamble for his clothes, he cries, "Father, forgive them, for they don't know what they are doing."[38] In the midst of crushing pain, to be able to see through one's suffering to the incomprehension of one's persecutors is nothing less than an act born of divine love. We, too, are called to forgive others for actions that arise from forces beyond their comprehension and to confess and accept forgiveness for our own actions born out of our shared, partial opacity.

Giving an Account: Extending Forgiveness in Direct Support

Forgiveness seemed to come easily to me when I worked direct support. I would regularly be kicked, punched, and scratched by people who were in pain, people who were dissatisfied with their support and lacked effective ways to communicate—more because of our own inability as theirs. "Forgive them, for they don't know what they're doing" could rightly capture my default posture in these circumstances. Perhaps more accurately, it's not that they didn't know what they were doing but that what they were doing was not ultimately *about me*. It was directed at systems, structures, pain, circumstances, and confusion that was in large part outside of our control. The mysterious aspects of their lives ("Why do I feel this pain?" "Why can't I do x, y, z?" "Why don't they understand me?" etc.) can become overwhelming.

There was one time, though, where it was different. I was supporting someone through his toilet routine. He would require extended time there because of bowel difficulties, and regular interventions were required as he would often experience pain and attempt self-injurious behavior in the close quarters of the small room. I was accustomed by that time to the kind of "dance" that would take place in intervening, then backing off, and believed that we had developed some rapport through these interactions. He understood when I would step in to prevent self-injury and when I would step back to give him space and as much privacy as we could. Through these times he would often grab our shirts or attempt to scratch us, pinch us, or pull our hair—especially those who had long hair.

Today was different, though. I had thought things had been going relatively well. But as I approached to prevent him from landing a blow to his face, he looked me straight in the eyes for a full second. This was unusual. Often, when he was in pain, he was too caught up in his own experience to look directly at us. When he was calm and comfortable, we would share time walking, listening to music, going for van rides, and other meaningful activities. Eye contact was not unusual in those times. Today was not one of those days. Yet he looked me directly in the eyes. And then punched me. Hard. In the face.

The anger, as much as the pain, was immediate and powerful. Usually, we understand that these interactions are not "about us." But this time he had looked directly at me. There was no doubt in my mind that this was exactly what he had intended. The situation seemed transparent. He had intended to hurt me. It was a betrayal of the rapport I thought we had built as much as it was an injury to my pride. And my face.

Thankfully, I recognized that I was upset. I called on a colleague to take over. I "walked it off." It took humility to forgive. I'm not sure I ever reached the point where I doubted his intention to hurt me. Yet all of this was caught up in an encounter that was structured more by his pain, his environment, and the professional-client relationship than it was by who we were as persons. In other words, it wasn't personal. Forgiveness—that's personal. And it was what I needed to extend that day to reclaim my humanity.

I went back in later, as much to demonstrate there were no hard feelings as to help my colleagues out. In this case, forgiveness looked like continuing to provide support as though nothing had happened. Almost literally, "turning the other cheek."[39]

In case you hadn't guessed it, this gentleman was Hiroshi. I went back in that day and countless days in the years that followed. Eventually, I moved on to another role within the organization, yet I stayed in touch with Hiroshi and saw him on multiple occasions. Thanks in part to continued, faithful direct support, reduction of his medication, and a strong community of care, Hiroshi no longer needs to wear a helmet as he did in those early days. His self-injurious behavior is now almost nonexistent. Perhaps most significantly, he can connect with people nearly all of the time in meaningful and rewarding sign conversations, both in public and private. To this day I'm not sure I have met anyone with such earnest and probing eyes. He has challenged me and changed me in ways I'll never be able to describe fully.

One's ability to remain calm and "professional" in situations where people exhibit challenging behavior comes just as much from habits of sincere care and appreciation for the person supported as it does from the hands-on training caregivers receive. The moral formation of practicing courageous humility and loving mercy, together with regular patterns of confession, leads us into relationships where extending forgiveness is an anticipatory posture rather than an intentional response.[40] In humility, we understand that the other person is not wholly the author of the pain they have caused or may not comprehend the full impact of their actions. In loving mercy, we *feel with* the other and begin to understand causes of action that may not be *about us*. Thus, regular practice of these virtues cultivates relationships of grace—relationships where those in power are first to confess to their misuse of this power, communities where miscommunication and pain might find healing in spaces of loving truth telling.

THE VIRTUES OF LAMENT AND MOURNING

In messy relationships, beset by circumstances and systems beyond our control, to mourn together is as important as finding joy with one another. In my work with people with disabilities as they are dying and the teams that support them through this process, it strikes me that processing loss defines our lives and relationships as much or more than our successes do. These times of grieving with people and teams often reveal great suffering. They are also some of the most meaningful moments in my work. People experience profound yet bittersweet joy as they recall the deceased person and the memories that have been shared. These memories are gifts to us that may fade, yet they leave a mark on who we are. There is a way in which our bodies remember everything, and our lives are composed by those who have formed us.

The virtues of mourning and lament are closely related to the practices of confession and forgiveness in community. We must confess and mourn all those times that we have caused pain to others, and even as we forgive one another we lament the pain that has been caused in our relationships. Whether or not forgiveness is granted following confession, the pain and the grief of caring for one another in a fallen world remains.

It is often only once we have confronted our own pain and loss that we are open to experiencing joy and celebration. It is when we have faced our fears that we are open to rejoicing in another's giftedness. Perhaps we do not know how to celebrate because we have not first learned to mourn.

Encountering Christ: Friendship with Lazarus

Jesus wept.

John 11:35

With these words, the biblical account conveys the profound, embodied pain of Jesus on behalf of his friend Lazarus and those who have known and have loved Lazarus. Jesus is surrounded by those who are mourning, and with loving mercy he enters into that pain. Here, Christ is also aware that the act of raising Lazarus from the dead will infuriate the religious leaders and lead him a step closer to the grave. At this point in Christ's ministry, even the disciples are aware that he is in danger. Before Jesus goes back to Bethany, his disciples remind him that the people in that region had only recently tried to stone him.[41] When they are about to set off, Thomas says to the other disciples, "Let's go, too—and die with Jesus."[42] Christ's friends are aware of the risks he is taking to bring Lazarus back to life. The weight of our own mortality is never far from our experience of a loss of another. We experience the death of a part of ourselves when a friend or loved one dies and are reminded of our own fate. We are woven together, and when one of our threads is cut it is easy to come unwound.

There is a mystery in this passage as to why Jesus is angry. His tears follow John's observation, "When Jesus saw her weeping and saw the other people wailing with her, a deep anger welled up within him, and he was deeply troubled."[43] Upon arriving at the tomb, "Jesus was still angry."[44] However, anger is often bound up with grief. Sometimes when we experience grief and anger, we are not even sure why we are angry. I am not sure that increased intelligence or even divine foreknowledge help us to grapple with these complex human emotions. The people with intellectual disabilities whom I support through grief are every bit as complex and mysterious as any other human being. In moments of profound grief, we all break, we all weep, and we all experience waves of mixed emotions such as anger, fear, hurt, love, gratitude, peace, anxiety, and pain. Questions and concerns surround us that do not find straightforward answers. As N. T. Wright observes, "This passage points us forward to the questions that will be asked at Jesus' own death. Couldn't the man who did so many signs have brought it about that he himself didn't have to die? Couldn't the one who saved so many have in the end saved himself?"[45] It is no wonder that Christ is caught up in grief and anger as questions and fears and the pain of those he loves surround him.

Memories and experiences of loss continue to haunt us in dark and compelling ways. These losses may be related to death, friendship, relationships, ability, or identity. Bringing these fears and traumas into the open with people we trust can be a source of healing and redemption. Will we ever completely understand the myriad ways that loss has touched our lives? I'm not convinced. However, in the practices of mourning together and in lament before God over losses conscious and unconscious, we find the possibility of moving beyond this grief toward hope in community.

Giving an Account: Grief in Direct Support

She called for what I thought was going to be a five-minute conversation to set up a time to meet for coffee. It ended up being an hour-long conversation.

Grace is a direct support professional who recently helped to perform CPR on someone she supported as they died. This can be a traumatic experience for anyone, but Grace had also experienced significant depression earlier in life and had recently lost other family and friends. She was off on medical leave, and I encouraged her to seek professional therapy, which she planned to do. For the moment, though, I was someone to talk to, someone to walk with through the mysterious complexity of her emotions.

As Grace cried and shared her pain, the resounding theme I heard was that she needed *permission to grieve*. Her supervisor had given her time off, grief supports had been provided, and yet Grace understood herself as a *giver*. She had cared for others and *felt* for others as long as she could remember. Caregiving was her calling, and she often repeated that God had a profound purpose for her life. That purpose, however, seemed to be defined by "doing great things." To spend time grieving was a setback, a weakness, and a failure to care for others in her view.

I attempt to not give a lot of advice when people are grieving. Generally, it's not what people need—they need quiet attentiveness. Also, we tend not to hear or process advice or instruction well in grief. However, toward the end of our conversation, I spoke to Grace about Henri Nouwen's observation that Christ's most significant work came not through action but his *passion*.[46] Nouwen writes, "All action ends in passion because the response to our action is out of our hands. That is the mystery of friendship, the mystery of community—they always involve waiting. And that is the mystery of Jesus' love."[47]

To grieve through suffering is to discover perfect strength because it is the gift of allowing ourselves to face the darkest and most mysterious aspects of our loss and brokenness. This strength does not come from our-selves, because we discover it in our weakness.[48] As Grace found encour-agement in listening to music, I suggested to her a song containing the phrase, "When the night is holding on to me, God is holding on."[49] To open ourselves to the experience of grief is to discover the radical equality that we are each sustained in the mysterious embrace of the divine.

Grief in professional caregiving is often disenfranchised. That is, because family or friends may not recognize support staff as needing to grieve, they do not readily find space to process this grief. Employment standards do not grant time following the death of someone supported to process grief. Profes-sional training does not generally know how to handle such emotions. After all, you are not their "friend," so why would this matter so much? However, it is in these times of grief that professionals and people supported come face to face with their shared humanity. Grief is often connected to loss of life, but it can just as well arise when someone has a setback toward personal goals, loses a job, experiences loss of ability or health, and so on. A principle from preaching applies here when relating to people who receive support: share from your scars, not your wounds. The virtue of lament and mourning does not mean that we turn to people we are supporting to make up for the loss we are feeling. Rather, we lament and mourn *together* in such a way that points to the possibility of hope and healing. We celebrate the love behind the loss, opening space for those around us to grieve, to mourn, and to recognize vulnerability not as a one-way plea but as a reciprocal opportunity to demon-strate care from the heart. Some of the most healing gestures of support I have encountered come not from professional staff but from people too often perceived as "receivers of care."

THE VIRTUE OF QUIET ATTENTIVENESS

> Attention is the rarest and purest form of generosity.
>
> **Simone Weil**[50]

What does it mean to *pay attention* to one another? Among its definitions is "observant care."[51] Attention is a form of care practiced simply by observa-tion, by patience, by listening and waiting. It is to learn to be "quick to listen, slow to speak and slow to become angry."[52]

The stories that we hear and the stories that we tell about ourselves are only gestures toward the "I" that I call myself. This "I" is ever receding, never grasped or captured in language. Insofar as it is "I" that is giving the account, it can never fully be the "I" that is represented *in* the account being given.

Indeed, as soon as I attempt to express myself in language I have already lost the singularity of the "I" that attempts to express itself. According to Derrida, "By suspending my absolute singularity in speaking, I renounce at the same time my liberty and my responsibility. Once I speak, I am never and no longer myself, alone and unique."[53]

We may give accounts of others or ourselves, yet these are never fully detached and objective. They are stories of which we are never fully the author. We heed the truth of Hannah Arendt's observation: "Storytelling reveals meaning without committing the error of defining it."[54] We convey meaning by what we say, yet to attempt to define every sense of meaning would be to overstep our ability, to become ensnared in the myths of transparency.

When we come to appreciate all the systems and structures of language that define our thought and our inability to communicate who we are or who another is fully, it is a wonder that we dare to speak at all. When we do, we must retain this sense of wonder at the mystery revealed by others and ourselves through our attempts to communicate. Whether or not it is possible to empty our thoughts, a sincere appreciation for the mysterious layers of meaning released in our mutual expression forms us in a default posture of quiet attentiveness toward God and toward one another. Quiet attention is nothing less than a subversive and revolutionary act in an age of idle chatter and hurry.

Encountering Christ: Silence as Disruption

> Here is my servant whom I have chosen,
>   the one I love, in whom I delight;
> I will put my Spirit on him,
>   and he will proclaim justice to the nations.
> He will not quarrel or cry out;
>   no one will hear his voice in the streets.
> A bruised reed he will not break,
>   and a smoldering wick he will not snuff out,
> till he has brought justice through to victory.
>   In his name the nations will put their hope.
> **Matthew 12:18-21, NIV**

Matthew here points to Christ as the fulfillment of the prophesy in Isaiah 42. Isaiah's words are profoundly subversive. The Messiah will "proclaim justice" to the nations, and yet "he will not quarrel or cry out; no one will hear his voice in the streets." Contrary to contemporary political climates where justice is sought by shouting in the loudest voice or garnering the largest audience, Christ's example is one of quiet love.

Isaiah reminds us, "He was oppressed and afflicted, yet he did not open his mouth; he was led like a lamb to the slaughter, and as a sheep before its shearers is silent, so he did not open his mouth."[55] Christ's example is one of profound *withness*.[56] He bore the torture of crucifixion, the violence of being commanded to *give an account* as one who had no voice, as one who was unable to speak up for himself. Christ demonstrates that there are times that responding to a violent system only legitimizes the authority that makes the demand. "The chief priests accused him of many things. So again, Pilate asked him, 'Aren't you going to answer? See how many things they are accusing you of.' But Jesus still made no reply, and Pilate was amazed."[57]

In Pilate's amazement, in his shock, we encounter a powerful moment of disruption. As though Christ is mute, his silence confronts the demands to give an account according to the terms of the chief priests. "My kingdom is not of this world. If it were, my servants would fight to prevent my arrest by the Jewish leaders. But now my kingdom is from another place," Jesus relays in John's gospel.[58] It is as though the whole regime of truth that the chief priests are relying on has been called into question. Christ gives no account, as the account that is demanded is rooted in the ethical violence of a system that has no comprehension of those who *give no account*. In Joe Arridy's case, the account he gave confronted the regime of an unjust system. In Christ's case, it is his silence.

Encountering Christ: Silence as Openness to Revelation

While gentle silence does not always disrupt, it always heals. As we take time to hear from God in silence, we are healed. In turn, we can pass this healing on to others as we demonstrate the care that is quiet attentiveness. Luke records that "Jesus often withdrew to lonely places and prayed."[59] This was not an occasional event but a regular practice for him.[60]

Before God, silence is often the most appropriate posture. Kierkegaard writes, "When prayer has properly become prayer, it has become silence."[61] When we encounter the mystery of the divine, our words often fail us. In reflecting on Christ's exhortation, "Look at the birds. . . . Consider the lilies of the field,"[62] Kierkegaard points to silence as a virtue we can learn from the lilies of the field:

> Out there with the lilies and the birds thou dost sense that *thou art before God*, a fact which is generally so entirely forgotten in speech and conversation with other men. For when there are two of us only that talk

together, not to say ten or more, it is so easily forgotten that thou and I, we two, or we ten, are before God. But the lily who is the teacher is profound. It does not enter into conversation with thee, it keeps silent, and by keeping silent it would signify to thee that thou art before God, that thou shouldst remember that thou art before God—that thou also in seriousness and truth mightest become silent before God.[63]

To speak hastily is to miss the revelation of being *before God* that is critical to Kierkegaard's foundation for radical equality. Similarly, when we are with one another, silence is often the most appropriate response. To listen to another in quiet attentiveness is to recognize their value, their worth, and to confess that there is much more to discover about them than we perhaps would like to admit. It is to understand in humility that they *are not* transparent to us and that we always have more to learn, to discover. To be silent is to wonder at the mystery of the other. To listen is to be open to revelation *from* one another. In these encounters, to speak hastily is to miss *the moment* in which we may give and receive mutual care:

> Only by keeping silent does one encounter the moment. When one speaks, even if one says only a single word, one misses the moment. Only in silence *is* the moment. And this is surely why it so rarely happens that a human being properly comes to understand when the moment is and how to make proper use of the moment.[64]

While he was not always silent, it is by virtue of Christ's posture of quiet attentiveness with those whom he encountered that he did not "break a bruised reed" or "snuff out a smoldering wick." In those moments when he took the time to see and listen to the people whom he encountered, he opened space for the strengthening of bruised reeds, the bright burning of wicks that had been smoldering. Indeed, just as Elijah had to remain silent to hear the still small voice of God, so we must be cautious of our inclination to speak before we have walked with others, listening to how they communicate. Sometimes this takes eyes to see. Sometimes this requires ears to hear. It always involves the virtue of quiet attentiveness, remaining open to the revelation that may come in a multitude of ways as we patiently and humbly journey with one another and with the divine.

Giving an Account: The Power of Quiet Attentiveness

Recently I hosted a support group and grief/loss activity session for a few people with intellectual disabilities who had recently lost a friend. One woman, Catherine, was in the process of sharing how much this loss had meant to her. Jane, who was sitting across the table from Catherine throughout her soliloquy, began to interject: "I'm your friend, Catherine." A minute later, "I'm a good friend, Catherine!" After a couple of these interruptions, a direct support professional asked Jane to be quiet. In subsequent remarks, one or another of the support staff would say "Shhh!" or "Catherine is talking now."

I put my hand on Jane's shoulder to acknowledge her contribution, waiting for a pause in Catherine's story to give Jane an opportunity to talk. "Jane," I said after thanking Catherine, "friendship is important as we experience grief together. I'm thankful that Catherine has good friends like you to help her through this time." In the next few minutes, as we gave Jane an opportunity to talk, I hope that I was able to model quiet attentiveness for her support staff.

Following this opportunity to express herself, Jane no longer felt the need to interject. She had been heard and understood. Rather than simply being told to be quiet, she was affirmed as a complex and contributing moral agent who wanted Catherine to know that she was there for her as a friend, someone who could be counted on. In her own way, she was demonstrating the virtue of *loving mercy* with her housemate.

FORMATION IN THE VIRTUES OF CARE

Virtues as Embodied Practice

> Jesus reveals his love slowly. Jesus takes time because love takes a certain kind of time.
>
> **John Swinton**[65]

Virtues cannot be separated from our physical embodiment. They require physical action and physical restraint. We must learn to *be with* one another, but this presence involves proximity (space) and patience (time). To eat together is to invest our lives in one another. It is not to rush but to linger. Where competencies too often entail being efficient in accomplishing a goal, virtues resemble fine wine. They take time to mature. To attempt to accomplish or achieve these virtues quickly is to miss the mark entirely.[66] Indeed, in being faithful in the presence of people who are different from us and in being open to the mystery of one another, we are formed together in the virtues of this community. Being conscious of the need for these virtues may aid in our moral formation, but it is difficult, if not impossible, to develop these virtues without presence in community.

The virtues of care are those of *compassionate presence*. They are for those moments when we believe that we cannot *do* much of anything. People are not problems that can be solved, and so the virtues that we need are for moments of misunderstanding, of revelation, of grief, of joy—moments when the overflow of the being of another overwhelms us—when we can no longer fit our neighbor into a neat mental compartment.

This list of five virtues is by no means exhaustive. Instead, it is an initial step toward those virtues often neglected because of myths of transparency. They are virtues established on a more holistic (yet also restrained) picture of the *imago Dei*, rich in both revelation and mystery. These virtues are not intended to replace competencies as dictated by professional caregiving environments. However, they may call them into question or help to reshape them. At very least, the grounding of divine love reframes our relationships with one another and opens a space of mutual generosity and compassion.

Virtues as Loving Habits

With Alasdair MacIntyre, we recognize that intellect and rationality alone are not sufficient to form an ethical deposition. Virtues involve the holistic range of what it means to be a human being, with all of our abilities and limitations. "Virtues are dispositions not only to act in particular ways, but also to feel in particular ways."[67]

This book began with the intent "to explore accounts of caregiving and related philosophical, theological, and biblical resources to locate the appropriate motivation for, and formation of, ethical Christian care provision." Through the pages that followed, responsibility to one another (ethical motivation) was discovered to be always already present in our *givenness* to one another and our radical interdependence. It is primarily our incomprehension of ourselves and others—the mysterious opacity in our experience and our experience of others—that binds us together in the *response-ability to love* one another.

Drawing on the rich tradition of Christian theology and social practice, I have pointed to the relational significance of the *imago Dei*. In Christian theological anthropology, dependence cuts even deeper than MacIntyre recognized. Vulnerability is not only a factor to be taken into consideration when deliberating ethical courses of action; it is the *source* of ethical obligation. It is only through prior *dispossession* of self—including our conceit of transparent narrative ethics—that we are *already* inclined toward moral responsibility. The flourishing of human society as a whole may rely upon the exercise of independent practical reasoning, yet it is only by being formed together in *virtues of care* that we flourish in our shared partial opacity with one another. Without learning to pause, to *be with* one another in loving presence, "human flourishing" leaves no opening toward experiencing the gifts of mutuality and interdependence. Arguably, it is in those moments together where we are free of the ethical violence of being summoned to *give an account* that we are most fully alive. These are moments of grace, moments when we rest in the givenness of our existence and are opened to celebrate each other's gifts.

With these reshaped priorities, we considered that the virtues are first transforming us not into rational account givers but into interdependent partners in care. Whatever gifts we have are directed toward one another, including the gift of reason. It is in this context that we are open not only to our own intellectual prowess but to the surpassing and surprising reality that breaks in from the outside—the mysterious revelation of our encounters with God and with one another.

> "No eye has seen, no ear has heard, and no mind has imagined what God has prepared for those who love him."[68]

"The wisdom we speak is of the mystery of God," yet it is not a power understood by earthly rulers or delivered by "clever and persuasive speeches."[69] This resurrection power is that which comes "in weakness—timid and trembling."[70] The message of the crucified Christ is the message, the wisdom, and the *logos* of love. It is the *mysterium tremendum*—"A frightful mystery, a secret to make you tremble."[71] It is frightful because, in its deep secret lie words that can never be spoken but only lived in grateful presence with one another. As we journey in care with one another, we will never be fully understood, yet perhaps we have never fully understood ourselves either. Perhaps this transparency was never the intent. We have ever only seen "things imperfectly, like puzzling reflections in a mirror, but then we will see everything with perfect clarity."[72] We will yet see "face to face. Now I know in part; then I shall know fully, even as I am fully known."[73]

Therefore, it is with bumbling steps and fear and trembling that we turn toward one another, *formed together* with each other. It is not primarily in rational knowledge that we move forward but in love. Yet to love God is to know God. Moreover, "if anyone loves God, he is known by God."[74] In the end, it is not our knowledge or even our gifting that matters. What matters is not to "know oneself" or to make one's actions *intelligible* to oneself or to the world. What matters is to be known by and loved by God.

Formation of the virtues, then, is the exercise and practice of love. "And let us consider how to stir up one another to love and good works, not neglecting to meet together, as is the habit of some, but encouraging one another, and all the more as you see the Day drawing near."[75] Love is as *eschatological* as it is *teleological*. In the end, it is faith, hope, and love that will remain, yet the greatest of these is love.[76]

According to MacIntyre, "Without an overriding conception of the *telos* of a whole human life, conceived as a unity, our conception of certain individual virtues has to remain partial and incomplete."[77] The paradox of human love is that it flourishes, or perhaps is only a possibility, in our shared "incompleteness." "If you have reasons to love someone, you don't love him/her," Slavoj Žižek once remarked.[78] At the very least, loving in the midst of unknowing is the litmus test of the strength of love. "Let love be your highest goal!"[79] Paul exclaims.

Many practical goals require a degree of planning or rational thought to achieve. In this way, they are only attainable by people with specific abilities or in partnership with others who have these abilities. Love is the gift that anyone can exercise, yet it is also the highest achievement and the fullest expression of what it means to be human. The *telos* of love does not require additional projects or steps along the way—indeed, these projects are often what prevent us from the calling to love one another. Within the teleology of love, MacIntyre's claim that "the exercise of independent practical reasoning is one essential constituent to full human flourishing" goes unfounded.[80] It is possible to *flourish fully* without being able to exercise independent practical reasoning. People with intellectual disabilities are complex moral agents who share the partial opacity to themselves and their own intentions that we all do.

Mysterious love grounds the initial *imago Dei* in which we are formed as well as the *telos* of the *imitatio Dei* discovered in Christ. In this way, moral formation is not found in the ability to establish a coherent and intelligible account of one's actions with the perspective of the unity of one's life from beginning to end. Instead, we discover moral flourishing in practicing the virtues of care with one another: "How do I make space for this person to feel heard and understood and loved in *this moment?*" Perhaps the account of the virtues in this book will aid in living into them. Ultimately, however, it is not knowledge of the virtues or of any system of ethics that forms us in love of our neighbor. Even the *imitatio Dei* can be fully embraced and lived out by people who would not necessarily be able to "give an account" of the life or ministry of Jesus. Indeed, my friends with intellectual disabilities have often been the greatest examples of God's incomprehensible love and the virtues of care in my life.

Epilogue

Responding to God's Call

ENDING AT THE BEGINNING

We end where we began. In seeking the appropriate motivation and formation of ethical Christian care, we discover that within this desire, within the call to care, our ethical motivation and the grounding of moral formation are already always present. Certainly, practices of care are aided by competencies and skills. This work is being carried out by many others. The particular contribution of this book is to profess that our *response-ability to love one another* is at the heart of ethical calling. It drives the caregiver forward, and it pulls the caregiver *toward* the other. It is a love that must never become overconfident in its power, ability, or knowledge. The radical relational dependency at the heart of what it means to be human has endowed us all with profound cognitive limitations. This same radical relational dependency drives us toward one another and has given us *to* one another in an overflow of gratitude. We are formed together in and through the partial opacity of the stories we share.

There are rich resources for exploring this ethical posture within the Christian tradition, wherein being created in the image of God means always beginning with an "us." Just as mystery and revelation are at the epicenter of God's interactions with human beings, so mystery and revelation are at the heart of our interactions with one another. Hypercognition and transparency myths have obscured the beauty of our mysterious connection and, in doing so, have undermined the virtues of care required to *love well*. Ethical Christian caregiving calls us to reclaim virtues born out of the mystery of the human experience. It calls us to question our own myths of transparency. It calls us to question any framework of professionalism that claims priority over the relational encounter of caregiving, because it is these encounters that sustain ethical care.

THE CALLING OF SELF-CARE

> Maman died today. Or yesterday maybe, I don't know. I got a telegram from the home: "Mother deceased. Funeral tomorrow. Faithfully yours." That doesn't mean anything. Maybe it was yesterday.
>
> **Meursault in Camus' *The Stranger*[1]**

As this book began with autobiographical reflections, so it concludes. I read Camus' *The Stranger* a few years ago. The phrase above stuck with me in a powerful way. In an existential novel that explores the height and depth of ethical transgression through the lens of an entirely indifferent protagonist, it was Meursault's relationship to his recently deceased mother that had the most significant impact.

"I don't know." How is it that one does not know when one's own mother has died? How could it be that this most basic of facts is not clear to her own son? Does she mean nothing to him? "Maman" is not so cold and distant as to convey detachment; neither is it so intimate as to indicate profound grief. What is the moral status of the one who *does not know* or *cannot remember*, especially as it relates to his own mother?

As the novel continues, Meursault becomes a strangely relatable character, yet by the end it is difficult to tease out his indifference from his final violent acts. Is there any sin so great as to *not care*? Does *not knowing* or *not remembering* equate to *not caring*?

Giving an Account: Mom

> For you created [formed] my inmost being; you knit me together in my mother's womb.
>
> **Psalm 139:13, NIV**

My mother was having painful headaches. Her naturopath was convinced it was hormonally related. I strongly encouraged her to have her symptoms checked out by a doctor. That much I remember, perhaps because my family has reminded me that this is how events occurred. I don't recall the year, though I know it was just before my oldest sister's wedding. At the wedding, most of mom's hair was gone, and stiches were visible across her scalp. She had wrestled with her own self-image and self-perception much of her life. Even if she hadn't, I imagine that it would have been difficult arriving at her oldest child's wedding with a glaring head incision.

Four weddings and a dozen grandchildren later, she was still with us. She had not been the same since her first surgery and the chemo that followed. She gained weight, I knew from the pictures from before. She didn't talk a lot, and when she did it was slowly and quietly. She could no longer do much around the house or attend to her beloved gardens. She became confused about dates and names and what was happening around her.

If you asked her questions, she did not often provide a coherent story. The hardest thing for me as her son is that I cannot remember what she was like *before*. My mother homeschooled us, invested every day of her life in us, and taught us most of what we know. I know this because we still have the workbooks with her incredibly neat printing across them.

But I can't remember.

I don't know if this is "normal." I do know that I have a shockingly poor memory, and perhaps I should have this checked out sometime. I rely on my wife and my friends and my family to remind me of the things I have said and done, where I have been, and the highlights and low points of my life. There are a few memories that stand out, it's true.

But to fail to remember your own mother, when she has forgotten much of her own story?

I don't know.

I cannot give an account.

It was not until a year before her death from a second tumor, faster growing than the first, that it struck me that my mother was cognitively disabled. To not be able to recount many experiences or memories from before her illness has become one of my greatest regrets. Of the fundamental relation that gave me life and raised me, I can give little account. My deep desire, and sense of duty as a son, is to sustain in my memory the mother who *once was*. While she was still with us, I wished beyond anything to be able to remind her of the joyful memories we had shared through the years, precisely at that time when she had difficulty remembering who she was or all she had accomplished. Yet here my memories failed me. She made me *who I am*, and yet I am unable to put this into words. How might I forgive myself for my failure to sustain her identity when she gave me mine?

I, too, seek transparency. There are times when I want more than anything to be able to *give an account* of the conditions of my own emergence, to give an account of all my mother gave to me. As I look to the God who formed me, though, I must claim the forgiveness that is offered through grace. I am learning to practice the virtues of care with myself. With courageous humility I must continue to embrace the memories I do have and not despair over the memories that have been lost. I must rest in the conviction that my mother is created in God's image, the image of a relational God who has *hidden* her identity in Christ.[2] Her character and worth are not dependent upon me to sustain them, just as my own identity is not sustained through my own efforts. It is in loving mercy that I leaned my head against her shoulder and stroked the hair beneath which her tumor grew. That much I remember. I must confess to all that I cannot be held accountable for and be reconciled to the grief of her passing. I must be quietly attentive with my family members as they continue to process her death. It is these virtues of care that give me the strength to care for those with whom I work, for my family, and for my brothers and sisters in Christ.

IN CONCLUSION?

> Care lies at the very heart of the vocation given to human beings
> by God.
>
> **John Swinton**[3]

I have discovered that the God whom I worship does not demand an account in the way that many of our ethical systems do. These laws, codes, and scripted obligations depend on myths of transparency that put our most vulnerable neighbors at risk. These neighbors and friends are often made vulnerable, put at risk by an inability to "give an account" in ways that are demanded of them. An ethic of transparent accountability erodes the trust of mutual care from the inside.

While this book began by investigating the moral motivation and formation of ethical Christian caregiving, its implications take us much further. We discover that the mysterious revelation at the heart of the relational *imago Dei* must be reclaimed if we are to walk with one another well as divine image-bearers. We must confront the violence of ethical systems that *demand an account* in order to practice loving listening in our encounters with one another. The virtues of care that flow from the mysterious and scandalous love of Christ call into question those competencies, practices, and postures that arise from systems of moral assessment and control. I have provided a rough sketch of some of these virtues, yet many others will be discovered in the journey of caregiving. Our work has only begun.

When we respond to the transcendent call to care, we respond to particular *others*, but we also respond to the call of *Another*. Every encounter with a neighbor is, at the same time, an encounter with the divine. As we accompany one another on the caregiving journey, compelled by the incomprehensible love of Christ, we respond to the ethical call of both God and neighbor.

Notes

INTRODUCTION: GIVING A CAREFUL ACCOUNT

1   Leo Tolstoy, *The Awakening: The Resurrection*, trans. William E. Smith (Auckland, New Zealand: Floating Press, 1899), 421.

2   The "cult of normalcy" cuts deep at the heart of our interwoven humanity. As Thomas Reynolds observes, society has a "set of rituals trained upon demarcating and policing the borders of a 'normal' way of being" (Thomas E. Reynolds, *Vulnerable Communion: A Theology of Disability and Hospitality* [Grand Rapids: Brazos Press, 2008], 60). This policing extends to the representation we give of ourselves to one another, coloring our accounts in subtle and frequently dehumanizing ways.

3   Henri J. M. Nouwen, *Adam: God's Beloved* (Maryknoll, N.Y.: Orbis Books, 1997), 58.

4   John 4:19, NIV.

5   Søren Kierkegaard, *The Present Age: On the Death of Rebellion*, trans. Alexander Dru (New York: Harper Perennial, 2010), 51.

6   Eva Feder Kittay aptly demonstrates the implications of subjectivity. We cannot separate Kittay's relation to her daughter Sesha from her writing on caregiving ethics. To do away with the "vital distinction" between her subjective relationship and her objective statements is to deny the inescapable effect that her role as a mother plays in her work as a philosopher. To take this a step further, not having a relationship with someone who is cognitively disabled does not "free" that person to undertake a more accurate objective ethical investigation. Kittay rightly challenges Peter Singer's unqualified pronouncements on the lives of people with intellectual disabilities from his seat in the ivory tower, detached from meaningful relationships. Instead, lack of relationships—and potentially friendship—with people with intellectual disabilities then shapes the philosopher's or theologian's ethical system (Eva Feder Kittay, "The Personal Is Philosophical Is Political: A Philosopher and Mother of a Cognitively Disabled Person Sends Notes from the Battlefield," *Metaphilosophy* 40, nos. 3/4 [2009], https://doi.org/10.1111/j.1467-9973.2009.01600.x).

7 This approach is open to scrutiny, as one might argue that other theologians and philosophers would serve these purposes better or that the thread connecting these sources is thin at best. I welcome this feedback and welcome others to join in the conversation and argue shared interests from different vantage points, with different sources.

8 Douglas Harper, "Motivation," *Online Etymology Dictionary*, accessed June 22, 2017, http://www.etymonline.com/.

9 Douglas Harper, "Formation," *Online Etymology Dictionary*, accessed June 22, 2017.

10 Mark 12:30.

11 Madeleine L'Engle, *The Rock That Is Higher: Story as Truth* (Wheaton, Ill.: Harold Shaw, 1993), 215. Alasdair MacIntyre puts this differently. "I can only answer the question 'What am I to do?' if I can answer the prior question 'Of what story or stories do I find myself a part?'" He goes on to describe humans as "story-telling animals" (Alasdair C. MacIntyre, *After Virtue: A Study in Moral Theory* [London: Bloomsbury Academic, 2013], 250).

1 VOCATION AND TRANSCENDENCE

1 Friedrich Wilhelm Nietzsche, *Beyond Good and Evil: Prelude to a Philosophy of the Future*, trans. Rolf-Peter Horstmann and Judith Norman (Cambridge: Cambridge University Press, 2002), 8.

2 Søren Kierkegaard, *Provocations: Spiritual Writings of Kierkegaard*, ed. Charles E. Moore (Farmington, Pa.: Plough, 2002), 86.

3 Henri J. M. Nouwen, *With Open Hands* (Notre Dame, Ind.: Ave Maria Press, 2006), 14.

4 Here, I follow Dietrich Bonhoeffer's observation as found in John Swinton's *Becoming Friends of Time: Disability, Timefullness, and Gentle Discipleship* (Waco, Tex.: Baylor University Press, 2016).

5 Robert Hickey, *A Profile of Direct Support Professionals and Their Work Experiences in Ontario's Developmental Services Sector* (report), June 30, 2013, i, www.professorhickey.com/publications.html.

6 Drawing here on the work of Charles Taylor, "The Immanent Frame," in *A Secular Age* (Cambridge, Mass.: Belknap Press of Harvard University Press, 2007), 539–93.

7 As one paper describes, "Because recent research (Duffy & Sedlacek, 2007) and calling's historical roots as a religious construct (Weber, 1930) suggest religiosity could affect the development of calling, the analyses controlled for participants' subjective, global assessment of the importance of religion in their lives" (Shoshana R. Dobrow, "Dynamics of Calling: A Longitudinal Study of Musicians," *Journal of Organizational Behavior* 34, no. 4 [2012]: 439).

8 Dobrow, "Dynamics of Calling," 431.

9 Dobrow, "Dynamics of Calling," 431.

10 Frederick Buechner, *Wishful Thinking: A Theological ABC* (New York: Harper & Row, 1973), 95.

11 Parker Palmer puts it this way: "Vocation does not mean a goal that I pursue. It means a calling that I hear. Before I can tell my life what I want to do with it, I must listen to my life telling me who I am" (Parker J. Palmer, *Let Your Life Speak: Listening for the Voice of Vocation* [San Francisco: Jossey-Bass, 2000], 4–5). Particularly when seen through the lens of religious vocation, John Swinton writes, "Our vocation occurs in God's time and is intended to fulfill God's purposes. Within such a context, vocation is never perceived as a personal achievement or goal; it is not an individual search for the fulfillment of our own

destiny" (Swinton, *Becoming Friends of Time*, 117). The nuances here between religious and secular views on vocation become pronounced. Religious vocation may very well feel as though a person is "fulfilling their destiny," though this comes about by seeking to respond to the call of the divine *first and foremost*. In other words, the Caller takes priority over the called.

12 "My life is not only about my strengths and virtues; it is also about my liabilities and my limits, my trespasses and my shadow" (Palmer, *Let Your Life Speak*, 29). Deborah Creamer's reference to "limitness" rather than *limitations* or *liabilities*, with their negative connotations, is relevant here. Our limits are an important factor, not a negative liability, in the human experience. We each have "embodied peculiarities" that we may dislike, yet often these are an intrinsic aspect of what it means to be human, what it means to be whole (Deborah Beth Creamer, *Disability and Christian Theology: Embodied Limits and Constructive Possibilities* [Oxford: Oxford University Press, 2009], 108). In the disability context, our physical or intellectual limits and abilities are key to this embodied peculiarity. Similarly, our epistemological limits in understanding our own story, in "listening to our life," must be embraced in the process of self-recognition, as will be explored later.

13 Dobrow, "Dynamics of Calling," 42.

14 "A relational perspective is particularly relevant to a discussion of callings, given the importance of relationships and interpersonal sense-making for understanding the meaningfulness of one's work" (M. T. Cardador and B. B. Caza, "Relational and Identity Perspectives on Healthy versus Unhealthy Pursuit of Callings," *Journal of Career Assessment* 20, no. 3 (2012): 340, doi:10.1177/1069072711436162). Buechner similarly references the intersubjective aspect of calling with "the world's deep hunger."

15 Cf. Max Weber, *The Protestant Ethic and the Spirit of Capitalism* (London: Routledge, 2001).

16 From Old French *vocacion* as "call, consecration; calling, profession." Douglas Harper, "Vocation," *Online Etymology Dictionary*, accessed March 30, 2015.

17 From Luther's commentary on Genesis 13:13, quoted in Alister McGrath, "Calvin and the Christian Calling," *First Things*, June/July 1999, accessed March 13, 2015, http://www .firstthings.com/article/1999/06/calvin-and-the-christian-calling.

18 McGrath, "Calvin and the Christian Calling." John Swinton observes that Luther viewed himself as restoring the "priesthood of all believers" from 1 Peter 2:5-9 to its rightful place. "Vocation had been taken out of the hands of the whole people of God and handed over to a spiritual elite: those who were ordained priests. . . . Luther considered the creation of such a spiritual hierarchy an abomination" (Swinton, *Becoming Friends of Time*, 118).

19 As Charles Taylor observes, "The denial of a special status to the monk was also an affirmation of ordinary life as more than profane, as itself hallowed and in no way second class" (Charles Taylor, *Sources of the Self: The Making of the Modern Identity* [Cambridge: Cambridge University Press, 1992], 217–18).

20 "Holy priesthood" references 1 Peter 2:9: "But you are a chosen people, a royal priesthood, a holy nation, God's special possession, that you may declare the praises of him who called you out of darkness into his wonderful light."

21 Valerie L. Myers suggests, "In the quest to fill gaps in the dominant conversation, scholars have yet to address—in a serious way—the voluminous literature and layers of meaning that have been woven into the definition of calling over hundreds of years" (Valerie

L. Myers, *Conversations about Calling: Advancing Management Perspectives* [New York: Routledge Taylor & Francis, 2014], 81).

22 Management scholars "have dismissed Weber's major claims (particularly that calling is moral or sacred)," yet how "calling" is utilized across fields is by no means homogeneous (Myers, *Conversations about Calling*).

23 Thinking here, for example, of the Enlightenment and the work of Immanuel Kant.

24 Swinton here follows Conyers, *Becoming Friends of Time*, 118.

25 See Cardador and Caza, "Relational and Identity Perspectives on Healthy versus Unhealthy Pursuit of Callings," 339.

26 Cardador and Caza, "Relational and Identity Perspectives on Healthy versus Unhealthy Pursuit of Callings," 339.

27 *Dictionary.com*, "Compassion Fatigue," s.v., accessed April 10, 2015. http://www.dictionary.com/browse/compassion-fatigue.

28 Hickey, *Profile of Direct Support Professionals*, i.

29 Hickey, *Profile of Direct Support Professionals*, 4.

30 Hickey, *Profile of Direct Support Professionals*, 18. To assess burnout levels, Hickey employed the Maslach Burnout Inventory to measure three distinct characteristics of burnout: emotional exhaustion, depersonalization, and lack of personal accomplishment.

31 I intend to use both male and female pronouns through this book, though the majority of caregivers whether in nursing or developmental services are female.

32 The full passage here is telling, "The expectation that we can be immersed in suffering and loss daily and not be touched by it is as unrealistic as expecting to be able to walk through water without getting wet. This sort of denial is no small matter. The way we deal with loss shapes our capacity to be present to life more than anything else. The way we protect ourselves from loss may be the way in which we distance ourselves from life and help. We burn out not because we don't care but because we don't grieve. We burn out because we've allowed our hearts to become so filled with loss that we have no room left to care" (Rachel Naomi Remen, *Kitchen Table Wisdom: Stories That Heal* [New York: Riverhead Books, 1997], 52).

33 Thomas Carlyle, *Past and Present* (London: Chapman and Hall, 1843), 137.

34 Weber, *The Protestant Ethic and the Spirit of Capitalism*, 44–45.

35 Weber, *The Protestant Ethic and the Spirit of Capitalism*, 44–45.

36 From the perspective of disability, John Swinton argues that it is important to understand providence as a "way of narrating our lives in light of God's larger purpose rather than as a way of explaining every event as caused by God" (Swinton, *Becoming Friends of Time*, 116). Too closely relating one's disabling conditions to God's causation can lead to difficult questions of theodicy, as Hans Reinders investigates in detail in *Disability, Providence, and Ethics: Bridging Gaps, Transforming Lives* (Waco, Tex.: Baylor University Press, 2014).

37 Swinton, *Becoming Friends of Time*, 118.

38 Luther reflects on Romans 13, "What can be the meaning of the phrase, 'It is God's servant,' except that the governing authority is by its very nature such that through it one may serve God?" (Martin Luther, "Temporal Authority: To What Extent It Should Be Obeyed," accessed April 29, 2015, http://pages.uoregon.edu/sshoemak/323/texts/luther~1.htm). This full work is also available in hard copy: Martin Luther, *The Christian in Society II*, ed. Walter I. Brandt (Philadelphia: Muhlenberg Press, 1962).

39 Luther, "Temporal Authority."

40 Luther does provide an exception to following a prince or authority when they are clearly in the wrong. The way in which he does this, though, is to imply that insofar as one is *not certain* that one's ruler is in the wrong, one may continue to obey the ruler without fear of guilt: "What if a prince is in the wrong? Are his people bound to follow him then too? Answer: No, for it is not one's duty to do wrong; we must obey God (who desires the right) rather than men [Acts 5:29]. What if the subjects do not know whether their prince is in the right or not? Answer: So long as they do not know, and cannot with all possible diligence find out, they may obey him without peril to their souls" (Luther, "Temporal Authority").

41 See, for instance, Thomas Mann's "Germany and the Germans" speech, where he asserts that Luther's writing minimizes political liberty (Thomas Mann, "Germany and the Germans" [an address delivered in the Coolidge Auditorium in the Library of Congress on the evening of May 29, 1945] [Washington, D.C.: Library of Congress, 1945], 20). Uwe Siemon-Netto, in *The Fabricated Luther: Refuting Nazi Connections and Other Modern* (St. Louis, Mo.: Concordia, 2007) would dispute this reading of Luther; however, even if it was unintended by Luther, it is difficult to read "Temporal Authority" without seeing the connection. For a summary of Uwe Siemon-Netto's work, see Uwe Siemon-Netto, "Vietnam, Luther, and the Doctrine of Vocation," *Religion & Liberty* 24, no. 1 (January 2014), accessed April 29, 2015, https://acton.org/sites/acton.org/files/issue-pdf/Winter%202014.pdf.

42 Karl Barth, *Eine Schweizer Stimme: 1938–1945* (Zollikon-Zürich: Evangelischer Verlag, 1945), 113. Perhaps the perceived compatibility of church and state is best observed in the rallying cry "Our religion is Christ, our politics Fatherland!" of Hans Schemm, who became Bavarian minister of education and culture for the Nazi Party (see Richard Steigmann-Gall, "Nazism and the Revival of Politicial Religion Theory," in *Fascism, Totalitarianism and Political Religion*, edited by Roger Griffin [London: Routledge, 2005], 97).

43 Robert N. Proctor, *Racial Hygiene: Medicine under the Nazis* (Cambridge, Mass.: Harvard University Press, 1998), 177.

44 As Swinton describes it, providence "should not be seen as God predetermining every human movement as if life occurred on some kind of giant, transcendent chessboard" (Swinton, *Becoming Friends of Time*, 116).

45 The language of belonging and distance here is borrowed from Miroslav Volf, who writes, "What should be the relation of the churches to the cultures they inhabit? The answer lies, I propose, in cultivating the proper relation between distance from the culture and belonging to it." According to Volf, positive engagement requires the ability not only to invest-in and belong-to a culture but also the ability to step back from cultural or political entanglements (Miroslav Volf, *Exclusion and Embrace: A Theological Exploration of Identity, Otherness, and Reconciliation* [Nashville: Abingdon, 1996], 37).

2 VOCATION AND IMMANENCE

1 It should be noted that the *imago Dei* is described in similar terms in chapter 4. Each is a different way of referencing the God-relation, as will be touched on in more detail there.

2 Dietrich Bonhoeffer, *Ethics* (New York: Macmillan, 1955), 157, emphasis mine.

3 Søren Kierkegaard, *Purity of Heart Is to Will One Thing: Spiritual Preparation for the Office of Confession*, trans. Douglas V. Steere (New York: Harper, 1956), 198.

4 Kierkegaard, *Purity of Heart Is to Will One Thing*, 198.

5   Kierkegaard, *Purity of Heart Is to Will One Thing*, 198.

6   Kierkegaard, *Purity of Heart Is to Will One Thing*, 202.

7   Eric Hoffer, *The Ordeal of Change* (Cutchogue, N.Y.: Buccaneer Books, 1976), 74.

8   In *Works of Love*, Søren Kierkegaard observes, "The neighbor is one who is equal. . . . The equality of a human being before God" (Søren Kierkegaard, *Works of Love: Some Christian Reflections in the Form of Discourse*, trans. Howard V. Hong, and Edna H. Hong [New York: Harper, 1962], 60). Kierkegaard wrote extensively on neighbor-love shortly after he began reading Luther. Embedded in a society of state Lutheranism in Denmark, Kierkegaard's writing protests the practice of Christianity simply being adopted because of "the place in which one finds oneself." One is not automatically a Christian because one is born in a "Christian country." Rather, each one must *become* Christian through a leap of faith. Surrounded by Lutheran Christianity, it is surprising that Kierkegaard reads Luther directly only late in his authorship. Kierkegaard appreciates much of what he reads in this fresh reading of Luther. He argues that the Lutheranism of his time has strayed far from Luther's writing. However, M. Jamie Ferreira observes in *Love's Grateful Striving* that "Kierkegaard is definitely ambivalent toward Luther" (M. Jamie Ferreira, *Love's Grateful Striving: A Commentary on Kierkegaard's Works of Love* [Oxford: Oxford University Press, 2001], 252).

9   Kierkegaard, *Works of Love*, 60.

10 One may wonder how Luther himself would answer, "Who is my neighbor?" (Luke 10:29). His writings in works such as *On the Jews and Their Lies* call into question his commitment to unconditional equality regarding his Jewish neighbors. Similarly, Luther reportedly suggested that a disabled twelve-year-old boy at Dessau be suffocated. This boy was only able to eat and to excrete and Luther was said to have reasoned, "I think he's simply a mass of flesh without a soul." For more on Luther's treatment of persons with disabilities, see M. Miles, "Martin Luther and Childhood Disability in 16th Century Germany," *Journal of Religion, Disability & Health* 5, no. 4 (2001): independentliving.org/docs7/miles2005b.html, accessed April 10, 2015, doi:10.1300/j095v05n04_02. See also M. P. Mostert, "Useless Eaters: Disability as Genocidal Marker in Nazi Germany," *Journal of Special Education* 36, no. 3 (2002): catholicculture.org/culture/library/view.cfm?recnum=7019, accessed April 10, 2015, doi:10.1177/00224669020360030601. Following these accounts and others, one may question whether Luther shared Kierkegaard's commitment to eternal equality with one's neighbor.

11 Galatians 3:28.

12 Søren Kierkegaard, *The Point of View for My Work as an Author: A Report to History, and Related Writings*, trans. Walter Lowrie, ed. Benjamin Nelson (New York: Harper, 1962), 118.

13 Kierkegaard, *The Point of View*, 58.

14 Nouwen, *Adam*, 42.

15 Nouwen, *Adam*, 42.

16 Nouwen, *Adam*, 43.

17 Nouwen, *Adam*, 43.

18 Nouwen, *Adam*, 46.

19 Nouwen, *Adam*, 47.

20 Michael Bonikowsky, "Called to Remain," *Nations*, June 2, 2019, https://nationsmedia .org/called-to-remain/.

21 Bonikowsky, "Called to Remain."

22 The stories of Nouwen and Bonikowsky carry this point of the journey of preferential care sufficiently, but it bears mentioning that this was my experience also. My first experience in providing care was with one of the men in the region who required extensive two-on-one supports, Hiroshi. This gentleman did not require total care in the way that Adam did but needed extra support because he would express himself in behavior that frequently put himself and support workers at risk. Two other men were hired in the house at the same time as I. Another potential worker who was significantly bigger in stature than I was intimidated by his experience with Hiroshi. I didn't see him again in my orientation and found out that he requested to work at another location, fearing that he would not be able to meet Hiroshi's needs. This, I concluded, was not a good sign. If he did not think that he could work with Hiroshi, what was I thinking?

As days and weeks went on, however, I came to know the people I supported in a new way. Hiroshi's behavior was no longer frightening. It was still often unpredictable, but with hindsight, we could usually figure out what had caused him to be upset or anxious. His needs were not so different from my own. For the people we support who are not able to communicate using words, or who have difficulty understanding and expressing their emotions, behavior may be one of their only avenues to communicate their needs and come to terms the world around them. Where I was initially anxious first for my own safety and then that I would demonstrate competence to my coworkers, challenging behavior began to make me worried for new reasons. I grew to care for the people I supported, and beneath each of the "outbursts," I came to appreciate a longing to be known, to be understood, and to communicate in ways that I had come to take for granted in my own relationships.

Later, as I worked in recruitment, I found that the number of applicants for the role of direct support professional who had siblings or a son or daughter with disabilities was significant. Where I initially assumed that people who were full-time caregivers in their personal lives would be looking for a "break" when applying for work, this was largely not the case. Rather, having been impacted by living closely with and supporting loved ones with disabilities, family members recognized the need for support in this area and had a desire to make a difference. They also knew of the profound rewards that come from getting to know and care for people in this way.

23 Nouwen, *Adam*, 47.

24 Kierkegaard, *Works of Love*, 267.

25 Nouwen, *Adam*, 58.

26 As Janie Butts and Karen Rich describe, "Health care professionals must acknowledge that they have something to learn from disabled people, that giving and receiving flows in both directions in flourishing communities" (Janie B. Butts and Karen L. Rich, "Acknowledging Dependence: A MacIntyrean Perspective on Relationships Involving Alzheimer's Disease," *Nursing Ethics* 11, no. 4 [2004]: 409, doi:10.1191/0969733004ne712oa).

27 Cardador and Caza, "Relational and Identity Perspectives on Healthy versus Unhealthy Pursuit of Callings," 346.

28 Cardador and Caza, "Relational and Identity Perspectives on Healthy versus Unhealthy Pursuit of Callings," 345.

29 Cardador and Caza, "Relational and Identity Perspectives on Healthy versus Unhealthy Pursuit of Callings," 345.

3 A THEOLOGICAL STORY

1 John McKnight, *The Careless Society: Community and Its Counterfeits* (New York: Basic Books, 1995), x.

2 Modern usage of "profess" carries this sense of *declare* with it.

3 From the mid-fourteenth century, "profession" referred to "any solemn declaration" and then, "occupation one professes to be skilled in" from early in the fifteenth century. Douglas Harper, "Profession," *Online Etymology Dictionary*, accessed March 30, 2015.

4 "The closest approach to a learned legal profession during the early Middle Ages lay in the ranks of the clergy . . . Churchmen were deeply involved in every aspect of the legal and institutional structures of the early Middle Ages . . . When Roman administrative structures began to crumble in the sixth century, clergymen moved in to fill the breach." James A. Brundage, *The Medieval Origins of the Legal Profession: Canonists, Civilians, and Courts* (Chicago: University of Chicago Press, 2008), 90.

5 I. K. Zola, "Healthism and Disabling Medicalization," in *Disabling Professions*, ed. I. Illich (London: M. Boyars, 1977), 41–69.

6 Rebecca Casey, "Burnout for Developmental Services Workers," *McGill Sociological Review* 2 (April 2011): 39–58, https://www.mcgill.ca/msr/volume2/article3.

7 "Spotlight on Transformation," Ontario Ministry of Social Services, February 2009, http://www.mcss.gov.on.ca/en/mcss/publications/developmentalServices/spotlight/sotFeb09.aspx.

8 "Spotlight on Transformation."

9 "Core Competencies Implementation" (lecture, Developmental Services Human Resources Strategy, Ottawa, Ont., 2013).

10 Now "Korn Ferry." "About Hay Group," Hay Group, accessed March 13, 2015, http://www.haygroup.com/ca/about/index.aspx?id=6502.

11 "Core Competencies Implementation."

12 "Core Competencies Dictionary," Hay Group, May 2013, http://pclkw.org/wp-content/uploads/2013/05/Core-Competency-Dictionary-October-1-2009.pdf, 1.

13 "Core Competencies Implementation."

14 Elliot Freidson notes the rise of these codes in professionalized services, "Part of the purpose of such codes is without doubt to persuade the public that the formulation of ethical standards justifies trust." (Elliot Freidson, *Professionalism: The Third Logic* [Chicago: University of Chicago Press, 2001], 214).

15 The Ministry of Community and Social Services has made it a key priority to "transform developmental services so individuals and families can benefit from greater choice and flexibility in services and be active members of an inclusive society" (Government of Ontario, "2015–2016 Published Plan," Ministry of Community and Social Services, accessed June 19, 2018, http://www.mcss.gov.on.ca/en/mcss/about/ppar/index.aspx, 2.e).

16 "Core Competencies Dictionary," 1.

17 The first assumption of the Hay Group methodology is "in every job, some people perform more effectively than others" ("Core Competencies Dictionary," 1).

18 MacIntyre, *After Virtue*, 88.

19 MacIntyre, *After Virtue*, 88.

20 "The manager treats ends as given, as outside his scope; his concern is with technique, with effectiveness in transforming raw materials into final products, unskilled labor into skilled labor, investment into profits" (MacIntyre, *After Virtue*, 35).

21 In "Excellence v. Effectiveness: MacIntyre's Critique of Business," Charles Horvath explains that, in MacIntyre's view, "managers have substituted external measures of 'winning' or 'effectiveness' for any internal concept of good" (Charles M. Horvath, "Excellence v. Effectiveness: Macintyre's Critique of Business," *Business Ethics Quarterly* 5, no. 3 [1995]: 499). In another place he describes it this way, "businesses have found a substitute ethical base in the concept of effectiveness" (514).

22 The Ministry of Community and Social Services identified a strategic plan to "transform developmental services" (Helena Jaczek, "Mandate Letter Progress: Community and Social Services," Ontario.ca, January 11, 2016, Transforming Developmental Services, https://www.ontario.ca/page/mandate-letter-progress-community-and-social-services).

23 This general approached is borrowed from Alasdair MacIntyre in *Dependent Rational Animals*. The first kind of goods is pleasurable goods (when something is good because it is pleasurable, i.e., because it satisfies felt bodily wants or felt wants generally). The second is instrumental goods, as MacIntyre describes good "only as a means." Specific skills or opportunities are good because they help advance another good. The third type of good is found within a practice. The goods of the practice dictate whether the agent is good at their role. "Whether there are (genuine goods) and what they are is characteristically and generally something to be learned only by being initiated into this or that particular activity." MacIntyre gives the examples of being a member of a fishing crew, or as a mother, or as a chess or soccer player. Finally, individual and communal human goods (when something is good because it is something that an individual person qua human being or society qua human should make a place for in their life). Individuals, while part of a particular society, need to determine the role that particular goods will play in their own lives. Human societies also determine particular goods, "for every society there is the question of whether it is good for that society that the goods of this or that particular practice should have this or that place in its common life" (Alasdair C. MacIntyre, *Dependent Rational Animals: Why Human Beings Need the Virtues* [Chicago, Ill.: Open Court, 1999], 65).

24 Daniel O. Dahlstrom, "Independence and the Virtuous Community," *Reason Papers* 43, no. 2 (October 2012), https://reasonpapers.com/pdf/342/rp_342_8.pdf.

25 Alasdair MacIntyre writes, "We cannot . . . characterize behavior independently of intentions, and we cannot characterize intentions independently of the settings which make those intentions intelligible both to agents themselves and to others" (MacIntyre, *After Virtue*, 240).

26 Linda Gilmore and Monica Cuskelly, "Vulnerability to Loneliness in People with Intellectual Disability: An Explanatory Model," *Journal of Policy and Practice in Intellectual Disabilities* 11, no. 3 (2014): 192–99, doi:10.1111/jppi.12089.

27 "Society has done a better job of increasing the community presence of people with an ID [intellectual disability] than in facilitating their 'living' within the community . . . research has found that people with IDD [intellectual or developmental disabilities] have few friends and mostly they name other disability service users, staff, and family members as their friends" (Angela Novak Amado et al., "Social Inclusion and Community Participation of Individuals with Intellectual/Developmental Disabilities," *Intellectual and Developmental Disabilities* 51, no. 5 [2013]: 362, doi:10.1352/1934-9556-51.5.360). See also J. S. Reinders on the limits of citizenship in light of the absence of friendships and meaningful relationships: "The Good Life for Citizens with Intellectual Disability," *Journal of Intellectual Disability Research* 46, no. 1 (2002): 1–5, doi:10.1046/j.1365–2788.2002.00386.

28 "Every activity, every enquiry, every practice aims at some good; for by 'the good' we mean that at which human beings characteristically aim" (MacIntyre, *After Virtue*, 147).

29 MacIntyre, *After Virtue*, 174.

30 "A virtue is an acquired human quality the possession and exercise of which tends to enable us to achieve those goods which are internal to practices and the lack of which effectively prevents us from achieving any such goods" (MacIntyre, *After Virtue*, 191).

31 MacIntyre, "Postscript to the Second Edition," *After Virtue*, 264.

32 Samuel Scheffler challenges MacIntyre's initial description in *After Virtue*, arguing that virtues identified within practices may not be virtuous once they cross over into other spheres of life and practice. For instance, if one were to take the qualities of ruthlessness and relentlessness apart from being able to distinguish when they were appropriate and when they were not, these qualities may be very effective within certain practices. MacIntyre takes a section of his postscript to the second edition to respond to Scheffler's critique and further defines what he means (MacIntyre, "Postscript to the Second Edition," *After Virtue*, 264).

33 Nouwen, *Adam*, 58.

4 TRACES OF THE DIVINE

1 Hans S. Reinders, *Receiving the Gift of Friendship: Profound Disability, Theological Anthropology, and Ethics* (Grand Rapids: Eerdmans, 2008), 2.

2 Genesis 1:28, NLT.

3 1 John 4:8.

4 Thomas J. Scirghi, "The Trinity: A Model for Belonging in Contemporary Society," *Ecumenical Review* 54, no. 3 (2002): 334, doi:10.1111/j.1758-6623.2002.tb00157.x.

5 Rainer Bucher quoting Adolf Hitler, *Mein Kampf* (vol. 2, chap. 1) in Rainer Bucher and Rebecca Pohl, *Hitler's Theology: A Study in Political Religion* (London: Continuum, 2011), 59.

6 John Locke, *Two Treatises of Government*, ed. Peter Laslett (Cambridge: Cambridge University Press, 1988), 1:30.

7 In practical matters, this meant that Locke's "economic-abilities view of the image of God led to the 'disinheritance of many' impoverished people during the Industrial Revolution." John Frederic Kilner, *Dignity and Destiny: Humanity in the Image of God* (Grand Rapids: Eerdmans, 2005), 19n95.

8 Stacy Clifford, "The Capacity Contract: Locke, Disability, and the Political Exclusion of 'Idiots,'" *Politics, Groups, and Identities* 2, no. 1 (2014): 93, doi:10.1080/21565503.2013.876918.

9 John Swinton, "Restoring the Image: Spirituality, Faith, and Cognitive Disability," *Journal of Religion and Health* 36, no. 1 (Spring 1997): 22. Quoting Peter Birchenall and Mary Birchenall, "Caring for Mentally Handicapped People: The Community and the Church," *Professional Nurse* 1 (March 1986): 6.

10 Augustine, *The Literal Meaning of Genesis*, trans. John Hammond Taylor (New York: Paulist Press, 1982), 6:193.

11 Thomas Aquinas, "Question 93: The End or Term of the Production of Man," in *The Summa Theologiæ of St. Thomas Aquinas*, trans. Fathers of the English Dominican Province (Kevin Knight, 2017), 1, Q. 93, co., http://www.newadvent.org/summa/1093.htm. It must be noted that Aquinas' response on this is much more nuanced and arguments have been made on both sides that Aquinas does (Miguel J. Romero, "Aquinas on the *Corporis*

Infirmitas: Broken Flesh and the Grammar of Grace," in *Disability in the Christian Tradition: A Reader*, ed. Brian Brock and John Swinton [Grand Rapids: Eerdmans, 2012], 101–51) and does not (H. Reinders, *Receiving the Gift of Friendship*, 2008) fully include people with intellectual disabilities in the "fullness" of this image. Regardless, the point here is that key theologians in the history of Christianity have argued for a substantive view of the image of God that has been construed or misconstrued in a variety of ways at the expense of people with intellectual and developmental disabilities.

12 *Summa Theologiæ*, 1.93.8, cited in Romero, "Aquinas on the *Corporis Infirmitas*," 129, cf. *De Trinitate*, XIV.6.

13 Jane S. Deland, "Images of God through the Lens of Disability," *Journal of Religion, Disability & Health* 3, no. 2 (1999), doi:10.1300/j095v03n02_06. This debate has also been raised by Molly C. Haslam in *A Constructive Theology of Intellectual Disability: Human Being as Mutuality and Response* (New York: Fordham University Press, 2012).

14 2 Corinthians 4:4, Colossians 1:15.

15 Romans 8:29.

16 1 Corinthians 11:7, 15:49; 2 Corinthians 3:18; Colossians 3:9-10; Ephesians 4:22-24.

17 1 Corinthians 11:1-6, James 3:9.

18 Reynolds, *Vulnerable Communion*, 178. Hans Reinders similarly writes, "The Bible does not seem to answer the question in which respects human beings reflect the image of their Creator" (Hans Reinders, "*Imago Dei* as a Basic Concept in Christian Ethics," in *Holy Scriptures in Judaism, Christianity and Islam: Hermeneutics, Values and Society*, ed. Hendrik M. Vroom and Gerald D. Gort [Atlanta: Rodopi, 1997], 189).

19 Reynolds, *Vulnerable Communion*, 177.

20 Emil Brunner, *Man in Revolt, A Christian Anthropology*, trans. Olive Wyon (Philadelphia: Westminster, 1947), 102.

21 Reynolds, *Vulnerable Communion*, 177.

22 1 John 4:8.

23 Kierkegaard, *Works of Love*, 62–63. Emphasis added.

24 It must be noted that Irenaeus initially articulated a similar distinction. Hans Reinders observes that Irenaeus relies on an overemphasis of the distinction between being created in God's "image" and God's "likeness" in Genesis 1:26: "In his anti-Gnostic treatise, *Adversus Haereses* Irenaeus explained the 'image' as referring to the substance that human beings can never lose without ceasing to be human. 'Likeness,' in contrast, refers to the original state in which man was created before the fall, the state of a *justitia originalis*." While Reinders goes on to note that modern scholarship reads "in our image, according to our likeness" as a phrase "wherein the second term is explanatory of the first" (H. Reinders, "*Imago Dei* as a Basic Concept in Christian Ethics," 191). Irenaeus' overall inclination does find a certain basis in the biblical text. Where the Genesis account of being created in God's image accords dignity and moral standing intertwined with the very nature of what it means to be human, the New Testament points to Christ as the "image of the invisible God," and calls Christians to imitate Christ in order to *live into* God's image. Reinders writes, "Evidently, these Paulinic sources contain very powerful notions for the doctrine of *imago dei*, but when considered together with the text in Genesis 1 one cannot help but conclude that the scriptural sources seem to pull in different directions. On the one hand, the image seems to be God's gift to humankind as he created them. On the other hand, however, the divine image is seen as real only in those human beings whom Christ has restored into conformity with God through his spirit" (195).

25 Emil Brunner, *Dogmatics*, vol. 2, *The Christian Doctrine of Creation and Redemption* (Philadelphia: Westminster, 1953), 55–56. Brunner once described Søren Kierkegaard as "the greatest Christian thinker of modern times" (Emil Brunner, *The Divine-Human Encounter*, trans. Amandus William Loos [Philadelphia: Westminster, 1943], 82).

26 In *The Sickness unto Death*, Kierkegaard refers to the self before God as "the theological self," a self whose criterion is God (Søren Kierkegaard, *The Sickness unto Death: A Christian Psychological Exposition for Upbuilding and Awakening*, trans. Howard V. Hong and Edna H. Hong [Princeton, N.J.: Princeton University Press, 1980], 79).

27 Stanley J. Grenz describes Brunner's distinction this way: "The formal dimension refers to the fact that we stand responsible to respond both to God and to others" (Stanley J. Grenz, *Theology for the Community of God* [Nashville: Broadman & Holman, 1994], 171).

28 Brunner, *Man in Revolt*, 104.

29 Deland, "Images of God through the Lens of Disability," 58.

30 George Pattison, *The Philosophy of Kierkegaard* (Montreal: McGill-Queen's University Press, 2005), 145. This is Pattison's translation of Kierkegaard's Danish text in *Upbuilding Discourses in Various Spirits*. One might argue, "Is not adoration itself an action, to *be* or to *do* something? In this way, is it not to exercise dominion over one's ability?" Yet Kierkegaard identifies that this is not to exercise dominion. The One whom one adores must entirely determine and define the kind of adoration Kierkegaard references. It is to be acted *upon*. Only within this framework might one "be nothing" in the act of adoration. The act is also strangely achieved through the "being" of the One who is adored. "To be able to adore" is itself the act of God, and it is this "ability" that "gives the invisible glory preeminence over the rest of creation." We are not accustomed to thinking of a person's ability as the ability of *Another*, yet this is what adoration of God is. It is a givenness, a receiving of the Other, before which one has no capacity except to receive, to be acted *upon*. We see that the love of God and the ability to return this love in no way depends on abilities or characteristics of the human beings created in God's image.

31 H. Reinders, *Receiving the Gift of Friendship*, 274.

32 H. Reinders, *Receiving the Gift of Friendship*, 119.

33 Brunner, *Man in Revolt*, 99.

34 Douglas John Hall, *Professing the Faith: Christian Theology in a North American Context* (Minneapolis, Minn.: Fortress, 1993), 215.

35 Martin Luther, "Lectures on Genesis, Chapters 1–5," in *Luther's Works*, ed. Jaroslav Pelikan, trans. George V. Schick (St. Louis: Concordia, 1958), 1:61.

36 Hall, *Professing the Faith*, 216.

37 John Calvin, *Commentaries on the First Book of Moses, Called Genesis*, trans. John King (Edinburgh: Edinburgh Printing, 1847), 1:94.

38 It is in search of this ethical equality despite limitation that leads Hans Reinders on a quest for a *relational ontology* that, building on Greek Orthodox theologian John D. Zizioulas, considers "how to think of human beings as constituted by external rather than internal relations" (H. Reinders, "*Imago Dei* as a Basic Concept in Christian Ethics," 191. See also *Receiving the Gift of Friendship* for development of this direction). Receiving God's love is not, strictly thinking, an *acting* or even a *being*, as Tom Reynolds describes, "as a capacity for love, the *imago Dei* is a capacity for God (*capax Dei*)" (Reynolds, *Vulnerable Communion*, 184). Love's "ability" is on the part of the One who loves first. "We love because he first loved us" (1 John 4:9).

39 Genesis 4:9.

40　The image of God is also referenced in Genesis 9:6 (NIV): "Whoever sheds human blood, by humans shall their blood be shed; for in the image of God has God made mankind." Again, the precise nature of what it means to be made in God's image is not articulated, yet its ethical implications are unmistakable. Profound respect is to be accorded those who have been created in this image.

41　David Novak observes, "Although Levinas assiduously avoids the traditional Hebrew term, *tselem Elohim*, and the traditional Latin term, *imago Dei* (probably because of his aversion to 'theology'), there can be no doubt that this is precisely his point of philosophical entrance" (David Novak, "The Human Person as the Image of God," in *Personhood and Health Care*, ed. David C. Thomasma, David N. Weisstub, and Christian Hervé [Dordrecht: Springer, 2011], 43).

42　Emmanuel Levinas, "God and Philosophy," in *Collected Philosophical Papers*, trans. Alphonso Lingis (Pittsburgh, Pa.: Duquesne University Press, 2006), 154.

43　Levinas, "God and Philosophy," 154.

44　Or, as Malebranche knew, "There is no idea of God, or God is his own idea" (Levinas, "God and Philosophy," 160). A similar move occurs as we observed previously with Kierkegaard on *adoration*. Just as adoration of God must be, in its truest sense, a reception of God's love as an act of God, so the "idea of the Infinite" can only be "put" in me by an "unequalled passivity."

45　For further exploration of this theme in Levinas, see Claudia Welz, *Humanity in God's Image an Interdisciplinary Exploration* (Oxford: Oxford University Press, 2016).

46　Edith Wyschogrod makes the connection between the *imago Dei* and Levinas' "trace" clear: "What comes to mind in Levinas's discussion of the trace is the classical conception of the *imago Dei*. This is indeed the perspective from which Levinas writes: the face is the image of God. But what does it *mean* to be in the image of God? It is not to be an 'icon' of God but 'to find oneself in his trace.' The God of the Judaeo-Christian tradition retains 'all the infinity of his absence.' He shows himself only through his trace as it is written in Exodus 33. . . . 'Thou shalt see what is behind me: but my face shall not be seen'" (Edith Wyschogrod, *Emmanuel Levinas: The Problem of Ethical Metaphysics* [New York: Fordham University Press, 2000], 163).

47　"It is then an idea signifying with a signifyingness prior to presence, to all presence, prior to every origin in consciousness and thus an-archical, accessible in its trace. . . . What can this antiquity mean if not the trauma of awakening—as though the idea of the Infinite, the Infinite in us, awakened a consciousness which is not awakened enough? As though the idea of the Infinite in us were a demand, and a signification in the sense that an order is signified in a demand" (Wyschogrod, *Emmanuel Levinas*, 161).

48　Wyschogrod, *Emmanuel Levinas*, 164.

49　Wyschogrod, *Emmanuel Levinas*, 164.

50　Wyschogrod, *Emmanuel Levinas*, 165.

51　Wyschogrod, *Emmanuel Levinas*, 167.

52　It should be noted that Levinas discusses in more detail the relation of the Infinite and love: "Love is possible only through the idea of the Infinite" (Levinas, "God and Philosophy," 164). We return to this connection between love and the face of the other in part 3.

53　Douglas Harper, "Encounter," *Online Etymology Dictionary*, accessed June 26, 2018. Continuing on, it will be noted that the initial sense of "to meet as adversaries" in an encounter is not entirely lost.

54 Brunner describes the formal image as "the human," that which distinguishes "man from all the rest of creation." However, Brunner oversteps his own description. He goes on to qualify the formal image, according it to human beings' *subjectivity* and *responsibility*. To be a subject for Brunner carries with it *rationality*, that is, "one with whom one can speak, with whom therefore God can also speak" (Emil Brunner and Karl Barth, *Natural Theology*, trans. John Baillie [London: G. Bles, 1956], 23). I have known many people through the years who would not pass this litmus test for "rational speech." Second, to be human for Brunner is to be *responsible*. Levinas captures the sense of this responsibility without the requirement of rationality and speech. Indeed, for Levinas it is one's inability to rationally articulate one's responsibility that points toward one's radical obligation. In this way, Levinas' *imago Dei* captures a kind of moral obligation that can be attributed to all human beings in a way that Brunner's own formal *imago* cannot.

55 Brunner, *Christian Doctrine of Creation and Redemption*, 60.

56 Reynolds, *Vulnerable Communion*, 179.

57 Brunner, *Christian Doctrine of Creation and Redemption*, 98.

58 Kierkegaard, *Works of Love*, 74.

59 Kierkegaard, *Works of Love*, 364.

60 Kierkegaard, *Works of Love*, 9–10.

61 1 John 4:19.

62 Kierkegaard, *Works of Love*, 55.

63 2 Peter 1:3.

64 Matthew 22:37-39.

65 Swinton, *Becoming Friends of Time*, 24.

66 Matthew 25:40, Mark 2:16.

67 1 John 4:9-11.

68 Romans 8:9. Thinking here of Saint Irenaeus of Lyons, "For the glory of God is a living man; and the life of man consists in beholding God," which is often rendered "For the glory of God is the human person fully alive." Irenaeus, *Against Heresies* (Whitefish, Mont.: Kessinger, 2007), Book 4, 20:7. Paul writes to the Ephesians to proclaim this "one new humanity" that Christ has proclaimed by making peace between the Jews and Gentiles (Eph 2:15), peace in which there is "neither Jew nor Gentile, neither slave nor free, nor is there male or female, for you are all one in Christ Jesus" (Gal 3:28). This is the true equality of which Kierkegaard writes, equality in which all are loved with an undying and unconditional love: the love of one's neighbor.

69 Recalling here Reynolds' "creativity with others, relation to others, and availability for others" (Reynolds, *Vulnerable Communion*, 177).

70 Brunner, *Man in Revolt*, 106.

71 Brunner, *Man in Revolt*, 102.

72 Luke 24:15-16.

73 Luke 24:31.

74 Luke 24:32.

5 SEEING YOU THROUGH ME

1 As quoted in Reynolds, *Vulnerable Communion*, 216.

2 Nouwen, *Adam*, 47.

3 Nouwen, *Adam*, 15.

4 Nouwen, *Adam*, 47.

5 Nouwen, *Adam*, 47.

6 Nouwen, *Adam*, 53.

7 Nouwen, *Adam*, 22.

8 Nouwen, *Adam*, 126.

9 Nouwen, *Adam*, 30.

10 Nouwen, *Adam*, 55.

11 Nouwen, *Adam*, 50.

12 H. Reinders, *Receiving the Gift of Friendship*, 373. See also 372, where Reinders points to Nouwen's Christology as an important point of illumination for Nouwen's interaction with Adam.

13 H. Reinders, *Receiving the Gift of Friendship*, 374.

14 Paul Tillich, *The New Being* (Lincoln: University of Nebraska Press, 2005), 127–28.

15 Gavin Francis, *Adventures in Human Being: A Grand Tour from the Cranium to the Calcaneum* (London: Profile Books, 2015), Audible audiobook.

16 Francis, *Adventures in Human Being*.

17 Anil K. Seth, "The Hard Problem of Consciousness Is a Distraction from the Real One," *Aeon*, November 2, 2016, https://aeon.co/essays/the-hard-problem-of-consciousness-is-a-distraction-from-the-real-one.

18 Seth, "Hard Problem of Consciousness Is a Distraction from the Real One."

19 Thomas Merton, *No Man Is an Island* (Boston: Shambhala, 2005), 177.

20 Eric Wargo, "How Many Seconds to a First Impression?" *Association for Psychological Science RSS*, July 2006, accessed September 16, 2016, http://www.psychologicalscience.org/index.php/publications/observer/2006/july-06/how-many-seconds-to-a-first-impression.html.

21 Timothy J. Basselin, *Flannery O'Connor: Writing a Theology of Disabled Humanity* (Waco, Tex.: Baylor University Press, 2013), 30.

22 Basselin, *Flannery O'Connor*, 30.

23 Basselin, *Flannery O'Connor*, 30.

24 Kathleen Lipovski-Helal, "Flannery O'Connor's Encounter with Mary Ann Long," *Flannery O'Connor Review* 11 (January 1, 2013), https://www.questia.com/library/journal/1P3-3123354531/flannery-o-connor-s-encounter-with-mary-ann-long.

25 From Flannery O'Connor's memoir, as quoted in Basselin, *Flannery O'Connor*, 5.

26 When considering Mary Ann or O'Connor herself, who was diagnosed with lupus just as she became a professional writer, we must be cautious to recognize the difference between illness and disability. Much damage has been done by equating the two. Disability does not always entail suffering, and many people with disabilities see it as an essential part of their identity rather than an aspect of their life that they are trying to "fix." Nonetheless, there can be overlap between perception of disability and that of illness. Many people with disabilities would share O'Connor's observation: "I believe that the basic experience of everyone is the experience of human limitation" (Basselin, *Flannery O'Connor*, 10). The particular contribution of O'Connor on the topic of disability, according to Basselin, is at this intersection of goodness and the grotesque. "Her grotesque characters challenge readers' perceptions of 'good' and 'bad,' exposing the perceived good—whether it be sympathy, human progress, or 'good' country people—as actually well-endowed with original sin" (33).

27 Basselin, *Flannery O'Connor*, 36.

28 Basselin, *Flannery O'Connor*, 39.

29 Basselin, *Flannery O'Connor*, 32.

30 Gilmore and Cuskelly, "Vulnerability to Loneliness in People with Intellectual Disability," 192.

31 Amado et al., "Social Inclusion and Community Participation of Individuals with Intellectual/Developmental Disabilities," 362.

32 Mike Fillon, "The Real Face of Jesus," *Popular Mechanics*, January 3, 2015, accessed August 2, 2016, http://www.popularmechanics.com/science/health/a234/1282186/.

33 Christopher Olivola and Alexander Todorov, "The Look of a Winner," *Scientific American*, April 28, 2009, accessed May 13, 2016, http://www.scientificamerican.com/article/the-look-of-a-winner/.

34 Fillon, "Real Face of Jesus," 2015.

35 Gert Stulp, Abraham P. Buunk, Simon Verhulst, and Thomas V. Pollet, "Tall Claims? Sense and Nonsense about the Importance of Height of US Presidents," *Leadership Quarterly* 24, no. 1 (2013): 159, https://doi.org/10.1016/j.leaqua.2012.09.002.

36 1 Samuel 16:7, ESV.

37 John 1:10.

38 Søren Kierkegaard, *Practice in Christianity*, trans. Howard V. Hong and Edna H. Hong (Princeton, N.J.: Princeton University Press, 1991), 127.

39 Kierkegaard, *Practice in Christianity*, 128.

40 Kierkegaard, *Practice in Christianity*, 126. In conversations around theology and disability, where people with severe cognitive disabilities are often perceived as being unable to intellectually grasp matters of faith, perhaps it is even easier for some to go beyond the "offense" to faith in Christ.

41 Kierkegaard, *Practice in Christianity*, 121.

42 Kierkegaard, *Works of Love*, 53.

43 Matthew 22:35-40, Mark 12:28-34, Luke 10:25-28.

44 Kierkegaard, *Works of Love*, 50.

45 Erving Goffman and Joel Best, *Interaction Ritual: Essays in Face to Face Behavior* (New Brunswick, N.J.: Aldine Transaction, 2005), 10.

46 Luke 10:29.

47 Reynolds, *Vulnerable Communion*, 221.

48 See Reynolds, *Vulnerable Communion*, 221.

49 Reynolds, *Vulnerable Communion*, 222.

50 Amos Yong observes, "The history of monstrosity, freakery, and disability tells us less about those who are so labeled than it does about the dominant majority doing the labeling" (Amos Yong, *Theology and Down Syndrome: Reimagining Disability in Late Modernity* [Waco, Tex.: Baylor University Press, 2007], 84).

51 Yong, *Theology and Down Syndrome*, 84.

52 Nietzsche, *Beyond Good and Evil*, aphorism 146.

53 Stacy Clifford Simplican, "Care, Disability, and Violence: Theorizing Complex Dependency in Eva Kittay and Judith Butler," *Hypatia* 30, no. 1 (2014): 226, doi:10.1111/hypa.12130.

54 It is identified as an ideal because even Kittay acknowledges this complete understanding of the other will never be fulfilled in the caregiving relationship, even where the person supported is one's child (Simplican, "Care, Disability, and Violence," 220).

55 Eva Feder Kittay, "Beyond Autonomy and Paternalism: The Caring Transparent Self," in *Autonomy and Paternalism: Reflections on the Theory and Practice of Health Care*, ed.

Thomas Nye, Yvonne Denier, and Toon Vandevelde (Leuven, Belgium: Peeters, 2007), 53, as quoted in Simplican, "Care, Disability, and Violence," 220.

56 There are far too many examples of this already, from institutional settings, through compassion fatigue or burnout, in the actions of disengaged staff, or within abusive relationships.

57 Kittay, "The Personal Is Philosophical Is Political," 406.

58 Kittay, "The Personal Is Philosophical Is Political," 405.

59 Eva Feder Kittay, *Love's Labor: Essays on Women, Equality, and Dependency* (New York: Routledge, 1999), 52, quoted in Simplican, "Care, Disability, and Violence," 220.

60 Trudy Steuernagel, quoted in Joanna Connors, "Kent State Professor Trudy Steuernagel's Fierce Protection of Her Autistic Son, Sky Walker, Costs Her Life: Sheltering Sky," *The Plain Dealer*, December 6, 2009, quoted in Simplican, "Care, Disability, and Violence," 2017.

61 Simplican, "Care, Disability, and Violence," 221.

62 Simplican, "Care, Disability, and Violence," 226.

6 THE STORIES I TELL

1 Thomas King, "The Truth about Stories: A Native Narrative," in *The 2003 CBC Massey Lectures*, Canadian Broadcasting Corporation, November 7, 2003, http://www.cbc.ca/radio/ideas/the-2003-cbc-massey-lectures-the-truth-about-stories-a-native-narrative-1.2946870.

2 Nietzsche, *Beyond Good and Evil*, 8.

3 MacIntyre, *After Virtue*, 242.

4 MacIntyre, *After Virtue*, 243.

5 See MacIntyre, *After Virtue*, 250; and Lia Mela, "MacIntyre on Personal Identity," *Public Reason* 3, no. 1 (June 2011): 103–13, http://www.publicreason.ro/articol/47.

6 "What the agent is able to do and say intelligibly as an actor is deeply affected by the fact that we are never more (and sometimes less) than the co-authors of our own narratives" (MacIntyre, *After Virtue*, 248). Or, "In evaluating a life what kind of unity are we ascribing to it? It is the unity of a narrative, often a complex narrative, of which the agent who enacts it is at once subject and author, or rather coauthor." Alasdair C. MacIntyre, *Ethics in the Conflicts of Modernity: An Essay on Desire, Practical Reasoning, and Narrative* (Cambridge: Cambridge University Press, 2017), 231.

7 MacIntyre, *After Virtue*, 248.

8 MacIntyre, *After Virtue*, 249.

9 MacIntyre, *After Virtue*, 150.

10 MacIntyre, *After Virtue*, 240.

11 MacIntyre, *After Virtue*, 241.

12 In a similar vein, MacIntyre later poses the question of an autobiography of the life of Thomas Becket: What genre does it belong to? Should it be medieval hagiography? Perhaps saga hero, or a tragedy? "Now it clearly makes sense to ask who is right, if anyone. . . . The answer appears to be clearly the last. The true genre of the life is neither hagiography nor saga, but tragedy." MacIntyre, *After Virtue*, 247.

13 MacIntyre would not claim that this same investigative practice needs to be undertaken regarding all intents, as our practices are determined by our independent practical reasoning and so much of our acting is done precisely without specifically questioning our

intentions. However, according to MacIntyre, in order to establish *the morality* of any of these accounts, the intent must be "clear."

14 This area of inquiry is known as attribution theory.

15 Matthew 7:1-5, NLT.

16 1 Corinthians 13:12, NASB.

17 Maurice Merleau-Ponty, *Le visible et l'invisible: Suivi de notes de travail* (Paris: Gallimard, 1964), 167, quoted in László Tengelyi, *The Wild Region in Life-History* (Evanston, Ill.: Northwestern University Press, 2004), 104.

18 Tengelyi, *Wild Region in Life-History*, xix.

19 MacIntyre, *Ethics in the Conflicts of Modernity*, 239. Note the similarity of "trace" language with Levinas.

20 MacIntyre, *Ethics in the Conflicts of Modernity*, 239.

21 MacIntyre, *Ethics in the Conflicts of Modernity*, 239.

22 This research has now made its way into popular books such as *Predictably Irrational*, by Dan Ariely; *You Are Not as Smart as You Think You Are*, by David McRaney; *The Happiness Hypothesis*, by Jonathan Haidt; and *Willpower Instinct*, by Kelly McGonigal, to name a few. As Machiavelli observed, "The great majority of mankind are satisfied with appearances, as though they were realities, and are often more influenced by the things that seem than by those that are" (as quoted in Jonathan Haidt, *The Happiness Hypothesis: Putting Ancient Wisdom and Philosophy to the Test of Modern Science* [London: Arrow, 2006], 61). This may not be significant if it were only certified narcissists and sociopaths who choose to bend reality to suit their own gain; however, as Jonathan Haidt writes, "from the person who cuts you off on the highway all the way to the Nazis who ran the concentration camps, most people think they are good people and that their actions are motivated by good reasons" (62).

23 Robert Wright, *The Moral Animal: Evolutionary Psychology and Everyday Life* (New York: Pantheon, 1994), 13, quoted in Haidt, *Happiness Hypothesis*, 65.

24 The objection might be made that in *Dependent Rational Animals*, MacIntyre goes to great lengths to consider the importance of vulnerability in the human experience and the implications of what it means to be "dependent rational animals." This work is, indeed, a vital contribution to his project and to philosophy as a whole. However, even here he emphasizes that "the exercise of independent practical reasoning is one essential constituent to full human flourishing," and that to be incapable of "reasoning soundly" at the level of practice is "a grave disability," and it is "a defect not to be independent in one's reasoning." Going further, "One cannot then be an independent practical reasoner without being able to give others an intelligible account of one's reasoning" (MacIntyre, *Dependent Rational Animals*, 105). Intelligibility remains his dominant criteria for ethical action and human flourishing.

25 Abraham Joshua Heschel, *Man Is Not Alone: A Philosophy of Religion* (New York: Farrar, Straus and Giroux, 1976), 43.

26 MacIntyre, *Dependent Rational Animals*, 83.

27 Judith Butler, *Giving an Account of Oneself* (New York: Fordham University Press, 2005), 19.

28 John M. Coetzee, *Doubling the Point: Essays and Interviews*, ed. David Attwell (Cambridge, Mass.: Harvard University Press, 1992), 391.

29 MacIntyre, *Dependent Rational Animals*, 97.

30 Butler, *Giving an Account of Oneself*, 82.

31 Butler, *Giving an Account of Oneself*, 8.

32 Butler, *Giving an Account of Oneself*, 21 (terms), 23 (norms).

33 Butler, *Giving an Account of Oneself*, 9.

34 Butler, *Giving an Account of Oneself*, 23.

35 Butler, *Giving an Account of Oneself*, 20.

36 Butler's project does not include reference to God or religion. The primary relations to which she refers are confined to the immanent sphere, though in such a way as to radicalize this sphere. Rather than being "transcendent" relations, these relations are almost subterranean, profound in their depth rather than their height. I point to Kierkegaard and Levinas in my use of being "before" one another. While Butler does not use this phrasing, the intent is similar. For both Kierkegaard and Levinas, however, reference to "height" or the transcendence of these relations (including God) is crucial.

37 This can be observed between the second and third stages of the rationality of traditions in Alasdair C. MacIntyre, *Whose Justice? Whose Rationality?* (Notre Dame, Ind.: University of Notre Dame Press, 2008), 80, 166. In *After Virtue*, contemporary moral debate is defined by incommensurable premises of rival arguments. For fruitful ethical discussion to take place, these places of incommensurability are opportunities to explore the "goods" toward which rival traditions are working. Rather than requiring an external, objective criterion that is unobtainable, ethical positions must be critiqued from within their tradition, and the clash with alternate traditions can be the site of useful reflection. In this sense, MacIntyre views moments of opacity or mystery as a "clash" that can lead to greater transparency.

38 Butler, *Giving an Account of Oneself*, 24.

39 These exceptions also highlight the existential vulnerability of our tentative place in the "regime of truth" (Butler, *Giving an Account of Oneself*, 23. She references Foucault here).

40 Søren Kierkegaard, *Papers and Journals: A Selection*, trans. Alastair Hannay (London: Penguin, 1996), 161.

41 MacIntyre, *After Virtue*, 214. Butler, *Giving an Account of Oneself*, 39.

42 Butler, *Giving an Account of Oneself*, 39.

43 Butler, *Giving an Account of Oneself*, 39.

44 Butler, *Giving an Account of Oneself*, 42. While Butler does not call attention to her word usage, even the language of discourse is upended when *blindness* finds itself as the catalyst for ethical responsibility, rather than as a metaphor for ethical transgression.

45 A seemingly innocent example of this can be seen in the "personal planning" process for people with intellectual and developmental disabilities. While anyone might benefit from this kind of a process, it is only people with intellectual and developmental disabilities who are called to "give an account" of their plans and goals each year and to provide ongoing updates to their service providers. While it could legitimately be argued that the alternative (not intentionally seeking out someone's dreams and goals) is a worse fate, the discrepancy between the account demanded of "normal" people living their lives and those with IDD must be acknowledged and impact our posture in these conversations.

46 Butler, *Giving an Account of Oneself*, 44.

47 Butler, *Giving an Account of Oneself*, 42. We recall the words of Christ, "Forgive them, for they don't know what they are doing" (Luke 23:34, NLT).

48 Marguerite Young, "The Clinic," in *Moderate Fable* (New York: Reynal and Hitchcock, 1944), 14.

49 As the Netflix original *Making a Murderer* brought to public consciousness, the way courts and the legal system handle intellectual disability still leaves much to be desired. In the case of Brendan Dassey, with an IQ of around 70, obtaining a confession by merely asking questions in a complicated or confusing way is very much a possibility (Laura Passin, "How 'Making a Murderer' Handles Intellectual Disability," *Rolling Stone*, January 11, 2016, http://www.rollingstone.com/politics/news/what-making-a-murderer-reveals-about-the-justice-system-and-intellectual-disability-20160111).

50 Butler, *Giving an Account of Oneself*, 136.

51 Butler, *Giving an Account of Oneself*, 84.

52 Butler almost sounds Kierkegaardian in that "we must recognize that ethics requires us to risk ourselves precisely at moments of unknowingness, when what forms us diverges from what lies before us, when our willingness to become undone in relation to others constitutes our chance of becoming human" (Butler, *Giving an Account of Oneself*, 136).

53 Acts 8:32-33, ESV.

54 Butler, *Giving an Account of Oneself*, 24.

55 1 Peter 4:8, NIV.

56 1 Corinthians 13:5.

57 1 Corinthians 13:12

58 Abraham Joshua Heschel, *Between God and Man* (New York: Free Press, 1997), 61.

59 One must pay particular attention to pseudonyms in Kierkegaard's writing. Works by Anti-Climacus are described by translators Edna and Howard Hong as pseudonymous in the sense that "they do not bear Kierkegaard's name as author, because his own existence did not correspond to the claims of higher ideality they express" (Søren Kierkegaard, *Journals and Papers*, trans. Howard Vincent Hong and Edna Hong [Bloomington: Indiana University Press, 1970], 4:761). Anti-Climacus reflects Kierkegaard's views that he does not believe that he attains or lives up to. This is very different from Johannes de Silentio, who was used by Kierkegaard to ventriloquize works by a writer who was unable to make the leap of faith. In this respect, Anti-Climacus' views can be taken to mirror Kierkegaard's own to a greater degree than those of Johannes de Silentio.

60 Kierkegaard, *Sickness unto Death*, 13.

61 Kierkegaard, *Sickness unto Death*, 13.

62 Kierkegaard, *Sickness unto Death*, 13.

63 Kierkegaard, *Sickness unto Death*, 13.

64 Kierkegaard, *Sickness unto Death*, 14.

65 Kierkegaard, *Journals and Papers*, 1:25–26.

66 Kierkegaard, *Sickness unto Death*, 69. One observes here a stark contrast with later French existentialists who presume that human beings need to create their own meaning in a world devoid of meaning. The self does not create itself; it is already established in relation to the divine.

67 Douglas Harper, "Author" and "Authority," *Online Etymology Dictionary*, accessed June 22, 2017. Note that in the case of authority, its etymology traces through a *scriptural* account to the original sense of authorship. Authority, too, is a word haunted by divine transcendence.

68 Precisely "in relating itself to itself and in willing to be itself, the self rests transparently in the power that established it" (Kierkegaard, *Sickness unto Death*, 49).

69 Kierkegaard, *Journals and Papers*, 1:22.

70 In *Point of View*, Kierkegaard reports that throughout his own life he has sensed his dependency on an Other: "From the very beginning I have been as it were under arrest and every instant have sensed the fact that it was not I that played the part of master, but that another was Master" (Kierkegaard, *Point of View*, 69). Kierkegaard also recognizes what has happened when he has tried to "take back the reins," so to speak: "Without God I am too strong for myself, and perhaps in the most agonizing of all ways am broken" (70).

71 1 Corinthians 6:19-20.

72 It is the reality that we are not our own that occasions the *giving of an account* in the first place. Selfhood is possible only as a dispossession from oneself in relation to the other. "It is only in dispossession that I can and do give any account of myself" (Butler, *Giving an Account of Oneself*, 37).

73 Butler, *Giving an Account of Oneself*, 37.

74 One must remember that I attempt here a constructive theology and do not claim that Butler, Kierkegaard, or Levinas would subscribe to the ways I have integrated their respective positions.

75 Butler, *Giving an Account of Oneself*, 42.

7 A MYSTERIOUS REVELATION

1 Augustine, *Sermons on the New Testament*, ed. John E. Rotelle, trans. Edmund Hill (52–94) (Brooklyn: New City Press, 2003), 3:57.

2 1 Timothy 2:4.

3 Exodus 33:19-23.

4 Reminiscent of Anselm's "that than which nothing greater can be thought" yet with the acknowledgment that nothing greater can be thought precisely because God exceeds thought.

5 1 Kings 19:11-13.

6 Abraham Joshua Heschel, *God in Search of Man* (New York: Harper Torchbooks, 1956), 186.

7 Job 26:14.

8 Deuteronomy 29:29.

9 Proverbs 10:19, HCSB.

10 Job 11:7.

11 Dionysius, *The Mystical Theology, and the Celestial Hierarchies of Dionysius the Areopagita: With Commentaries by the Editors of the Shrine of Wisdom and Poem by St. John of the Cross* (Fintry, U.K.: Shrine of Wisdom, 1965), 16.

12 *The Writings of Tertullian*, ed. Anthony Uyl (Woodstock, Ont.: Devoted, 2017), 1:36.

13 Ludwig Wittgenstein, *Tractatus Logico-Philosophicus*, trans. David Pears and Brian McGuinness (London: Routledge, 2001), 3.

14 Dionysius, *Mystical Theology*, 14. In the Dionysian/Thomist view perspective of Vatican I, we read that God is "incomprehensible, essentially different from the world, in and of himself most blessed and unspeakably exalted above everything else which can be thought of" (First Vatican Council, s.3, c.1, quoted in Robert Miner, "Thomas Aquinas and Hans Urs von Balthasar: A Dialogue on Love and Charity," *New Blackfriars* 95, no. 1059 [2014]: 507, doi:10.1111/nbfr.12087).

15 Job 38:2.

16 C. S. Lewis, *The Pilgrim's Regress: An Allegorical Apology for Christianity, Reason, and Romanticism* (Grand Rapids: Eerdmans, 2014), 163.

17 One might even suggest that Lewis' use of disability metaphors (deaf, limping, etc.) call for forgiveness even as he relates to people, let alone in speaking to God.

18 Callid Keefe-Perry, "T Is for Theopoetics," *Homebrewed Christianity*, August 1, 2014, https://homebrewedchristianity.com/2014/08/01/t-is-for-theopoetics/.

19 Keefe-Perry, "T Is for Theopoetics."

·20 Colossians 1:15, NIV.

21 Kierkegaard, *Works of Love*, 62–63.

22 Colossians 1:15.

23 Romans 16:25.

24 Ephesians 1:9.

25 Hebrews 1:3.

26 1 Corinthians 1:18-21.

27 Borrowing here from Martin Luther's theology of the cross. Luther draws inspiration from the same passages in 1 Corinthians, writing, "Because men misused the knowledge of God through works, God wished again to be recognized in suffering, and to condemn wisdom concerning invisible things by means of 'wisdom concerning visible things,' so that those who did not honor God as manifested in his works should honor him as he is hidden in his suffering [*absconditum in passionibus*]" (Martin Luther, "The Heidelberg Disputation," in *Luther's Works*, vol. 31, *Career of the Reformer I*, ed. Jaroslav Pelikan [Philadelphia: Fortress, 1957], 52–53).

28 1 Corinthians 2:2-4.

29 1 Corinthians 2:7.

30 1 Corinthians 2:10.

31 1 Corinthians 2:10-13.

32 Søren Kierkegaard, *Concluding Unscientific Postscript*, trans. Howard V. Hong and Edna H. Hong (Princeton, N.J.: Princeton University Press, 1846), 203.

33 Søren Kierkegaard, *Eighteen Upbuilding Discourses*, trans. Howard V. Hong and Edna H. Hong (Princeton, N.J.: Princeton University Press, 1990), 171.

34 Karl Barth, *The Epistle to the Romans*, trans. Edwyn C. Hoskyns (New York: Oxford University Press, 1980), 98.

35 Barth, *Epistle to the Romans*.

36 Hebrews 11:1, HCSB.

37 I attempt here, again, to employ blindness as a positive metaphor that subverts metaphors of blindness as negative limitation, loss, and ignorance. In this context blindness is prerequisite to ethics.

38 N. T. Wright, "Wouldn't You Love to Know: Towards a Christian View of Reality," *BioLogos*, December 6, 2016, http://biologos.org/blogs/jim-stump-faith-and-science-seeking-understanding/wouldnt-you-love-to-know-towards-a-christian-view-of-reality.

39 Source unknown.

40 John 3:16, NIV.

41 Reynolds, *Vulnerable Communion*, 204.

42 1 Corinthians 2:9, NLT.

43 Jürgen Moltmann, *The Crucified God: The Cross of Christ as the Foundation and Criticism of Christian Theology*, trans. R. A. Wilson and John Bowden (Philadelphia: Fortress, 1974), 212, quoted in Reynolds, *Vulnerable Communion*, 205.

44 Philippians 3:10.

45 1 John 4:19.

46 Hans Urs Von Balthasar, *Love Alone Is Credible*, trans. Alexander Dru (New York: Herder and Herder, 1969), 48, quoted in Miner, "Thomas Aquinas and Hans Urs von Balthasar," 508.

8 FORMED TOGETHER IN LOVE

1 Kittay, "The Personal Is Philosophical Is Political," 16.

2 MacIntyre, *After Virtue*, 191

3 MacIntyre, "Postscript to the Second Edition," *After Virtue*, 264.

4 MacIntyre, "Postscript to the Second Edition," *After Virtue*, 264.

5 The word "anthropoetics" occurs to me here. Just as *theopoetics* acknowledges the importance of poetry and "weak" language to gesture at the nature of the divine, so we hint at, guess at, and gesture toward our own accounts and the accounts of others.

6 Søren Kierkegaard, *Fear and Trembling, and Repetition*, trans. Howard Vincent Hong and Edna Hatlestad Hong (Princeton, N.J.: Princeton University Press, 1983), 115, quoted in Jacques Derrida, *The Gift of Death*, trans. David Wills (Chicago: University of Chicago Press, 1995), 61.

7 Jean Vanier, *Gospel of John, the Gospel of Relationship* (Cincinnati, Ohio: Franciscan Media, 2015), Kindle, loc. 863.

8 Derrida, *Gift of Death*, 60.

9 Vanier, *Gospel of John*, loc. 863.

10 Colossians 3:3.

11 1 John 4:8.

12 Kierkegaard, *Works of Love*, 9–10.

13 Kierkegaard, *Works of Love*, 160.

14 Balthasar, *Love Alone Is Credible*, 48, quoted in Miner, "Thomas Aquinas and Hans Urs von Balthasar," 508.

15 Matthew 5:44.

16 Balthasar, *Love Alone Is Credible*, 51, quoted in Miner, "Thomas Aquinas and Hans Urs von Balthasar," 508.

17 Or, as the apostle John conveys, "We love each other because he loved us first" (1 John 4:19).

18 Miner, "Thomas Aquinas and Hans Urs von Balthasar," 514.

19 Kierkegaard, *Works of Love*, 50.

20 Kierkegaard, *Works of Love*, 373.

21 Kierkegaard, *Works of Love*, 47.

22 Kierkegaard, *Fear and Trembling, and Repetition*, 86.

23 Derrida, *Gift of Death*, 65.

24 Derrida, *Gift of Death*, 68.

25 Derrida, *Gift of Death*, 68.

26 According to Derrida, Søren Kierkegaard and Emmanuel Levinas essentially stress the same obligation in different ways. Whether one is referencing the "infinite alterity" of every human other (Levinas) or God (Kierkegaard), one suspends other ethical

obligations in order to *give* to either. In this way, Levinas' philosophy is just as religious as Kierkegaard's. "For his part, in taking into account absolute singularity, that is, the absolute alterity obtaining in relations between one human and another, Levinas is no longer able to distinguish between the infinite alterity of God and that of every human. His ethics is already a religious one. In the two cases the border between the ethical and religious discourses becomes more than problematic, as do all attendant discourses" (Derrida, *Gift of Death*, 84).

27 Derrida, *Gift of Death*, 68.
28 Brunner, *Man in Revolt*, 104.
29 Noting here that the biblical Greek for Paul's reference to "spiritual gifts" in 1 Corinthians 12:4 is "charisma" out of the root *charis* (grace).
30 Note that "response-ability" is used here to draw a helpful distinction yet is necessarily supported directly by the etymology of "responsibility," although the condition of being responsible does in a sense also imply the ability to respond. The suffix "-ity" does not.
31 Butler, *Giving an Account of Oneself*, 80.

9 THE VIRTUES OF CARE

1 C. S. Lewis, *Mere Christianity* (New York: Macmillan, 1952), 53–54. Lewis' language of "being their own masters" recalls Kierkegaard's emphasis on relating to one's establishing power in *Sickness unto Death* and his related writing in his journals.
2 Genesis 3:5, NLT.
3 We recall here Deborah Creamer's limits model of disability as referenced in chapter 1.
4 Henri J. M. Nouwen, *The Wounded Healer: Ministry in Contemporary Society* (London: Darton, Longman & Todd, 2014), 77.
5 Kierkegaard, *Works of Love*, 154.
6 Kierkegaard, *Works of Love*, 155.
7 Kierkegaard, *Works of Love*, 156.
8 Kierkegaard, *Works of Love*, 159.
9 Kierkegaard, *Works of Love*, 174. Christ in this way is the pattern for the "humble courage" of faith that Johannes de Silentio uses to describe Abraham in *Fear and Trembling* and Johannes Climacus describes in *Sickness unto Death* (FT 41/SKS 4 143, SUD 85/SKS 11 199).
10 Teresa of Calcutta, *Come Be My Light: The Revealing Private Writings of the Nobel Peace Prize Winner*, ed. Brian Kolodiejchuk (London: Rider, 2007), 34.
11 MacIntyre, *Dependent Rational Animals*, 123. We see similarities here with Kierkegaard's reflections on neighbor-love, in that it is a mercy that goes beyond caring for one's own "in-group." MacIntyre believes that "communal life itself needs this virtue that goes beyond the boundaries of communal life" (124). The difference being *misericordia* relies on recognition of a profound and significant need and, as we will see, upon a perceived or recognized commonality.
12 Robert C. Miner, "The Difficulties of Mercy: Reading Thomas Aquinas on *Misericordia*," *Studies in Christian Ethics* 28, no. 1 (2015): 71, doi:10.1177/0953946814555325.
13 Miner, "Difficulties of Mercy," 73. Robert Miner goes on to describe its origin as follows: "'For *misericordia* is named from the fact that someone has a wretched heart (*miserum cor*) over the wretchedness of another' (30.1 co). If one has a 'wretched heart,' caused by another's wretchedness, one 'suffers with' the other; one has compassion for her, in the literal sense of *compassion*."

14 Miner, "Difficulties of Mercy," 75.

15 Miner, "Difficulties of Mercy," 76.

16 Nancy L. Eiesland, *The Disabled God: Toward a Liberatory Theology of Disability* (Nashville: Abingdon, 1994).

17 Thomas Aquinas, *Questions on Love and Charity: Summa Theologiae, Secunda Secundae, Questions 23–46*, trans. Robert C. Miner (New Haven, Conn.: Yale University Press, 2016), Q 24 a2, 40.

18 MacIntyre argues that *misericordia* is still capable of being a secular virtue. He does so by quickly observing that "charity in the form of *Misericordia* is recognizably at work in the secular world and the authorities whom Aquinas cites on its nature, and whose disagreements he aspires to resolve. . . . *Misericordia* then has its place in the catalogue of the virtues, independently of its theological grounding" (MacIntyre, *Dependent Rational Animals*, 124). Robert Miner seeks to clarify MacIntyre's hasty dismissal that *misericordia* can operate without its "theological grounding." Miner points out, "Cut off from divinely infused charity, *misericordia* is no virtue; it is only a passion, and a questionable one at that. Any satisfying reading of Thomas must observe the dependence of *misericordia* on caritas, noting that without the latter, the former stands as the matter for virtue, awaiting full formation by caritas" (Miner, "Difficulties of Mercy," 80).

19 Miner, "Difficulties of Mercy," 81.

20 The error of believing that one must be cognitively aware of these concepts "presumes that the operation of divine grace within a person is determined or otherwise limited by her conceptual apparatus. But Thomas would not make this presumption. He knows that membership in the church and residence in the *civitas Dei* never coincide perfectly. The spirit blows where it will" (Miner, "Difficulties of Mercy," 81).

21 Matthew 15:32, NASB.

22 Mark 6:34.

23 Matthew 20:34, NASB.

24 Isaiah 43:3.

25 Stanley Hauerwas, "Timeful Friends: Living with the Handicapped," in *Critical Reflections on Stanley Hauerwas' Theology of Disability: Disabling Society, Enabling Theology*, ed. John Swinton (New York: Routledge, 2008), 23.

26 Miner, "Difficulties of Mercy," 75.

27 Miner, "Difficulties of Mercy," 81. He is here building on the work of Herbert McCabe.

28 John 15:15, NLT.

29 H. Reinders, *Receiving the Gift of Friendship*, 30.

30 H. Reinders, *Receiving the Gift of Friendship*, 273.

31 H. Reinders, *Receiving the Gift of Friendship*, 301.

32 H. Reinders, *Receiving the Gift of Friendship*, 301.

33 H. Reinders, *Receiving the Gift of Friendship*, 374.

34 Henri Nouwen, "Forgiveness: The Name of Love in a Wounded World," *Weavings* 7, no. 2 (1992): 15.

35 Butler, *Giving an Account of Oneself*, 43.

36 Vanier, *Gospel of John*, loc. 1533.

37 Ephesians 4:15.

38 Luke 23:34, NLT.

39 Matthew 5:38. While I do not believe that this gentleman was an "evil person," there are moments when any of us may see another as an evil person. In that moment, I read in his

eyes an evil intent. Whether I was correct does not ultimately matter. It is the attribution of evil rather than the intention itself that structures our posture toward another. We will never know the true intent, and oftentimes the other person will not come to fully understand their own intent either. Christ's words here are for our interactions with the Evil Person—that is, the person we have deemed to be evil or in that moment we perceive to be our enemy. To turn the other cheek is to love one's neighbor, who may also be one's enemy.

40 Again, it should be noted that this may or not be conscious and intentional development of these virtues. Moral formation takes place whether or not it is clear to us that this is what's happening. Certainly, in my own story it is only in looking back that I come to appreciate the formation of moral virtues.

41 John 11:8.

42 John 11:16.

43 John 11:33.

44 John 11:38.

45 N. T. Wright, *John for Everyone*, part 2, *Chapters 11–21* (London: SPCK, 2004), 11.

46 Henri J. M. Nouwen, "Spirituality of Waiting," in *The Weavings Reader: Living with God in the World*, ed. John S. Mogabgab (Nashville: Upper Room Books, 1993), 72–74.

47 Nouwen, "Spirituality of Waiting," 72.

48 2 Corinthians 12:9.

49 "King of My Heart," by John Mark McMillan and Sarah McMillan, © 2015 Meaux Jeaux Music (SESAC) Raucous Ruckus Publishing (SESAC) (adm. at CapitolCMGPublishing .com) / Sarah McMillan Publishing (SESAC) (adm. at WatershedMusicPublishing.com).

50 Simone Weil and Joë Bousquet, *Correspondance: Simone Weil, Joë Bousquet*, ed. Jil Silberstein (Lausanne: Ed. l'Age d'Homme, 1982), 18.

51 Douglas Harper, "Attention," *Online Etymology Dictionary*, accessed June 22, 2017.

52 James 1:19.

53 Derrida, *Gift of Death*, 60. While the emphasis of this section focuses on verbal account giving, one may observe similar parallels in nonverbal accounts and expressions—in oneself and related to others. In the writing of Levinas, for example, we read that "expression, or the face, overflows images" (Emmanuel Levinas, *Totality and Infinity: An Essay on Exteriority*, trans. Alphonso Lingis [Pittsburgh, Pa.: Duquesne University Press, 2005], 297). The face cannot be "possessed" and "refuses to be contained" (297, 194). "The face of the Other at each moment destroys and overflows the plastic image it leaves me, the idea existing to my own measure. . . . It expresses itself." (50, 51). This expression is both "a source from which all meaning appears" and that which exceeds all definition or interpretation (297).

54 Hannah Arendt, "Isak Dinesen: 1885–1963," in *Men in Dark Times* (New York: Harcourt Brace, 1983), 105.

55 Isaiah 53:7.

56 Dr. Neil Cudney at Christian Horizons was the first to draw attention to the relation of "witness" and "withness" for me.

57 Mark 15:3-5.

58 John 18:36.

59 Luke 5:15-16, see also Mark 1:45.

60 Matthew 13:1-3, 14:13, 23, 15:29 Mark 1:35, 3:7, 4:1, 4:31-32, 46, 8:27, Luke 9:18, etc.

61 Søren Kierkegaard, *The Lily of the Field and the Bird of the Air*, trans. Bruce H. Kirmmse (Princeton, N.J.: Princeton University Press, 2016), 20.

62 Matthew 6:26 and 6:28.

63 Kierkegaard, *Lily of the Field and the Bird of the Air*, 24.

64 Kierkegaard, *Lily of the Field and the Bird of the Air*, 25.

65 Swinton, *Becoming Friends of Time*, 81.

66 For a more in-depth understanding of the relation of time and being with others, see Swinton's *Becoming Friends of Time*.

67 MacIntyre, *After Virtue*, 175.

68 1 Corinthians 2:9.

69 1 Corinthians 2:7; 2:4.

70 1 Corinthians 2:3.

71 Derrida, *The Gift of Death*, 53.

72 1 Corinthians 13:12, NLT.

73 1 Corinthians 13:12, NLT.

74 1 Corinthians 8:3.

75 Hebrews 10:24-25, ESV.

76 1 Corinthians 13:13.

77 MacIntyre, *After Virtue*, 235.

78 Slavoj Žižek, "If You Have Reasons to Love Someone, You Don't Love Her/Him," Twitter, November 20, 2013, https://twitter.com/Slavojiek/status/403149945337044992. This follows the logic of Kierkegaard, for whom faith cannot rest on logical "proof" or else is not faith.

79 1 Corinthians 14:1.

80 MacIntyre, *After Virtue*, 105.

EPILOGUE: RESPONDING TO GOD'S CALL

1 Albert Camus, *The Stranger*, trans. Matthew Ward (New York: Vintage International, 1989), 3.

2 "For you died, and your life is now hidden with Christ in God. When Christ, who is your life, appears, then you also will appear with him in glory" (Col 3:3, 4).

3 John Swinton, *Dementia: Living in the Memories of God* (Grand Rapids: Eerdmans, 2012), 171.

Bibliography

"About Hay Group." Hay Group. Accessed March 13, 2015. http://www.haygroup.com/ca/about/index.aspx?id=6502.

Amado, Angela Novak, Roger J. Stancliffe, Mary Mccarron, and Philip Mccallion. "Social Inclusion and Community Participation of Individuals with Intellectual/Developmental Disabilities." *Intellectual and Developmental Disabilities* 51, no. 5 (2013): 360–75. doi:10.135 2/1934-9556-51.5.360.

Aquinas, Thomas. "Question 93: The End or Term of the Production of Man." In *The Summa Theologiæ of St. Thomas Aquinas*, translated by Fathers of the English Dominican Province. Kevin Knight, 2017. http://www.newadvent.org/summa/1093.htm.

———. *Questions on Love and Charity: Summa Theologiae, Secunda Secundae, Questions 23–46.* Translated by Robert C. Miner. New Haven, Conn.: Yale University Press, 2016.

Arendt, Hannah. "Isak Dinesen: 1885–1963." In *Men in Dark Times*. New York: Harcourt Brace, 1983.

Augustine. "Chapter 12." In *The Literal Meaning of Genesis*, translated by John Hammond Taylor, vol. 6. New York: Paulist Press, 1982.

———. *Sermons on the New Testament*. Edited by John E. Rotelle. Translated by Edmund Hill. Vol. 3. Brooklyn: New City Press, 2003.

Balthasar, Hans Urs Von. *Love Alone Is Credible*. Translated by Alexander Dru. New York: Herder and Herder, 1969.

Barth, Karl. *Eine Schweizer Stimme: 1938–1945*. Zollikon-Zurich: Evangelischer Verlag, 1945.

———. *The Epistle to the Romans*. Translated by Edwyn C. Hoskyns. New York: Oxford University Press, 1980.

Basselin, Timothy J. *Flannery O'Connor: Writing a Theology of Disabled Humanity*. Waco, Tex.: Baylor University Press, 2013.

Birchenall, Peter, and Mary Birchenall. "Caring for Mentally Handicapped People: The Community and the Church." *Professional Nurse* 1 (March 1986): 148–50.

Bonhoeffer, Dietrich. *Ethics*. New York: Macmillan, 1955.

Bonikowsky, Michael. "Called to Remain." *Nations*, June 2, 2019. https://nationsmedia.org/called-to-remain/.

Brundage, James A. *The Medieval Origins of the Legal Profession: Canonists, Civilians, and Courts*. Chicago: University of Chicago Press, 2008.

Brunner, Emil. *The Divine-Human Encounter*. Translated by Amandus William Loos. Philadelphia: Westminster, 1943.

―――. *Dogmatics*. Vol. 2, *The Christian Doctrine of Creation and Redemption*. Philadelphia: Westminster, 1953.

―――. *Man in Revolt: A Christian Anthropology*. Translated by Olive Wyon. Philadelphia: Westminster, 1947.

Brunner, Emil, and Karl Barth. *Natural Theology*. Translated by John Baillie. London: G. Bles, 1956.

Bucher, Rainer, and Rebecca Pohl. *Hitler's Theology: A Study in Political Religion*. London: Continuum, 2011.

Buechner, Frederick. *Wishful Thinking: A Theological ABC*. New York: Harper & Row, 1973.

Butler, Judith. *Giving an Account of Oneself*. New York: Fordham University Press, 2005.

Butts, Janie B., and Karen L. Rich. "Acknowledging Dependence: A MacIntyrean Perspective on Relationships Involving Alzheimer's Disease." *Nursing Ethics* 11, no. 4 (2004): 400–10. doi:10.1191/0969733004ne712oa.

Calvin, John. *Commentaries on the First Book of Moses, Called Genesis*. Translated by John King. Vol. 1. Edinburgh: Edinburgh Printing, 1847.

Camus, Albert. *The Stranger*. Translated by Matthew Ward. New York: Vintage International, 1989.

Cardador, M. T., and B. B. Caza. "Relational and Identity Perspectives on Healthy versus Unhealthy Pursuit of Callings." *Journal of Career Assessment* 20, no. 3 (2012): 338–53. doi:10.1177/1069072711436162.

Carlyle, Thomas. *Past and Present*. London: Chapman and Hall, 1843.

Casey, Rebecca. "Burnout for Developmental Services Workers." *McGill Sociological Review* 2 (April 2011): 39–58. Accessed February 4, 2016. https://www.mcgill.ca/msr/volume2/article3.

Clifford, Stacy. "The Capacity Contract: Locke, Disability, and the Political Exclusion of 'Idiots.'" *Politics, Groups, and Identities* 2, no. 1 (2014): 90–103. doi:10.1080/21565503.2013.876918.

Coetzee, John M. *Doubling the Point: Essays and Interviews*. Edited by David Attwell. Cambridge, Mass.: Harvard University Press, 1992.

"Compassion Fatigue." *Dictionary.com*. Accessed April 10, 2015. http://www.dictionary.com/browse/compassion-fatigue.

Connors, Joanna. "Kent State Professor Trudy Steuernagel's Fierce Protection of Her Autistic Son, Sky Walker, Costs Her Life: Sheltering Sky." *The Plain Dealer*, December 6, 2009.

"Core Competencies Dictionary." Hay Group. May 2013. Accessed February 4, 2016. http://pclkw.org/wp-content/uploads/2013/05/Core-Competency-Dictionary-October-1-2009.pdf.

"Core Competencies Implementation." Lecture by the Hay Group, Developmental Services Human Resources Strategy, Ottawa, Ont., 2013.

Creamer, Deborah Beth. *Disability and Christian Theology: Embodied Limits and Constructive Possibilities*. Oxford: Oxford University Press, 2009.

Dahlstrom, Daniel O. "Independence and the Virtuous Community." *Reason Papers* 43, no. 2 (October 2012): 70–83. https://reasonpapers.com/pdf/342/rp_342_8.pdf.

Deland, Jane S. "Images of God through the Lens of Disability." *Journal of Religion, Disability & Health* 3, no. 2 (1999): 47–81. doi:10.1300/j095v03n02_06.

Derrida, Jacques. *The Gift of Death*. Chicago: University of Chicago Press, 1995.

Dionysius. *The Mystical Theology, and the Celestial Hierarchies of Dionysius the Areopagita: With Commentaries by the Editors of the Shrine of Wisdom and Poem by St. John of the Cross*. Fintry, U.K.: Shrine of Wisdom, 1965.

Dobrow, Shoshana R. "Dynamics of Calling: A Longitudinal Study of Musicians." *Journal of Organizational Behavior* 34, no. 4 (2012): 431–52.

Eiesland, Nancy L. *The Disabled God: Toward a Liberatory Theology of Disability*. Nashville: Abingdon, 1994.

Ferreira, M. Jamie. *Love's Grateful Striving: A Commentary on Kierkegaard's Works of Love*. Oxford: Oxford University Press, 2001.

Fillon, Mike. "The Real Face of Jesus." *Popular Mechanics*, August 11, 2016. Accessed May 13, 2016. http://www.popularmechanics.com/science/health/a234/1282186/.

Francis, Gavin. *Adventures in Human Being: A Grand Tour from the Cranium to the Calcaneum*. London: Profile Books, 2015. Audible audiobook.

Freidson, Eliot. *Professionalism: The Third Logic*. Chicago: University of Chicago Press, 2001.

Gilmore, Linda, and Monica Cuskelly. "Vulnerability to Loneliness in People with Intellectual Disability: An Explanatory Model." *Journal of Policy and Practice in Intellectual Disabilities* 11, no. 3 (2014): 192–99. doi:10.1111/jppi.12089.

Goffman, Erving, and Joel Best. *Interaction Ritual: Essays in Face to Face Behavior*. New Brunswick, N.J.: Aldine Transaction, 2005.

Government of Ontario. "2015–2016 Published Plan." Ministry of Community and Social Services. Accessed June 19, 2018. http://www.mcss.gov.on.ca/en/mcss/about/ppar/index.aspx.

Grenz, Stanley J. *Theology for the Community of God*. Nashville: Broadman & Holman, 1994.

Haidt, Jonathan. *The Happiness Hypothesis: Putting Ancient Wisdom and Philosophy to the Test of Modern Science*. London: Arrow, 2006.

Hall, Douglas John. *Professing the Faith: Christian Theology in a North American Context*. Minneapolis: Fortress, 1993.

Harper, Douglas. *Online Etymology Dictionary*. Accessed September 6, 2017. http://www.etymonline.com/.

Haslam, Molly C. *A Constructive Theology of Intellectual Disability: Human Being as Mutuality and Response*. New York: Fordham University Press, 2012.

Hauerwas, Stanley. "Timeful Friends: Living with the Handicapped." In *Critical Reflections on Stanley Hauerwas' Theology of Disability: Disabling Society, Enabling Theology*, edited by John Swinton, 11–26. New York: Routledge, 2008.

Heschel, Abraham Joshua. *Between God and Man*. New York: Free Press, 1997.

———. *God in Search of Man*. New York: Harper Torchbooks, 1956.

———. *Man Is Not Alone: A Philosophy of Religion*. New York: Farrar, Straus and Giroux, 1976.

Hickey, Robert. *A Profile of Direct Support Professionals and Their Work Experiences in Ontario's Developmental Services Sector*. Report. June 30, 2013. Accessed April 13, 2015. https://mir.queensu.ca/default/assets/File/(8)%20Hickey%20Devleopmental%20Services.pdf.

Hoffer, Eric. *The Ordeal of Change*. Cutchogue, N.Y.: Buccaneer Books, 1976.

Horvath, Charles M. "Excellence v. Effectiveness: Macintyre's Critique of Business." *Business Ethics Quarterly* 5, no. 3 (1995): 499.

Irenaeus. *Against Heresies*. Whitefish, Mont.: Kessinger, 2007.

Jaczek, Helena. "Mandate Letter Progress: Community and Social Services." Ontario.ca. January 11, 2016. https://www.ontario.ca/page/mandate-letter-progress-community-and-social -services.

Keefe-Perry, Callid. "T Is for Theopoetics." *Homebrewed Christianity*. August 1, 2014. https:// homebrewedchristianity.com/2014/08/01/t-is-for-theopoetics/.

Kierkegaard, Søren. *Concluding Unscientific Postscript*. Translated by Howard V. Hong and Edna H. Hong. Princeton, N.J.: Princeton University Press, 1846.

———. *Eighteen Upbuilding Discourses*. Translated by Howard V. Hong and Edna H. Hong. Princeton, N.J.: Princeton University Press, 1990.

———. *Fear and Trembling, and Repetition*. Translated by Howard Vincent Hong and Edna Hatlestad Hong. Princeton, N.J.: Princeton University Press, 1983.

———. *Journals and Papers*. Translated by Howard Vincent Hong and Edna Hong. Bloomington: Indiana University Press, 1970.

———. *The Lily of the Field and the Bird of the Air*. Translated by Bruce H. Kirmmse. Princeton, N.J.: Princeton University Press, 2016.

———. *Papers and Journals: A Selection*. Translated by Alastair Hannay. London: Penguin, 1996.

———. *The Point of View for My Work as an Author: A Report to History, and Related Writings*. Translated by Walter Lowrie. Edited by Benjamin Nelson. New York: Harper, 1962.

———. *Practice in Christianity*. Translated by Howard V. Hong and Edna H. Hong. Princeton, N.J.: Princeton University Press, 1991.

———. *The Present Age: On the Death of Rebellion*. Translated by Alexander Dru. New York: Harper Perennial, 2010.

———. *Provocations: Spiritual Writings of Kierkegaard*. Edited by Charles E Moore. Farmington, Pa.: Plough, 2002.

———. *Purity of Heart Is to Will One Thing: Spiritual Preparation for the Office of Confession*. Translated by Douglas V. Steere. New York: Harper, 1956.

———. *The Sickness unto Death: A Christian Psychological Exposition for Upbuilding and Awakening*. Translated by Howard V. Hong and Edna H. Hong. Princeton, N.J.: Princeton University Press, 1980.

———. *Works of Love: Some Christian Reflections in the Form of Discourses*. Translated by Howard V. Hong and Edna H. Hong. New York: Harper, 1962.

Kilner, John Frederic. *Dignity and Destiny: Humanity in the Image of God*. Grand Rapids: Eerdmans, 2005.

King, Thomas. "The Truth about Stories: A Native Narrative." In *The 2003 CBC Massey Lectures*. Canadian Broadcasting Corporation. November 7, 2003. http://www.cbc.ca/radio/ ideas/the-2003-cbc-massey-lectures-the-truth-about-stories-a-native-narrative-1.2946870.

Kittay, Eva Feder. "Beyond Autonomy and Paternalism: The Caring Transparent Self." In *Autonomy and Paternalism: Reflections on the Theory and Practice of Health Care*, edited by Thomas Nye, Yvonne Denier, and Toon Vandevelde, 23–70. Leuven, Belgium: Peeters, 2007.

———. *Love's Labor: Essays on Women, Equality, and Dependency*. New York: Routledge, 1999.

———. "The Personal Is Philosophical Is Political: A Philosopher and Mother of a Cognitively Disabled Person Sends Notes from the Battlefield." *Metaphilosophy* 40, nos. 3/4 (2009): 606–27. https://doi.org/10.1111/j.1467-9973.2009.01600.x.

L'Engle, Madeleine. *The Rock That Is Higher: Story as Truth*. Wheaton, Ill.: Harold Shaw, 1993.

Levinas, Emmanuel. "God and Philosophy." In *Collected Philosophical Papers*, translated by Alphonso Lingis, 153–74. Pittsburgh, Pa.: Duquesne University Press, 2006.

———. *Totality and Infinity: An Essay on Exteriority*. Translated by Alphonso Lingis. Pittsburgh, Pa.: Duquesne University Press, 2005.

Lewis, C. S. *Mere Christianity*. New York: Macmillan, 1952.

———. *The Pilgrim's Regress: An Allegorical Apology for Christianity, Reason, and Romanticism*. Grand Rapids: Eerdmans, 2014.

Lipovski-Helal, Kathleen. "Flannery O'Connor's Encounter with Mary Ann Long." *Flannery O'Connor Review* 11 (January 1, 2013). Accessed September 13, 2016. https://www.questia .com/library/journal/1P3-3123354531/flannery-o-connor-s-encounter-with-mary-ann -long.

Locke, John. *Two Treatises of Government*. Edited by Peter Laslett. Cambridge: Cambridge University Press, 1988.

Luther, Martin. *The Christian in Society II*. Edited by Walter I. Brandt. Philadelphia: Muhlenberg Press, 1962.

———. *Luther's Works*. Edited by Jaroslav Pelikan and Helmut T. Lehmann. 56 vols. St. Louis: Concordia; Philadelphia: Fortress, 1855–1986.

———. *On the Jews and Their Lies*. Translated by Martin H. Bertram. Sebeka, Minn.: Coleman Rydie, 2009.

———. *Temporal Authority: To What Extent It Should Be Obeyed*. Accessed April 29, 2015. http:// pages.uoregon.edu/sshoemak/323/texts/luther~1.htm.

MacIntyre, Alasdair C. *After Virtue: A Study in Moral Theory*. London: Bloomsbury Academic, 2013.

———. *Dependent Rational Animals: Why Human Beings Need the Virtues*. Chicago, Ill.: Open Court, 1999.

———. *Ethics in the Conflicts of Modernity: An Essay on Desire, Practical Reasoning, and Narrative*. Cambridge: Cambridge University Press, 2017.

———. *Whose Justice? Whose Rationality?* Notre Dame, Ind.: University of Notre Dame Press, 2008.

Mann, Thomas. "Germany and the Germans." An address delivered in the Coolidge Auditorium in the Library of Congress on the evening of May 29, 1945. Washington, D.C.: Library of Congress, 1945.

McGrath, Alister. "Calvin and the Christian Calling." *First Things*. June/July 1999. Accessed March 13, 2015. http://www.firstthings.com/article/1999/06/calvin-and-the-christian -calling.

McKnight, John. *The Careless Society: Community and Its Counterfeits*. New York: Basic Books, 1995.

Mela, Lia. "MacIntyre on Personal Identity." *Public Reason* 3, no. 1 (June 2011): 103–13. http:// www.publicreason.ro/articol/47.

Merleau-Ponty, Maurice. *Le visible et l'invisible: Suivi de "Notes de Travail."* Paris: Gallimard, 1964.

Merton, Thomas. *No Man Is an Island*. Boston: Shambhala, 2005.

Miles, M. "Martin Luther and Childhood Disability in 16th Century Germany." *Journal of Religion, Disability & Health* 5, no. 4 (2001): 5–36. doi:10.1300/j095v05n04_02.

Miner, Robert C. "The Difficulties of Mercy: Reading Thomas Aquinas on *Misericordia*." *Studies in Christian Ethics* 28, no. 1 (2015): 70–85. doi:10.1177/0953946814555325.

————. "Thomas Aquinas and Hans Urs von Balthasar: A Dialogue on Love and Charity." *New Blackfriars* 95, no. 1059 (2014): 504–24. doi:10.1111/nbfr.12087.

Moltmann, Jürgen. *The Crucified God: The Cross of Christ as the Foundation and Criticism of Christian Theology*. Translated by R. A. Wilson and John Bowden. Philadelphia: Fortress, 1974.

Mostert, M. P. "Useless Eaters: Disability as Genocidal Marker in Nazi Germany." *Journal of Special Education* 36, no. 3 (2002): 157–70. doi:10.1177/00224669020360030601.

Myers, Valerie L. *Conversations about Calling: Advancing Management Perspectives*. New York: Routledge Taylor & Francis, 2014.

Nietzsche, Friedrich Wilhelm. *Beyond Good and Evil: Prelude to a Philosophy of the Future*. Translated by Rolf-Peter Horstmann, and Judith Norman. Cambridge: Cambridge University Press, 2002.

Nouwen, Henri J. M. *Adam: God's Beloved*. Maryknoll, N.Y.: Orbis Books, 1997.

————. "Forgiveness: The Name of Love in a Wounded World." *Weavings* 7, no. 2 (1992): 6–15.

————. "Spirituality of Waiting." In *The Weavings Reader: Living with God in the World*, edited by John S. Mogabgab, 65–74. Nashville: Upper Room Books, 1993.

————. *With Open Hands*. Notre Dame, Ind.: Ave Maria Press, 2006.

————. *The Wounded Healer: Ministry in Contemporary Society*. London: Darton, Longman & Todd, 2014.

Novak, David. "The Human Person as the Image of God." In *Personhood and Health Care*, edited by David C. Thomasma, David N. Weisstub, and Christian Hervé, 43–54. Dordrecht: Springer, 2011.

Olivola, Christopher, and Alexander Todorov. "The Look of a Winner." *Scientific American*, April 28, 2009. Accessed September 16, 2016. http://www.scientificamerican.com/article/the-look-of-a-winner/.

Palmer, Parker J. *Let Your Life Speak: Listening for the Voice of Vocation*. San Francisco: Jossey-Bass, 2000.

Passin, Laura. "How 'Making a Murderer' Handles Intellectual Disability." *Rolling Stone*, January 11, 2016. http://www.rollingstone.com/politics/news/what-making-a-murderer-reveals-about-the-justice-system-and-intellectual-disability-20160111.

Pattison, George. *The Philosophy of Kierkegaard*. Montreal: McGill-Queen's University Press, 2005.

Proctor, Robert N. *Racial Hygiene: Medicine under the Nazis*. Cambridge, Mass.: Harvard University Press, 1998.

Reinders, Hans. *Disability, Providence, and Ethics: Bridging Gaps, Transforming Lives*. Waco, Tex.: Baylor University Press, 2014.

————. "*Imago Dei* as a Basic Concept in Christian Ethics." In *Holy Scriptures in Judaism, Christianity and Islam: Hermeneutics, Values and Society*, edited by Hendrik M. Vroom and Gerald D. Gort, 187–204. Atlanta: Rodopi, 1997.

————. *Receiving the Gift of Friendship: Profound Disability, Theological Anthropology, and Ethics*. Grand Rapids: Eerdmans, 2008.

Reinders, J. S. "The Good Life for Citizens with Intellectual Disability." *Journal of Intellectual Disability Research* 46, no. 1 (2002): 1–5. doi:10.1046/j.1365–2788.2002.00386.x.

Remen, Rachel Naomi. *Kitchen Table Wisdom: Stories That Heal*. New York: Riverhead Books, 1997.

Reynolds, Thomas E. *Vulnerable Communion: A Theology of Disability and Hospitality*. Grand Rapids: Brazos Press, 2008.

Romero, Miguel J. "Aquinas on the *Corporis Infirmitas*: Broken Flesh and the Grammar of Grace." In *Disability in the Christian Tradition: A Reader*, edited by Brian Brock and John Swinton, 101–51. Grand Rapids: Eerdmans, 2012.

Scirghi, Thomas J. "The Trinity: A Model for Belonging in Contemporary Society." *Ecumenical Review* 54, no. 3 (2002): 333–42. doi:10.1111/j.1758-6623.2002.tb00157.x.

Seth, Anil K. "The Hard Problem of Consciousness Is a Distraction from the Real One." *Aeon*, November 2, 2016. Accessed November 4, 2016. https://aeon.co/essays/the-hard-problem -of-consciousness-is-a-distraction-from-the-real-one.

Siemon-Netto, Uwe. *The Fabricated Luther: Refuting Nazi Connections and Other Modern Myths*. St. Louis, Mo.: Concordia, 2007.

———. "Vietnam, Luther, and the Doctrine of Vocation." *Religion & Liberty* 24, no. 1 (January 2014): 3. Accessed April 29, 2015. https://www.acton.org/vietnam-luther-and-doctrine -vocation.

Simplican, Stacy Clifford. "Care, Disability, and Violence: Theorizing Complex Dependency in Eva Kittay and Judith Butler." *Hypatia* 30, no. 1 (2014): 217–33. doi:10.1111/hypa.12130.

"Spotlight on Transformation." Ontario Ministry of Social Services. February 2009. Accessed February 10, 2016. http://www.mcss.gov.on.ca/en/mcss/publications/developmentalServices/ spotlight/sotFeb09.aspx.

Steigmann-Gall, Richard. "Nazism and the Revival of Politicial Religion Theory." In *Fascism, Totalitarianism and Political Religion*, edited by Roger Griffin, 82–102. London: Routledge, 2005.

Stulp, Gert, Abraham P. Buunk, Simon Verhulst, and Thomas V. Pollet. "Tall Claims? Sense and Nonsense about the Importance of Height of US Presidents." *Leadership Quarterly* 24, no. 1 (2013): 159–71. https://doi.org/10.1016/j.leaqua.2012.09.002.

Swinton, John. *Becoming Friends of Time: Disability, Timefullness, and Gentle Discipleship*. Waco, Tex.: Baylor University Press, 2016.

———. *Dementia: Living in the Memories of God*. Grand Rapids: Eerdmans, 2012.

———. "Restoring the Image: Spirituality, Faith, and Cognitive Disability." *Journal of Religion and Health* 36, no. 1 (Spring 1997): 21–28.

Taylor, Charles. "The Immanent Frame." In *A Secular Age*, 539–93. Cambridge, Mass.: Belknap Press of Harvard University Press, 2007.

———. *Sources of the Self: The Making of the Modern Identity*. Cambridge: Cambridge University Press, 1992.

Tengelyi, László. *The Wild Region in Life-History*. Evanston, Ill.: Northwestern University Press, 2004.

Tertullian. *The Writings of Tertullian*. Edited by Anthony Uyl. Vol. 1. Woodstock, Ont.: Devoted, 2017.

Teresa of Calcutta. *Come Be My Light: The Revealing Private Writings of the Nobel Peace Prize Winner*. Edited by Brian Kolodiejchuk. London: Rider, 2007.

Tillich, Paul. *The New Being*. Lincoln: University of Nebraska Press, 2005.

Tolstoy, Leo. *The Awakening: The Resurrection*. Translated by William E. Smith. Auckland, New Zealand: Floating Press, 1899.

Vanier, Jean. *Gospel of John, the Gospel of Relationship*. Cincinnati, Ohio: Franciscan Media, 2015. Kindle.

———. *Our Journey Home: Rediscovering a Common Humanity beyond Our Differences*. Ottawa, Ont.: Novalis, 1997.

Volf, Miroslav. *Exclusion and Embrace: A Theological Exploration of Identity, Otherness, and Reconciliation*. Nashville: Abingdon, 1996.

Wargo, Eric. "How Many Seconds to a First Impression?" *Association for Psychological Science RSS*, July 2006. Accessed September 16, 2016. http://www.psychologicalscience.org/index .php/publications/observer/2006/july-06/how-many-seconds-to-a-first-impression.html.

Weber, Max. *The Protestant Ethic and the Spirit of Capitalism*. London: Routledge, 2001.

Welz, Claudia. *Humanity in God's Image an Interdisciplinary Exploration*. Oxford: Oxford University Press, 2016.

Weil, Simone, and Joë Bousquet. *Correspondance: Simone Weil, Joë Bousquet*. Edited by Jil Silberstein. Lausanne: Ed. l'Age d'Homme, 1982.

Wittgenstein, Ludwig. *Tractatus Logico-Philosophicus*. Translated by David Pears and Brian McGuinness. London: Routledge, 2001.

Wright, N. T. *John for Everyone*. Part 2, *Chapters 11–21*. London: SPCK, 2004.

———. "Wouldn't You Love to Know: Towards a Christian View of Reality." *BioLogos*, December 6, 2016. Accessed December 7, 2016. http://biologos.org/blogs/jim-stump-faith -and-science-seeking-understanding/wouldnt-you-love-to-know-towards-a-christian -view-of-reality.

Wright, Robert. *The Moral Animal: Evolutionary Psychology and Everyday Life*. New York: Pantheon, 1994.

Wyschogrod, Edith. *Emmanuel Levinas: The Problem of Ethical Metaphysics*. New York: Fordham University Press, 2000.

Yong, Amos. *Theology and Down Syndrome: Reimagining Disability in Late Modernity*. Waco, Tex.: Baylor Univ. Press, 2007.

Young, Marguerite. "The Clinic." In *Moderate Fable*. New York: Reynal and Hitchcock, 1944.

Žižek, Slavoj. "If You Have Reasons to Love Someone, You Don't Love Her/Him." Twitter. November 20, 2013. https://twitter.com/Slavojiek/status/403149945337044992.

Zola, I. K. "Healthism and Disabling Medicalization." In *Disabling Professions*, edited by I. Illich, 41–69. London: M. Boyars, 1977.

Index

Also Available in the SRTD Series